THE DEATH OF JESUS:
THE DIABOLICAL FORCE
AND THE MINISTERING ANGEL

LUKE 23, 44-49

ISSN 0575-0741

CAHIERS DE LA REVUE BIBLIQUE

43

THE DEATH OF JESUS: THE DIABOLICAL FORCE AND THE MINISTERING ANGEL

LUKE 23, 44-49

by

Michael PATELLA, O.S.B.

PARIS
J. GABALDA et Cie Éditeurs
Rue Pierre et Marie Curie, 18
—
1999

ISBN : 2-85021-113-3
ISSN : 0575-0741

To my parents

Thomas, in loving memory

Anne, in loving gratitude

Special thanks to the Dominican community at the Couvent de Saint Étienne, whose hospitality sustained me during my sojourn in Jerusalem, and to the faculty and staff at the École biblique et archéologique française de Jérusalem where this topic first took shape. The ready assistance of librarians Anthony Ward, SM; Kevin McCaffrey, OP; and Antoun Hazou helped considerably in my research. The insight and comments of Marie-Émile Boismard, OP, and Jerome Murphy-O'Connor, OP, concerning my *mémoire*, figured greatly in its development into a dissertation. I am especially grateful to my doctoral advisor, Justin Taylor, SM.

Among colleagues at Saint John's University, I would like to thank Dietrich Reinhart, OSB, President of Saint John's University; Dale Launderville, OSB, Dean of the Saint John's School of Theology; and Carmela Franklin, former Chair of the Department of History, for their initial and continual interest in my work, as well as Margaret Cook of the Department of Modern and Classical Languages. I am indebted to my colleagues at the Saint John's School of Theology who were most helpful in commenting and providing suggestions when presented with this work at a faculty colloquium. Likewise, I am grateful to Ursula Klie, Mark Nussberger, Danielle Nussberger, and Erin Ryan for their assistance in preparing the manuscript as well as to Edmund Little of the Diocese of Wellington for advice on formatting the text.

I would like to extend my gratitude to my monastic community at Saint John's Abbey for their fraternal support of my research in Rome, Jerusalem, and Collegeville. In this regard, I would like to remember Abbot Primate Jerome Theisen, OSB who encouraged my study of Scripture; I deeply regret that he died before the completion of this work. I would expressly like to thank Abbot Timothy Kelly, OSB for his support and encouragement through my years of study.

And to my family, I offer deep and heartfelt gratefulness.

2DH	Two-Document Hypothesis
a	A primitive death narrative
AnBib	Analecta Biblica
Apoc. Elijah	*Apocalypse of Elijah*
Apoc. Paul	*Apocalypse of Paul* (*Nag Hammadi Codices*)
APOT	*Apocrypha and Pseudepigrapha of the Old Testament*
b	A primitive death narrative
BAGD	Bauer, Arndt, Gingrich, and Danker. *A Greek-English Lexicon of the New Testament and Other Early Christian Literature*
BDB	Brown, Driver, Briggs, Gesenius. *Hebrew and English Lexicon*
BDF	Blass, Debrunner, and Funk. *A Greek Grammar of the New Testament*
BEvT	Beiträge zur evangelischen Theologie
Bib	*Biblica*
BZ	*Biblische Zeitschrift*
CahRB	*Cahiers de la Revue Biblique*
CBQ	*Catholic Biblical Quarterly*
EBib	Études bibliques
ExpTim	*Expository Times*
GH	Griesbach Hypothesis
Gos. Pet.	*The Akhmim Fragment of the Apocryphal Gospel of Peter*
Gos. Thom.	*Gospel According to Thomas*
HR	Hatch and Redpath, *Concordance to the Septuagint*
J	Johannine redaction
J Ant	Josephus, *Jewish Antiquities*
JSNT	*Journal for the Study of the New Testament*

JSNTSup	Journal for the Study of the New Testament-Supplement Series
JSOT	*Journal for the Study of the Old Testament*
JTS	*Journal of Theological Studies*
J War	Josephus, *Jewish War*
Jub.	*Jubilees*
KB	Koehler and Baumgartner. *Lexicon in Veteris Testamenti libros*
L	Lucan redaction
L-A	Luke-Acts
LCL	Loeb Classical Library
LS	Liddel and Scott. *A Greek-English Lexicon*
LXX	Septuagint, the Greek Old Testament (Rahlfs)
Mart. Isa.	*Martrydom and Ascension of Isaiah*
ms, mss	manuscript(s)
MT	Massoretic text (*Biblica Hebraica Stuttgartensia*)
NA^{27}	*Nestle-Aland Novum Testamentum Graece, 27th Edition*
NHS	Nag Hammadi Studies
NovTSup	Novum Testamentum, Supplements
NRSV	*New Revised Standard Version*
NT	New Testament
NTS	*New Testament Studies*
OT	Old Testament
OTPseud	*Old Testament Pseudepigrapha*, vols. 1 and 2 (Charlesworth)
PN	Passion narrative
Q	(*Quelle*) source material common to Matthew and Luke but absent from Mark
RB	*Revue Biblique*

RSR	*Recherches de science religieuse*
SBL	Society of Biblical Literature
SC	*Sources chrétiennes*
SNTSMS	Society for New Testament Studies Monograph Series
T. 12 Patr.	*Testaments of the Twelve Patriarchs*
T. Ash.	*Testament of Asher*
T. Benj.	*Testament of Benjamin*
T. Dan	*Testament of Dan*
T. Levi	*Testament of Levi*
T. Naph.	*Testament of Naphtali*
T. Reub.	*Testament of Reuben*
T. Sim.	*Testament of Simeon*
T. Zeb.	*Testament of Zebulon*
TTZ	*Trierer theologische Zeitschrift*
VC	*Vigiliae christianae*
VKGNT	*Vollständige Konkordanz zum Griechischen Neuen Testament*
UBSGNT[3]	*United Bible Societies Greek New Testament, 3rd Revised Edition*
UBSGNT[4]	*United Bible Societies Greek New Testament, 4th Revised Edition*
WUNT	*Wissenschaftliche Untersuchungen zum Neuen Testament*
ZRT	*Zeitschrift für Religionswissenschaft und Theologie*
ZNW	*Zeitschrift für die neutestamentliche Wissenschaft*

Abbreviations for biblical and pseudepigraphic books as well as the Dead Sea Scrolls and related texts are according to the directives of the *CBQ* (46 [1984] 397-8).

Introduction

In Acts 2,23-24 Peter speaks of Jesus as one "delivered up according to the definite plan and foreknowledge of God, [whom] you crucified and killed by the hands of lawless men. But God raised him up..." Thus beginning with Peter's Pentecost oration, the passion, death, and resurrection of Christ become the object of preaching throughout the remainder of Acts.

Erich Auerbach speaks of the contents of this preaching, and of the whole gospel, as "...something which neither the poets nor the historians of antiquity ever set out to portray: the birth of a spiritual movement in the depths of the common people, from within the everyday occurrences of contemporary life, which thus assumes an importance it could never have assumed in antique literature".[1] But why would the ignominious death of a Palestinian Jew be a topic of preaching, let alone the cause of a new religious movement? Obviously, there had to be something in the passion and death which would have appeal to any listener. The salvific content in the gospel is the source of this attraction, but in order for this content to inspire the minds and hearts of its hearers, it had to resonate with their expectations.

The Lucan corpus has two volumes, the Gospel and the Acts. Thus, the possibility for detecting the literary strains which went into the Christian kerygma is greater in the third gospel than in Matthew, Mark, or John. Moreover, the redactional history of Luke serves to strengthen this assumption.[2] It has been demonstrated that the kerygma was transmitted orally before its achieving canonical, written form.[3] The salvific strains contained in the kerygma, and how and why they were redacted into a final Lucan version of the death of Jesus constitute the major examination of this study.

This investigation into Lucan soteriology has three parts. Part One scans the background of the whole Lucan passion narrative beginning with the prediction of Peter's denial (22,31-34) and concluding with the burial (23,56), Chapter One. In addition to the main argument set forth in the chapter, this section also contains a secondary discussion, set off by italics, incorporating the findings of many other scholars. I hope that such a style will enhance the presentation without clouding the central thesis. Hence, the research in Chapter One delineates ten themes which run through the passion narrative and selects one for further investigation in Chapter Two, the Satan motif. The results of this analysis show that, although Luke relies on *diabolical force* and *ministering angel* traditions existing in several OT, pseudepigraphic, and intertestamental works, he reinterprets these traditions in composing his gospel.

Part Two deals with the four death narratives and concludes that the most

---

[1] Erich Auerbach, *Mimesis, the Representation of Reality in Western Literature* (Princeton: Princeton University Press, 1953) 42-43.

[2] Cf. M.-É. Boismard, O.P., *En Quête du proto-Luc* (EBib 37; Paris: J. Gabalda et Cie, 1997).

[3] Étienne Nodet, O.P. and Justin Taylor, S.M., *The Origins of Christianity, an Exploration* (Collegeville, Minnesota: The Liturgical Press, 1998) 3-9.

primitive levels of the death narrative are visible in Luke 23,44-49 and John 19,25-30. Early versions of these two gospels influenced the formation of the parallel accounts in both Matthew and Mark. This hypothesis is demonstrated first through a textual criticism of Matt 27,45-56 and Mark 15,33-41 along with the respective pericopes in Luke and John (Chapter Three). A literary and source analysis of these same parallel passages (Chapter Four) indicates that the final redaction of the Lucan death account was reached after the early traditions had undergone several stages in their development.

Part Three concentrates solely on the Lucan death narrative and integrates the various issues discussed in the first four chapters. The synthesis manifests a Lucan soteriology, one that views Christ's death as a transfiguration into glory, and one which also promises to humanity the same transformation. This last point, the notion of Christian *theosis*, is a tenet often not considered in exegetical discussions, and it is my desire that this monograph will help to uncover some of its scriptural foundations with the hope that it will resurface as a quality vitally integral to the Christian life.

Collegeville, Christmas 1998   Michael Patella

Part One

Background to the Lucan Death Account

The first part of this study, composed of two chapters, traces the various themes of the Lucan passion narrative. Chapter One investigates the narrative structure and also indicates several motifs in this framework: Jesus as prophet, suffering servant, confessor, teacher of disciples, just one, intercessor, martyr, pardoner, and conqueror of Satan. Chapter Two analyzes the last motif and shows that it is part of the *diabolical force* and *ministering angel* themes which originate in OT and intertestamental literature. In the early stages of the gospel tradition these themes developed into "fixed points" which the final Lucan redactor employed in the formation of the third gospel.

Chapter One

The Passion Narrative: major themes

The Lucan passion narrative contains information not found in any other gospel. This circumstance has advanced two major theories of composition.

The first, the Two-Document Hypothesis, stresses Marcan priority supplemented by Q sayings. On this basis, the composition of the Lucan passion narrative can be explained by maintaining that in the PN, Luke, relying solely on Mark, transposed, altered, or created various, diverse passages. Principal digression from this theory holds that Luke combined a separate source with the Marcan account.[1]

---

[1] Those maintaining that Luke had no source outside Mark for the PN include Raymond E. Brown, S.S. *The Death of the Messiah* (1 and 2; New York: Doubleday, 1994); Anton Büchele, *Der Tod Jesu im Lukasevangelium* (Frankfurt: Josef Knecht, 1978); Joseph A. Fitzmyer, S.J. *The Gospel According to Luke 10-24, vol. 2* (Anchor Bible 28a; Garden City, New York: Doubleday and Company, 1985); Frank J. Matera, "The Death of Jesus According to Luke," *CBQ* 47 (1985) 469-485; Gerhard Schneider, *Die Passion Jesu nach den drei älteren Evangelien* (München: Kösel-Verlag, 1973); for additional authors in this category, cf. Brown (*Messiah* 1; 67 n 72). Among those opting for a separate Lucan PN in addition to Mark include John Amedee Bailey, *The Traditions Common to the Gospels of Luke and John* (Leiden: E.J. Brill, 1963); M.-É. Boismard, O.P. *Synopse des Quatre Évangiles* (2; Paris: Les Éditions du Cerf, 1972) and *L'Évangile de Marc, sa préhistoire* (EBib 26; Paris: J. Gabalda et Cie, 1994); Lloyd Gaston, *No Stone on Another* (NovTSup 23; Leiden: E.J. Brill, 1970); Joel B. Green, *The Death of Jesus* (WUNT 2/33; Tübingen: J.C.B. Mohr [Paul Siebeck] 1988); M.-J. Lagrange, O.P. *Évangile selon Saint Luc* (EBib 15; Paris: J. Gabalda et Cie, 1921); I.H. Marshall, *Luke: Historian and Theologian* (Exeter: The Paternoster Press, 1978); Friedrich Rehkopf, *Die lukanische Sonderquelle, ihr Umfang und Sprachgebrauch* (Tübingen: J.C.B. Mohr [Paul Siebeck] 1959); Julius Schniewind, *Die Parallelperikopen bei Lukas und Johannes* (Hildesheim: Georg Olms Verlagsbuchhandlung, 1958); B.H. Streeter, "On the Trial of Our Lord before Herod, a Suggestion," *Oxford Studies in the*

The second major theory, the Griesbach Hypothesis, sees Matthew as the earliest gospel from which Luke borrows. In this theory, Mark draws from both Luke and Matthew.[2] Opponents of this hypothesis generally prefer the 2DH. To examine the source issue fully is well beyond the scope of the present study, but the existence of this problem points to a difficulty.

If the source question is not addressed, can a study of any gospel narrative be sound? Joseph B. Tyson believes that, because the issue of sources is "at present, unresolved," a holistic approach is to be preferred.[3] Jerome Neyrey examines the Lucan PN under the lens of redaction criticism, but prefaces this by citing his work as a departure from "concern...with questions of Luke's sources and issues of historicity".[4] Robert J. Karris studies Luke's artistry as a "vehicle for his theology" by examining major motifs in the third gospel;[5] there is no examination of sources or redaction. Robert C. Tannehill, addressing the narrative structure of Luke-Acts, explicitly states that he is concerned with Luke-Acts in its finished form, not with pre-Lucan tradition.[6]

Although these various approaches to the study of Luke's gospel are valid and beneficial, to ignore the source question will have some deleterious effects on the interpretation, foremost among which is a dehistoricized reading. On the other hand, critics of those who invest their time solely in examining the *minutiae* of a particular text are correct in their assessment that such study can result in a truncated interpretation disconnected from the larger whole. I would like to avoid both extremes.

Source question

The final Lucan redaction determines the line for the discussion in this

---

Synoptic Problem (ed. W. Sanday, Oxford: Clarendon Press, 1911) 229-31; Vincent Taylor, *The Passion Narrative of St Luke* (SNTSMS 19; Cambridge: University Press, 1972); for additional authors in this category, cf. Brown (*Messiah* 1; 66 n 70).

[2] Cf. W.R. Farmer, *The Synoptic Problem: A Critical Analysis* (New York: Macmillan Company, 1964). For an overview of the opinions of various exegetes on the GH as well as a brief critique of the hypothesis itself, cf. Sherman E. Johnson, *The Griesbach Hypothesis and Redaction Criticism* (Atlanta: Scholars Press, 1991) 1-5.

[3] Joseph B. Tyson, *The Death of Jesus in Luke-Acts* (Columbia: University of South Carolina Press, 1986) 9.

[4] Jerome Neyrey, S.J., *The Passion According to Luke* (New York: Paulist Press, 1985) 1.

[5] Robert J. Karris, O.F.M., *Luke: Artist and Theologian* (New York: Paulist Press, 1985) 1.

[6] The author affirms, however, the two-source theory of Mark and Q in a note (Robert C. Tannehill, *The Narrative Unity of Luke-Acts, A Literary Interpretation* [Philadelphia: Fortress Press, 1986] 6 n 3).

chapter.[7] Where Luke departs from the other gospels, the understanding is that, despite Luke's dependence on Mark/Matthew or any non-Marcan/Matthean PN, the end result is a PN with Luke's own theological imprint. Thus, for the present, attention to the Lucan PN will be confined to elaborating how various episodes in Luke, particularly in the PN, are interrelated with the death account (23,44-49). One of these theological themes, Satan's hour and the power of darkness, is the subject of investigation in a succeeding chapter.

As for the source question, it would be impossible in the space of this monograph to tackle every verse of the PN with the same degree of thoroughness that is applied to the death account.[8] I will limit that approach to the hour and the power of darkness, now and also in a succeeding chapter. Nonetheless, a thorough reading of the Lucan PN reveals that Matthew and Mark often agree against Luke and John.[9] Thus, in the narrative and contextual discussion in this chapter, the Matthean and Marcan PNs form the predominant point of comparison for the discussion. Most of these parallels are noted as they arise, while others necessitating deeper discussion receive further treatment in successive chapters.

What becomes evident in the research is that neither the 2DH nor the GH sufficiently explains the source for the Lucan death account (23,44-49). In addition, the echoes and parallels Luke has with John strongly suggest a common tradition shared by these two evangelists. For example, the presence of the disciples at the crucifixion (Luke 23,49) shows a similarity to John 19,25. Moreover, some passages, such as the sword incident (Luke 22,49-51; Matt 26,51-52 and John 18,10-11), the tradition of the strengthening angel (22,43-44; John 12,28ff but cf. Matt 26,53), the tomb description (23,53b; cf. Matt 27,60 and John 19,41) and the Lucan and Matthean use of ἑκατόνταρχης/ἑκατόνταρχος (Luke 23,47; Matt 27,54; cf. Mark 15,39), all show substantial concord between Lucan, Matthean, or Johannine PNs, not the Marcan narrative.

Many, but certainly not all, of the Lucan departures from Mark/Matthew can be explained by the third evangelist's desire to render an "orderly account" (Luke 1,3) from a Marcan or Matthean source.[10] Hence, a number of Lucan readings can be considered transpositions, substitutions, and omissions of material of Marcan/Matthean origin.

Lucan readings which appear as "additions" to a Marcan/Matthean source, however, demand further explanation for two reasons. First, the great majority of the additions are not needed to clarify anything. Rather, they serve to develop or underscore a certain historical or theological point. Second, although I am not addressing questions of source criticism here, the debate on whether Luke used another PN in addition to Mark, Matthew, or John still continues. Because Luke is one of the synoptic texts, if the third gospel's PN actually is the fusion of two

---

[7] A more diachronic approach is taken in successive chapters.

[8] Cf. Chapters Three and Four, below.

[9] Cf. particularly Chapters Three and Four below.

[10] The death account itself, Luke 23,44-49, and its parallel accounts have another explanation. Cf. below, Chapter Four.

or more different passion stories, this melding would be most evident in any
additions to the Marcan/Matthean account.   When probing these additions,
however, a new way of viewing the PN emerges. The research shows that Mark
and Matthew agree against Luke and John at nearly every verse. The two notable
exceptions are Luke 23,47/Matt 26,54b and Luke 22,51/Matt 26,52-54. These
Lucan and Matthean verses also contain echoes of material found in John, and
neither the 2DH or GH can adequately explain these phenomena. Opening up to
the more fluid theory of "stages of development" results in a richer appreciation
of the Lucan redaction.

The approach

Regardless of whether Luke created these additions or relied on a non-
Marcan/Matthean source or tradition, the Lucan PN nonetheless relates a story
which is sensitive to certain themes while simultaneously maintaining stylistic
coherence.

Raymond Brown furnishes a framework of acts and scenes which
dramatize the gospel passion accounts.[11]   Brown defines the Lucan PN as
beginning with the Mount of Olives episode (22,39) and ending with the burial
(23,56).[12] Brown's schema, however, is constructed on a Marcan outline, hence
his design of acts and scenes does not hold up well under the weight of an
individual, in this case, Lucan scrutiny. For this reason, I prefer verse citations
supplemented by subject headings. In so doing, the discussion will be clearer and
more precise. Although the prediction of Peter's denial stands outside the PN, it
gains importance by the fact that it foreshadows an event in the passion.   I
therefore treat Luke 22,31-34 before addressing the PN proper.

Prediction of Peter's denial; Luke 22,31-34

The prediction of Peter's denial at the Last Supper (Luke 22,31-34) is
within the context of a dispute among the individual disciples concerning their
respective greatness.[13] Luke presents the account (vv 31-34) in a manner which
suggests that Peter has peppered the argument with a great deal of bravado,
making Jesus address him personally. Karris points out that whereas formerly the
transgressors in Luke were unconverted tax collectors and sinners, they are now
the disciples.[14] The address to Peter in v 32, however, is actually a prayer which

---

[11] Brown, *Messiah* 1; 68-75.

[12] As Brown notes, the change of scene from the Last Supper to the Mount of
Olives episode is clearer in Luke than in the other two synoptics (Brown, *Messiah*
1; 39).

[13] David Crump emphasizes that Jesus' prayer is not for Peter alone -- nb.
ὑμεῖς (v 31) and σύ (v 32) -- but for all the disciples. Peter is singled out first, as
a literary premonition of the denial, and second, as the group representative who
will restore the others (*Jesus the Intercessor* [WUNT 2/49; Tübingen: J.C.B.
Mohr (Paul Siebeck), 1992] 161).

tempers the prediction of the denial, and by extension, the denial itself (22,55-62); it simultaneously prepares for Peter's role in Acts[15] as it foreshadows the impending events.[16] Furthermore, Boismard notes that in Luke, Peter's denial establishes a parallel between David's comments to Ittai (2 Sam 15,19-21) and Jesus' words to Peter.[17] The prediction also continues a PN Satan motif first sounded at 22,3.

Neyrey considers the Last Supper (22,14-38) to be within the genre of the "Farewell Speech," something rooted in biblical traditions.[18] The "Farewell Speech," given by a leader to children or disciples, includes a prediction of danger to the immediate circle.[19] If this is the case, Luke's context of the discussion on greatness places the danger within the circle itself; indeed, Judas' betrayal confirms this notion, as does the following dialogue about the two swords (v 38).[20]

The agony on the Mount of Olives; Luke 22,39-46

Mark's selection of Peter, James, and John from among the group at Gethsemane (Mark 14,33) is connected to the fleeing of the disciples in Mark 14,50-52. The Marcan PN has ordered a graduated intensity of desertion. Since Peter, James, and John receive privileged place in Mark's gospel,[21] their flight along with the rest of the disciples now at the hour of the Lord's greatest need[22] underscores Jesus' abandonment, which reaches its climax with Peter's denial

---

[14] Karris, *Artist* 70. I imagine Karris means that the bickering disciples show that they are not yet converted.

[15] David L. Tiede makes a good point that though the mention of Satan (v 31) may indicate a struggle transcending human choice, it still does not exempt Peter from culpability in the denial (*Prophecy and History in Luke-Acts* [Philadelphia: Fortress Press, 1980] 107).

[16] Crump, *Jesus* 154.

[17] Boismard also applies this understanding to John 13,36-37 (*Synopse* 2; 387).

[18] Neyrey, *Passion* 6.

[19] Neyrey, *Passion* 7. These verses also remind the disciples that no one is invulnerable to Satan (Tyson, *Death* 54).

[20] In the Marcan account (14,26-30), on the other hand, the prediction of the denial seems to be an afterthought, something to be stated before the arrest.

[21] Cf. Mark 3,16-17 but Matt 10,2 and Luke 6,14. Cf. also Mark 9,2; Matt 17,1; Luke 9,28.

[22] John T. Squires stresses that on the Mount of Olives, Jesus, confronting the will of the Father, knows that it will lead to his own death (*The Plan of God in Luke-Acts* [SNTSMS 76; Cambridge: Cambridge University Press, 1993] 170).

(14,66-72). Luke, unlike Mark or Matthew, does not record the flight of the disciples. Indeed they are present to the end (23,49).[23] Therefore, there is no reason for the third evangelist to choose Peter, James, and John from among the others on the Mount of Olives (22,40-41). Tyson sees Luke's use of πειρασμός (v 40) as a signal for the final conflict with the devil.[24]

    Neyrey views the pericope as Lucan redaction of Marcan material.[25] Within this schema, Neyrey notes the omission of Jesus' emotion (grief) with the corresponding attribution of that emotion to the disciples in v 45 (ἀπὸ τῆς λύπης).[26] After studying several classical septuagintal works, Neyrey summarizes that grief is one of the four cardinal passions reckoned as a typical form of punishment for sin, and an indication of guilt.[27] The opposite quality, courage, is the virtue which the Lucan Jesus displays.[28] Neyrey's argument is not convincing. Is courage the opposite of grief, is not Jesus grieving in his agony?
    Brown and others[29] see a likeness between Jesus' going out (ἐξέρχομαι), crossing the Kidron to the Mount of Olives and David's doing the same in 2 Sam 15,30 (LXX 2 Kgs 15,16.30). The similarity of action, locale, and even personages (is Judas a latter-day Absalom?) certainly press for such an analogy, but it is necessary to mark the difference: David flees from his persecutors to safety while Jesus does not.[30] More germane to the PN is that throughout Luke's gospel, as Fitzmyer comments, a mountain has the connotation of prayer, divine presence, and revelation.[31] This should receive the emphasis.

---

    [23] Brown notes that in Luke 22,28-29, the evangelist has Jesus commend the disciples for their fidelity (*Messiah* 1; 126).

    [24] Tyson, *Death* 53. So also Squires (*Plan* 56).

    [25] Neyrey, *Passion* 49.

    [26] Neyrey, *Passion* 49. So also Tannehill (*Narrative* 270-1).

    [27] Neyrey, *Passion* 52-3.

    [28] Cf. the Lucan phrase "..if you are willing..." (v 42) vis-à-vis the Marcan version (14,36); in Luke, Jesus conforms his will to the Father's (Neyrey, *Passion* 54).

    [29] Cf. Brown's discussion, *Messiah* 1; 125-6; cf. also Boismard (*Synopse* 2; 387-8).

    [30] Cf. LXX 2 Kgs 15,14ff; 16,13-14.

    [31] Luke 9,28; 19,29; 21,37; 22,39 (Joseph A. Fitzmyer, *The Gospel According to Luke, 1-9, vol. 1* (Anchor Bible, 28; Garden City, New York: Doubleday and Company, 1981; 616 notes). I would add 3,5; 6,12; Acts 1,12; 7,30.38 as well as two apocalyptic references, Luke 21,21 and 23,30.

Luke 22,43-44

The presence of the strengthening angel at the Mount of Olives as well as Jesus' sweating drops of blood during his agony, is not only unique to Luke,[32] it is also contested in being original to the third gospel itself. The textual tradition is varied.[33]

[[ὤφθη δὲ αὐτῷ ἄγγελος ἀπ᾽ οὐρανοῦ ἐνισχύων αὐτόν. καὶ γενόμενος ἐν ἀγωνίᾳ ἐκτενέστερον προσηύχετο· καὶ ἐγένετο ὁ ἱδρὼς αὐτοῦ ὡσεὶ θρόμβοι αἵματος καταβαίνοντες ἐπὶ τὴν γῆν]]

[[   ]] P (69vid).75 ℵ1 A B N T W 579 1071* *l* 844 *Lect*1/2 it^f syr^s cop^sa,bo'pt arm geo some Greek mss^acc.to Anastasius-Sinaita; Greek and Latin mss^acc to Hilary Ambrose Jerome

Text ℵ*.2 D L Δ* Θ Ψ 0171 0233 *f*1 13^c 157 180 205 565 597 700 828^1/2 892* 1006 1010 1071^c 1241 1243 1292 1342 1424 1505 *Byz* [E F G H Q] *l* 1841^1/2 it^a,aur,b,c,d,e,ff2,i,l,q,r'1 vg syr^c,p,h,pal cop^bo'pt eth slav Diatessaron^arm Justin Irenaeus^gr Hippolytus^acc.to Theodoret Origen^dub Ps-Dionysius Arius^acc.to Epiphanius Eusebian Canons Didymus^dub Epiphanius Chrysostom Theodore Nestorius Theodoret all versions and most Greek mss^acc. to Anastasius-Sinaita John-Damascus; Hilary Greek and Latin mss^acc. to Jerome Augustine Quodvultdeus

including with asterisks or obeli Δ^c 0171^vid 892^c

transposed to after Mt 26,39 *f*13 [13* 828^1/2]

transposed vv 43-45a (καὶ…ποσευχῆς) after Matt 26,39 *Lect*1/2 [*l* 1841/2]

That the Alexandrine witnesses, most importantly ℵ and B, do not agree on reading vv 43-44 as part of the Lucan PN, weakens the ground for considering these verses as part of the text. The strongest case for their inclusion on a textual basis lies, first, in the agreement between Sinaiticus' original hand and its second corrector; and second, in the concord between the Alexandrine Sinaiticus and the Western Bezae. Speaking about the omission of the verses, Lagrange recalls that the witnesses against the reading represent only certain parts of Egypt; Dionysius of Alexandria, who was not using a Western text, includes them.[34]

The inclusion of these lines has additional support. Certain manuscripts show these two verses transposed to Matt 26,39 while other witnesses have them

---

[32] But cf. John 12,27ff; also Mark 14,35ff.

[33] The apparatus is based on *UBSGNT*4. For a list of major exegetes who would include or exclude these two verses, cf. Crump (*Jesus* 116-7 n 25).

[34] Lagrange, *Luc* 562. Lagrange's opinion is reinforced by the early P75 and the late Bohairic mss, both Alexandrian witnesses originating in Egypt. The former omits while the latter includes.

with asterisks or *obeli*. Papyrus 0171, Fayum in origin, contains v 44, and it is "among the earliest surviving Greek manuscript witnesses for so-called 'Western' readings".[35]   This text establishes at least one mutual witness between Alexandrine ℵ*.2 and "Western" Bezae. The emendation in Matthew by *f*[13] and *Lect* raises the issue of a parallel account. There is certainly none in either the synoptic or the Johannine gospels, but both Matt 26,53 and John 12,28b-29 contain readings which show a thematic correspondence to these Lucan verses. This allows for the possibility that an angel tradition existed in the earliest passion material.   Furthermore, the attestation of these verses in the Diatesseron and patristic sources indicate their venerability early in the composition of the PN.

In expressing doubt for the inclusion of these verses in the text, the committees of both the *UBSGNT*[3] and *UBSGNT*[4] double-bracket them. Thus, the *UBSGNT*[3] ranks them as *C*, i.e., there is considerable doubt whether the text or apparatus contains the superior reading.[36]   The editors of *USBGNT*[4], however, nonetheless rank their inclusion as *A*, i.e., "certain".[37]   Fitzmyer, on the other hand, excludes them because 1) *lectio brevior potior*; 2) they lack synoptic parallels; 3) they contain emotions not in accord with Luke's sober presentation; 4) they are absent from the oldest Lucan ms (P[75]); and 5) they evidence concerns of a later period.[38]

B.D. Ehrman's and M.A. Plunkett's thorough examination of the textual problem of vv 43-44 concludes that, on the basis of the textual evidence, the balance tips for their exclusion.[39]   The authors base their conclusion on three factors: external, transcriptional, and intrinsic probability.[40]

The most dependable textual grouping, the Alexandrian family, has weak witness for the inclusion of the verses.   Ehrman and Plunkett are correct in concluding that the external evidence offers no solid textual support for reading 22,43-44 as part of the original Lucan PN.[41]   Hence, the deletion of these verses

---

[35] Anonymous, "Short Notes," *The New Testament Textual Research Update* 2 (1994) 43.

[36] Bruce M. Metzger, *A Textual Commentary on the Greek New Testament* (New York: United Bible Societies, 1971) 177.

[37] *UBSGNT*[4] 3*. In his updated commentary, Bruce M. Metzger explains that this rating is a result of the antiquity and importance of these disputed verses within the textual tradition (*A Textual Commentary on the Greek New Testament*, 2nd *Edition* [New York: American Bible Society, 1994] 151).

[38] Fitzmyer, *Luke* 2; 1444. For a more complete discussion of the problem, cf Brown (*Messiah* 1; 179-90).   For a full list of other scholars and their opinions, cf. Brown (*Messiah* 1; 180 n 2).

[39] B.D. Ehrman and M.A. Plunkett, "The Angel and the Agony: The Textual Problem of Luke 22:43-44," *CBQ* 45 (1983) 401-16.

[40] Ehrman, "Angel" 416.

[41] Ehrman, "Angel" 416.

in the tradition is due most probably to a transcriptional cause. The authors believe that because omissions from the Lucan text are first evident in P[69vid].[75] and Clement (AD 200-230), and earliest inclusion is evident in Justin (AD 160), verses 43-44 were transcribed into the Lucan PN as part of anti-docetic polemic.[42]

Ehrman's and Plunkett's conclusion, however, is based only on a reading of the Greek manuscripts. In addition to Justin's inclusion of the verses, certain Latin and Syriac manuscripts do likewise. Jean Duplacy proposes that these verses were deleted, perhaps in Egypt, in an attempt to harmonize the gospels,[43] and his opinion provides a clue explaining their exclusion. Besides vv 43-44, the Alexandrine ℵ[*.2] bo[pt] and the "Western" D lat sy[c.p.h] also include 23,34a[44] against its omission by P[75] and B; hence, if vv 43-44 were deleted in Egypt, as Duplacy suggests, the support given to ℵ by the "Western" readings weighs the question in favor of their inclusion at the earliest level of the textual tradition.

Turning then to intrinsic evidence, Ehrman and Plunkett hold that these verses are not in accord with the portrayal of a restrained, self-controlled Jesus as seen in other parts of the Lucan PN.[45] Additionally, these verses intrude into a neat chiastic structure:[46]

A   temptation (22,40)   A' temptation (22,45c-46)
B   he withdrew (22,41a)   B' he came (22,45b)
C   he knelt (22,41b)   C' he rose (22,45a)
                     D   he prayed (22,41c-42)

There can be no argument with Ehrman and Plunkett on the external evidence. The manuscript tradition is evenly split, with perhaps slightly more weight given to excluding vv 43-44. Stating that the verses probably entered the text by anti-docetists, however, is problematic. The textual problem is not solved by conjecturing that the anti-docetists *inserted* the episode into the text. It is an equally plausible conjecture that the docetists *removed* it from the original. If one text was emended in Luke, an unanswered question is why texts in the other three gospels were left intact. In addressing the intrinsic evidence, the authors' conclusions are even less solid.

To maintain that 22,43-44 cannot be original to Luke because it destroys a chiasm is a weak reason for excluding the reading. It is easy to perceive chiasms in texts but less easy to prove that they were intended as such by the author. Here specifically, Ehrman and Plunkett's "concise chiasmus" would still stand by extending D to include the strengthening angel and sweating of blood. Furthermore, as Green comments, these verses give better sense to v 45,[47] and are essential to Luke's portrayal of Jesus as the Servant of the Lord.[48]

---

[42] Ehrman, "Angel" 403.416.

[43] Jean Duplacy, "La préhistoire du texte en Luc 22:43-44," *New Testament Textual Criticism: Essays in Honour of Bruce M. Metzger* (ed. Eldon Jay Epp and Gordon D. Fee, Oxford: Clarendon Press, 1981) 86.

[44] Here it is the first hand of D; at 23,34 it is the second corrector of D.

[45] Ehrman, "Angel" 416.

[46] Ehrman, "Angel" 413.

That these verses are out of harmony with Luke's general depiction of Jesus necessitates further examination. Ehrman and Plunkett state that, though the vocabulary used in vv 43-44 may seem to be Lucan, the terms are used in a non-Lucan manner.[49] For example, although Luke employs angels throughout L-A, nowhere does the phrase ἄγγελος ἀπ᾽οὐρανοῦ appear. In addition, every other Lucan angel speaks; this one does not.[50]

In Lyder Brun's seminal study of the problem,[51] the author points out that the Lucan agony scene is not an intentional mitigation of Mark.[52] Jesus is undergoing a struggle of the soul; but because that struggle takes place in the context of prayer, it is a calm struggle not a frenetic one.[53]

Brun proposes that vv 43-44 be viewed in light of the entire agony pericope as well as the whole Lucan PN.[54] For a point of comparison, Brun cites the occurrence of ἐκτενής (Acts 12,5) and its comparative ἐκτενέστερον (Luke 22,44) as both involving earnest prayer to strengthen someone undergoing an ordeal. In Acts 12,5 the church prays for the imprisoned Peter. In like manner, Brun compares the two occurrences of ἐνισχύω in the Lucan corpus (Luke 22,43; Acts 9,19).[55] Although, in the latter, Paul receives strength from food, not from an angel, it is a divine intervention which directs Ananias to Saul in any case.[56]

Despite Ehrman and Plunkett's opinion, Brown convincingly demonstrates that the vocabulary in vv 43-44 is Lucan, or at least cannot be proven to be non-Lucan[57] and continues to show that the vocabulary is used in a characteristically Lucan style.[58]

---

[47] Joel B. Green, "Jesus on the Mount of Olives," *JSNT* 26 (1986) 36.

[48] Green, "Jesus" 42.

[49] Ehrman, "Angel" 408-9.

[50] Ehrman, "Angel" 409.

[51] Lyder Brun, "Engel und Blutschweiß, Lc 22,43-44," *ZNW* 32 (1933) 265-76.

[52] Brun, "Engel" 267-8.

[53] Brun, "Engel" 268.

[54] Brun, "Engel" 265.

[55] Brun, "Engel" 267.

[56] Acts 9,10-16.

[57] Brown, *Messiah* 1; 181-82.

[58] Brown, *Messiah* 1; 182. Ludger Feldkämper compares the appearance of the angel on the Mount of Olives to the exhausted Elijah under the broom tree in LXX 3 Kgs 19,5-8 (*Der betende Jesus als Heilsmittler nach Lukas* (Veröffentlichungen des Missionspriesterseminars St. Augustin bei Bonn 29; St. Augustin: Stelyer Verlag, 1978] 243-4). Related by theme but even more so by

Crucial to this contextual understanding are ἀγωνία and πειρασμός. The Greek ἀγωνία, *anxiety, agony*, has its root in ἀγών, *athletic contest, struggle, fight*.[59] When coupled with πειρασμός, *test, trial*,[60] the meaning of 22,43-44 becomes clearer. Like an athlete, Jesus is tense before a great contest, and the angel strengthens him for the trial, i.e. drinking from the cup the Father has set before him[61] in the hour and power of darkness (22,53; 23,44).

Luke has arranged the PN carefully. The Lucan temptation scene (4,1-13) clarifies the strengthening angel's role in 22,43 especially when read against Matt (4,1-11) and Mark (1,12-13); as Brown indicates,[62] unlike the other two synoptics, Luke does not have ministering angels in the wilderness.[63] Instead, at the conclusion of the desert temptation scene, Luke writes that the devil departed until an opportune time (4,13). Hence, the importance of πειρασμός in Luke 22,40.46. It is the culmination of all temptations in Luke.[64] The agony on the Mount of Olives is the opportune time. Luke has taken the ministering angels from Mark's temptation scene (1,13),[65] and transposed them to Jesus' agony (22,43) by writing them as a single angel. This is Brown's opinion.[66]

Joel B. Green, opting for the inclusion of the verses, recognizes Luke's aversion to doublets and thus holds that Luke substituted vv 43-44 for Mark 14,33-34.[67] In this redaction, Green believes that Luke made use of two traditions, the Marcan story and a non-Marcan, pre-Lucan Quelle.[68] Vincent

---

vocabulary, the comparison reflects Luke's reliance on the LXX as well as the third evangelist's tendency to present Jesus as a prophet.

[59] BAGD 15.

[60] BAGD 640-1.

[61] Brown, *Messiah* 1; 189-90.

[62] Brown, *Messiah* 1; 186.

[63] Cf. Matt 4,11; Mark 1,13.

[64] In addition to the agony scene, πειρασμός carries the notion of trial with, or test by evil forces at several points in Luke's gospel: 4,2 (participle) and 4,13, the temptation in the desert; 8,13, the sower and the seed parable; 11,4, the Lord's Prayer.

[65] N.b. John 12,28-29.

[66] Brown, *Messiah* 1; 186.

[67] Green, *Death* 55. Neyrey also affirms the inclusion of vv 43-44 but for reasons that the verses are part of Lucan soteriology; ie, Jesus shows his humanity and thus is the second Adam (*Passion* 57). So also Crump (*Jesus* 121-3).

[68] Green, *Jesus* 43.

Taylor, however, views all of 22,39-46a as non-Marcan, an embellishment of an oral or written, pre-Lucan source.[69]

Behind the transposition of Mark's and Matthew's ministering angels at the temptation to Luke's single one at the Mount of Olives lies the possibility that Luke combined the Marcan/Matthean source with one outside that tradition. The "legions of angels" in Matt 26,53, and the angelic voice in John 12,28b-29 point to a non-Marcan source in which angels figure in the PN. Luke edited the ministering angels of the Marcan/Matthean temptation scene and the "passion angels" of the non-Marcan source to produce the strengthening angel of Luke 23,43. In so doing, Luke took the "sorrowful, even to death" of Mark 14,34 and Matt 26,38, and using his skills as an artist,[70] refashioned the verse into the highly intense scene of bloody sweat (22,44). By not resisting the temptation to escape over the Mount of Olives, and strengthened by the angel in his resolve, Jesus meets the power of darkness head on (22,53), a power which, in the words of Fitzmyer, "will hold sway and even stifle the good".[71] Substantiating that point, Boismard champions a strong link in source material between the agony, the temptation, and the arrest visible in the Johannine themes present here: "hour," "power of darkness" (cf. John 12,31; 14,30; 16,11).[72] This encounter with the "power of darkness" gains further import from the setting; the Mount of Olives becomes the place of the Lord's visitation.[73]

This understanding is strengthened by Barbara Reid's study of the transfiguration.[74] Reid believes that Luke combined the predictive angelophany in special Lucan material with details from the Marcan tradition, thereby reworking the narrative into a pronouncement story.[75] The conflation has resulted in a transfiguration pericope with strong links to the agony scene especially with its accent on Jesus' prayer (9,28-29; 22,40-41.44-46), the sleepiness of the disciples (9,32; 22,45), and the impending passion (9,31; 22,40.42).[76]

---

[69] Taylor, *Passion* 71-2.

[70] Along with his medical knowledge (Col 4,14)?

[71] Fitzmyer, *Luke* 2; 1452.

[72] Boismard, *Synopse* 2; 396-7.

[73] Cf. below, Chapter Two.

[74] Barbara Reid, O.P. *The Transfiguration: A Source- and Redaction- Critical Study of Luke 9,28-36* (CahRB 32; Paris: J. Gabalda et Cie, 1993).

[75] Reid, *Transfiguration* 85-6.

[76] Reid, *Transfiguration* 96. Jerome Murphy-O'Connor, O.P. reaches similar conclusions ("What Really Happened at the Transfiguration," *Bible Review* 3/3 [1987] 21).

But why were these verses missing in so many important witnesses? The argument that copyists and scribes found them scandalous seems to be the answer, and textual harmonization provided a worthy pretext for their removal. The dispute over the inclusion of vv 43-44 arises from their content. Sweating drops of blood paints a picture of utmost despair. This state of mind is all the more heightened by the fact that Jesus undergoes his most intense agony while an angel is strengthening him. It seems that, for many scribes and adherents to the gospel, these verses would present a double scandal. On the one hand, Jesus behaves in an all too human fashion; there is none of the equanimity in the face of adversity that one would prefer to see from one's Savior. On the other hand, the divine aspects are not presented in a positive light either; if Jesus sweats blood, the strengthening angel is not very effective.

It appears that these two verses are describing ultimate abandonment. The evangelist is saying that even God in heaven cannot, or chooses not to, rescue Jesus from the passion and death which he must undergo. The thought is too horrific for redactor, scribe, and listener; hence, it was excised early in the tradition. But in that horror lies the purpose of this scene and of these disputed verses. To be kept in mind is that the choice still exists for Jesus to face execution or to flee from it; to run over the Mount of Olives to safety, as David did,[77] is all he need do. The agony is over a decision, and the immediate context of the decision is prayer. In 22,40.46, Jesus commands his disciples to pray in order not to enter into temptation, and that is exactly the intent of Jesus' prayer in v 42-44.

Sleeping disciples; Luke 22,45-46

In addition to being an abbreviated version of Marcan/Matthean agony in Gethsemane,[78] the corresponding Lucan scene on the Mount of Olives features the disciples asleep because of "grief" (22,45) rather than "heavy eyes" as it appears in Mark 14,40 and Matt 26,43. If Luke replaced καταβαρύνομαι with λύπη, why did he do so? Since in Mark 14,50-52 and Matt 26,56 the disciples flee, it is not out of character for them to sleep here in Gethsemane. In a sense they desert Jesus through negligence. Their drowsiness at night is perfectly understandable, especially given the meal they have just finished.

This explanation, however, does not work in the Lucan PN, where the disciples are loyal to the point of remaining at Skull Place. In addition, many of them are eager to put up a fight at the moment of arrest (22,49), whereas in Mark and Matthew, only one person lashes out with a sword. Green comments that the grief of the apostles should be understood in relation to the agony of Jesus; if Jesus needed a strengthening angel to pray, it is no wonder that the disciples sleep.[79] True, but from grief? Luke had to substitute *grief* for *heavy eyes* to ensure that the disciples always appear in a loyal light despite the fact that one of

---

[77] Cf. above.

[78] Some Lucan omissions help to present a finer narrative. Luke finds unnecessary the repetitions in Mark/Matthew, i.e., two reprimands to the disciples (Mark 14,40-41; Matt 26,43-45).

[79] Green, *Death* 58.

the qualities of grief is insomnia, as Luke the doctor should have known.[80]

The betrayal; Luke 22,47-48

Luke's presentation is more economical than that of Mark or Matthew. Information about the intended sign of the kiss is transmitted through Jesus' address to Judas (22,48), but the kiss[81] does not take place. At the arrest, the listener knows that the chief priests, temple police, and elders come with swords and clubs through the narrator's introductory comments (22,52).

Neyrey draws attention to the verb προέρχομαι (v 47); Luke stresses that Judas led the arresting party, a fact confirmed in Acts 1,16.[82] *Boismard holds that the betrayal itself is evident in John where Judas leads the soldiers and officers to Jesus.*[83] *Tyson notes that specifically at this scene (vv 47-53), the role of the Jewish public changes; Jesus loses all support.*[84] *Fitzmyer observes that this dialogue, and the following one with the sword-wielding disciple, are Lucan dramatic touches.*[85]

The sword incident; Luke 22,49-51

Luke's account has greater similarity with the Matthean and Johannine parallels (26,51-52; 18,10-11).[86] In Luke the followers ask and then presume permission to join in combat; the right ear is severed. Jesus' reprimand follows as he heals this casualty. This touch is an act of forgiveness toward those arresting him and hence one of reconciliation even as the rest of the passion awaits Jesus.

---

[80] Col 4,14. Crump places the sleeping disciples on the same plane as Peter's denial (Crump, *Jesus* 160-1). Surely, it contributes to the general abandonment of Jesus, but whereas Peter's denial is from fear, the sleep of the other eleven is from weakness and a lack of understanding.

[81] Boismard believes that the kiss is only a greeting (*Synopse* 2; 395). Cf. also Brown who traces the action of the kiss throughout the OT (*Messiah* 1; 254-5).

[82] Neyrey, *Passion* 20.

[83] Boismard, *Synopse* 2; 395.

[84] Tyson, *Death* 37-8.

[85] Fitzmyer, *Luke* 2; 1447.

[86] But cf. Mark 14,47-48 where no dialogue exists and thus severing the ear of the slave appears to be done with Jesus' tacit approval. N.b. the reference to angelic help in Matt 26,53, an echo of Luke 22,43; cf. also John 12,28ff.

The disciples fail to understand the admonition against falling into temptation (22,40.46), and as Brown indicates, when the slave is attacked at the arrest, Jesus must be more forceful in the reprimand than he was at the supper.[87] Benedict Viviano, referring to the Marcan parallel (14,47) demonstrates that the term ὁ δοῦλος τοῦ ἀρχιερέως can mean *segan hacohanim*, the prefect of the priests.[88] Thus what Mark describes has a theological purpose; the mutilation renders the *segan* unfit for temple service. Hence, the Marcan account is an "action parable"[89] which criticizes the collaborationist Sadducean priesthood.[90]

Viviano holds that στρατηγός in Luke 22,4.52 refers to the *segan*.[91] In this case, the theological understanding of the sword incident in Luke is similar to that in Mark, but with one crucial difference: In Luke, Jesus heals the ear. Jesus' act then balances any judgment on the temple and priesthood with one of healing and forgiveness. Thus, in this pericope, Luke's double attitude toward the temple, criticism on the one hand, mitigation on the other, is maintained;[92] simultaneously, the first of three examples of the forgiveness motif surfaces.[93]

Since damaging the right side is more shameful than the left, Luke is probably intensifying the drama by this detail.[94] Squires maintains that Jesus "provokes" his arrest by encouraging Judas to kiss him.[95]

---

[87] Brown, *Messiah* 1; 280. At the supper Luke foreshadows the use of the sword at the arrest through Jesus' ironic response to the disciples, "It is enough" (22,36-38), a comment directed at the whole mentality of the disciples (Fitzmyer, *Luke* 2; 1434). The irony, however, is lost on them not only at the supper but also here.

[88] Benedict T. Viviano, O.P., "The High Priest's Servant's Ear: Mark 14:47," *RB* 96 (1989) 73.

[89] Viviano, "High" 74.

[90] Viviano, "High" 78. Brown counters Viviano on grounds that if Mark must explain to readers Jewish purification rites (7,3-5), they would never comprehend any criticism about the temple priesthood present in this verse (*Messiah* 1; 273-4). It is doubtful, however, that such an explanation would have been necessary if, as Viviano specifies, severing one or both ears because of its concomittant social stigma, was a common form of punishment in the ancient world ("High" 78).

[91] Viviano, however, does not sufficiently explain why Luke would use δοῦλος in 22,50 and στρατηγός in 22,4.52 ("High" 73).

[92] Cf. below, Chapter Five.

[93] Cf. 23,34.43.

[94] Brown, *Messiah* 1; 272.

[95] Squires, *Plan* 183.

The arrest; Luke 22,52-53

The Lucan presentation of the arrest fits into the lean pattern developed in the third gospel. In two of the three passion predictions, the Lucan Jesus does not say that he will be delivered into the hands of scribes.[96] Mark and Matthew, on the other hand, show Jesus specifying the scribes for two of the three predictions.[97] When these predictions are read in parallel, it becomes apparent that in his third prediction, Luke departs from Mark and Matthew in specifying that Jesus will be turned over *only* to the Gentiles. It seems, then, that at 18,31-32, Luke wishes to harmonize the account with what is portrayed in his PN, but for some reason, perhaps negligence, he did not do it for the first prediction (9,22). This harmonization is also continued in Judas' consultation with the chief priests and officers (22,4).[98]

The Lucan attention to historical detail is evident with the inclusion of the temple police among those arresting Jesus.[99] Jesus is not alone on the Mount of Olives; his disciples are with him. To describe the arrest of one as popular as he by only "chief priest, scribes, and elders" as in Mark (14,43) and Matthew (26,47), stretches the imagination; a police force is more formidable.

Neyrey believes that the role of the devil (4,13), Satan (22,3.31), and darkness (22,53) form a frame within the Lucan narrative.[100] What is even more noteworthy is how Luke differentiates among these terms. Outside the desert temptation (4,2-3.5-6.13), διάβολος has only three more occurrences in L-A.[101] Satan, on the other hand, instances seven times in L-A, and takes on a tone more menacing than the generic "devil".[102] The arrest ushers in the power of darkness which will hold sway until the resurrection.[103] Satan is the force behind the death of Jesus (22,3.53).[104]

---

[96] Luke 9,43b-44, hands of men; 18,31-32, to the Gentiles; but cf. 9,22, elders, chief priests, and scribes.

[97] Mark 8,31 and Matt 16,21, elders, chief priests, and scribes; Mark 10,33 and Matt 20,18-19, chief priest, scribes, and Gentiles; Mark 9,31 and Matt 17,22, the hands of men (so also Luke 9,44).

[98] Although in 22,4 στρατηγός is not further modified by τοῦ ἱεροῦ as it is in 22,52. But n.b. Luke 22,2 where the chief priests and scribes seek to put him to death.

[99] But cf. Mark 14,43 and John 18,3.

[100] Neyrey, *Passion* 31; cf. also below, Chapter Two. There is also an analogy between darkness/light and Satan/God in Acts 26,18.

[101] The parable of the sower and the seed, Luke 8,12; Peter's summary of Jesus' life Acts, 10,38; and Paul's castigation of Elymas, Acts 13,10.

[102] In addition to the events leading to the passion (22,3.31) which Neyrey demontrates (*Passion* 31), Satan also occurs at Jesus' exclamation to the seventy (Luke 10,18), in the Beelzebul controversy (Luke 11,18), the healing of a crippled woman on the Sabbath (Luke 13,16), the episode of Ananias and Sapphira (Acts 5,3), and in Paul's description of his conversion (Acts 26,18).

Neyrey's findings coincide with those of Fitzmyer who comments that there are three elements to the arrest episode: Jesus' reaction to his captors and the kiss, Jesus' response to the one taking up the sword, and Jesus' serene demeanor, an element which relates the present evil to the Father's salvific plan.[105] *Likewise, Brown sees expressed in this verse both the hour of Jesus as he begins to hand over his spirit to the Father as well as the hour of Satan who is responsible for his death.*[106]

Neyrey maintains that Satan's return at the opportune time includes Jesus' crucifixion.[107] *Can the chief priests, captains of the temple, and elders be considered agents of Satan? Tiede notes that they are given their "grim due" by acknowledging their alliance with the powers of darkness.*[108] *Crump calls the reference to the "power of darkness" the "final assault by Satan's forces".*[109] *For this reason Karris is wrong in holding vv 47-53 as those which "describe Jesus on the brink of his passion".*[110] *The passion begins at the agony (22,39-46), a fact substantiated by Boismard's source analysis. Boismard holds that instead of a Matthean or Marcan tradition as the basis for the Lucan agony and arrest scene, there are actually two traditions: a single Matthean-Marcan tradition, which could have been Matthean in origin, and a Lucan tradition which has some contacts with John.*[111] *For the arrest, the Marcan-Lucan redactor, depending on a Matthean tradition, inserted the account in the Marcan narrative.*[112]

---

[103] The effects of the resurrection are manifest in Luke's use of Satan and devil. "Satan" shows only twice in Acts (5,3; 26,18) but five times in Luke (10,18; 11,18; 13,16; 22,3.31). Likewise, "devil" appears two times in Acts (10,38; 13,10) but has six occurrences in Luke (4,2-3.5-6.13; 8,12).

[104] Neyrey, *Passion* 178.

[105] Fitzmyer, *Luke* 2; 1449.

[106] Brown, *Messiah* 1; 293.

[107] Neyrey, *Passion* 180.

[108] Tiede, *Prophecy* 110.

[109] Crump, *Jesus* 162.

[110] Karris, *Artist* 36.

[111] Boismard, *Marc* 206-8. For example, both Luke 22,50 and John 18,10 specify the right ear as the one which the high priest's slave severs (*Marc* 208).

[112] Boismard, *Marc* 207. In addition to Luke 22,50 and John 18,10, for the Lucan tradition's link with John, cf. Luke 22,49 and John 18,4 (*Marc* 208).

Peter's denial; Luke 22,55-62

    Peter's denial itself provides a transition from the arrest (22,47-54a) to the inquiry on the next morning (22,66-71). The intervening mockery (22,63-65), including the charge of blasphemy, serves to intensify the drama. Mark (14,66-72) and Matthew (26,69-75), however, feature an anticlimactic denial after the council's interrogation (Mark 14,53-65; Matt 26,57-68).

    The Lord's glance at Peter at the denial (22,61) is not only a dramatic flourish but is also connected to the role of the disciples in the Lucan PN. The gaze constitutes the last communication of Jesus to a disciple until the resurrection; hereafter, disciples follow him but stand off from afar. Indeed, Peter is both the last of the apostles mentioned before the death (22,61) and the first one cited in the resurrection account (24,12).

    Jesus casts a "knowing glance" at Peter, an action with such import that it causes Peter to go out and weep bitterly. The glance at Peter etches the importance of this scene in the narrative; it is personal betrayal.[113] Peter's reaction (22,62) is the first of three (23,27.48) where people, wanting to remain faithful, are overcome by circumstances beyond their control. They represent Luke's "tragic vision" in depicting those who recognize the consequences of their participation once it is too late.[114] The proof of Peter's faith lies, however, in his prompt conversion or repentance following Jesus' glance.[115] Peter's denial, or particularly his reaction to the Lord's glance, also has a hortative function; it admonishes vigilance to future disciples.[116]

    Luke is the only synoptic account which has an order of denial, mockery, and Sanhedrin inquiry. The others show the reverse: trial, mockery, denial; John relates the denial at two different points[117] while not recording a mockery.[118] The third gospel reads a vocative addressed to the accuser in all three denials,[119] and, unlike the other synoptics, Peter denies knowing Jesus in the first denial.[120]

---

[113] Tannehill, *Narrative* 265.

[114] Tiede, *Prophecy* 104-5.

[115] Schneider, *Passion* 81-2.

[116] Gerhard Schneider, *Verleugnung, Verspottung und Verhör Jesu* (München: Kösel-Verlag, 1969) 171.

[117] Cf. John 18,12-14, Jesus bound; vv 15-18, denial; vv 19-24, Sanhedrin trial; vv 25-27, denial.

[118] Cf. Matt 26,57-75; Mark 14,53-72; John 18,13-28 but note vv 22-23.

[119] 22,57 γύναι; 22,58.60 ἄνθρωπε.

[120] Luke 22,57 but cf. John 18,17.

In the second and third denials, Luke switches the accuser from a woman to a man (vv 58.59). This leads Brown to suggest that Luke wishes to make Peter's stance "legally more grave".[121] On the other hand, whereas the other two synoptics have the successive denials mount in intensity,[122] Luke does not.

Brown sees the Lucan version as an attempt to modify Mark's harshness.[123] *By having Jesus present in the courtyard with Peter instead of having an indoor/upstairs setting for Jesus countered by an outdoor/downstairs one for Peter, Brown notes that Luke has fashioned a more dramatic scene.*[124] *Because of its unanimity among the gospels, the three-fold denial, according to Fitzmyer, is probably the "one piece of historical truth" in the PN.*[125]

The mockery; Luke 22,63-65

The mockery scene in Luke, when compared to the parallel accounts,[126] features several transpositions. First, it takes place before the inquiry. It occurs in the courtyard of the high priest and is perpetrated by the "men who were holding" Jesus.[127] In keeping with his distaste for superfluity, Luke does not include spitting or slapping in this scene. Brown believes that these were extraneous to the mocking game which consisted of covering Jesus, beating him, and taunting him with "Prophesy!"[128] This removes the allusions to the suffering servant of Isaiah 50,6, but Brown cautiously suggests that Luke supplies the reference in Acts 8,26-39 where the Ethiopian eunuch reads Isaiah 53,7-8.[129]

Brown's understanding seems plausible, but that Luke may have wished to portray another quality in Jesus' passion has better claim for this abbreviated scene. Jesus is resolute and steadfast, an ideal martyr, but Peter, in the previous scene, capitulated. This is a flashback to the agony on the Mount of Olives where Jesus told the disciples to pray in order not to enter temptation.

---

[121] Brown, *Messiah* 1; 602.

[122] Both Matt and Mark have Peter physically distancing himself from Jesus as well as swearing and cursing (Matt 26,71.74; Mark 14,68.71).

[123] Brown, *Messiah* 1; 605.

[124] Brown, *Messiah* 1; 622.

[125] Fitzmyer, *Luke* 2; 1459.

[126] Mark 14,64-65; Matt 26,67-68; but cf. John 18,22-23.

[127] Fitzmyer states that those holding Jesus are not the Jewish authorities but their underlings (*Luke* 2; 1461), yet Brown counters that there is no proof of such and that this is a seam in Luke's redaction (Brown, *Messiah* 1; 582).

[128] Brown, *Messiah* 1; 583-4.

[129] Brown, *Messiah* 1; 584.

Lagrange notes the extremely rare example of the verb συνέχω (v 63) used for "to imprison";[130] it has a like meaning in 1 Macc 13,15. This reference substantiates Brown's thesis that the Lucan PN portrays Jesus as a prophet and martyr.[131]

Jesus' role as prophet is the element which Neyrey sees highlighted here.[132] Neyrey observes a prophet theme which goes through the gospel beginning at Nazareth (4,24-29) and ending at the mockery when Jesus is taunted to prophesy (22,64).[133] In between these two pericopes are passages demonstrating Israel's rejection of God's prophet.[134] As for the placement of the mockery here, Neyrey considers it a parallel to the Herod scene (23,11).[135] Schneider, however, concentrates on the act itself. Such suffering as displayed in the mockery is a necessity; it attacks Jesus as Messiah without contradicting Christian faith in the Messiah.[136]

Setting this scene into its immediate context, particularly with the trial that follows, produces a steady dramatic progression. Jesus is cited as being a prophet and often compared to one throughout the Lucan gospel.[137] He is mocked as a prophet by men who do not realize that minutes before their taunt, Peter denied him, a fact which Jesus had prophesied. In the following scene the Sanhedrin demand whether Jesus is the Messiah and the Son of God. In this ascending portrayal of disbelief, Jesus' enemies ironically grow closer to the truth.[138]

---

[130] Lagrange, *Luc* 570.

[131] Brown, *Messiah* 1; 31. Cf also 4 Macc 6,6.11; 7,8.

[132] Neyrey, *Passion* 70.

[133] προφήτης occurs 30 times in Luke (31 with variant at 7,28) and 30 times in Acts (*VKGNT* 1/2; 1183-4). Of these προφήτης refers to Jesus at Luke 4,24; 7,16.39; 9,19; 13,33 and Acts 3,22.23; 7,37.52.

[134] Cf. Luke 6,22-23; 11,47-51; 13,33-34; Acts 7,51-52. Neyrey also considers Luke 20,10-15 to fall into the same category (*Passion* 70).

[135] Neyrey, *Passion* 78.

[136] Schneider, *Verleugnung* 171-2.

[137] Cf. 4,24.27; 7,16.39; 9,8.19; 13,33-34; 24,19 (*VKGNT* 1/2 1183-4).

[138] Brown, *Messiah* 1; 584-5.

The interrogation;[139] *Luke 22,66-71*

Because Luke does not have the testimony of witnesses, these proceedings cannot be called a trial. In light of Luke 24,20 and Acts 13,27-28, however, it is obvious that a trial was the Lucan interpretation of the event. Luke has departed from the legal format in order to focus the blame on the elders, chief priests, and scribes; they officiated at a travesty of justice, a fact which underscores Jesus' innocence.

Luke places scenes where they chronologically fit and make sense. There is a daytime interrogation instead of a Marcan/Matthean nighttime one (14,53-65; 26,57-68) which, as Brown indicates, matches the pattern in Acts 4,3.5 where Peter and John are held through the night until the next morning.[140] A striking difference between Luke and the other two synoptics is the realized eschatology evident in v 69, the coming Son of Man (ἀπὸ τοῦ νῦν).[141]

Function and interpretation

That the Lucan description of the interrogation does not include witnesses who falsely testify that Jesus had spoken against the temple sanctuary is a difference between Luke and the other synoptics. Brown holds that Luke shifted the false witnesses from the PN to the accusations against Stephen (Acts 6,12-14), and that Luke's theological outlook and desire for order necessitated the switch.[142] Luke is clarifying that Jesus was not against the temple, though he did warn about divine judgment even if he would not usher it in.[143] Placing the accusation in Acts highlights the temple destruction at a time after it had taken place and depicts its destruction as punishment for the persecution of Peter, Stephen, and Paul.[144]

Brown's explanation reads too much into the text. Luke may have transferred the false witnesses to Acts where it makes chronological sense *vis-à-*

---

[139] Neyrey (*Passion* 71) and Brown (*Messiah* 1; 389 n 142) both read a trial into the Lucan version of the Sanhedrin episode. Since there is no sentence in Luke, however, I would prefer to call the proceedings an interrogation.

[140] Brown, *Messiah* 1; 423. Whether Luke modifies Mark 15,1 to clarify that there was a single morning session, or whether he believes Mark refers to two sessions of Sanhedrin (14,55; 15,1) is unclear (*Messiah* 1; 629-32). Fitzmyer states that Luke's account of the trial is most likely the better recollection of when the interrogation took place, in the morning (*Luke* 2; 1456).

[141] Cf. Mark 14,62 with ὁράω in the future tense and especially Matt 26,64 where the future tense of ὁράω is coupled with the adverbial phrase ἀπ' ἄρτι.

[142] Brown, *Messiah* 1; 436.

[143] Luke 13,35; 19,44; 23,28-31. In Luke, references to Jerusalem are related thematically to the temple. Cf. below, Chapter Five.

[144] Brown, *Messiah* 1; 436-7.

vis the historical destruction, but Luke is ambivalent in his treatment of the temple, and he does not always interpret temple destruction as punishment either for Christ's death or for the persecution of disciples.[145]

There are four thematic points which arise in this scene.[146] First, Jesus bears witness to God's prophet as the Christ, Son of God, and Son of Man, hence serving as a model to the apostles in Acts; second, like all Israel's prophets, he is rejected; thus third, Jesus' trial is a trial of Israel itself; fourth, Jesus predicts his vindication (22,69), a prophecy fulfilled in his resurrection.[147]

Neyrey sees a parallel between Jesus' trial and those of Paul in Acts.[148] Tyson notes the parallel as well, but he also indicates the differences, i.e., Paul's vigorous self-defense against his accusers, support for him from the Pharisees, his rescue by the Roman tribune, the authority which also summons the Sanhedrin.[149]

Tannehill adds that the appearance of the "council of elders" (22,66) suggests that this body is acting on behalf of the people.[150]

According to Tyson, the function of 22,66-71 is based on its position in the narrative as a whole; it is the fulfillment of what had been anticipated in the passion predictions (9,22.44; 17,25; 18,31-34).[151] The passion predictions are only partially fulfilled in the interrogation pericope, however. Particularly with reference to 18,33-34, Jesus has not yet been scourged or killed, nor obviously has he risen. On this basis, the interrogation, in addition to fulfilling previous predictions, is also a prediction of future glorification; it recalls what has been predicted previously and thus, reminds the listener of what is still to come.

In the Sanhedrin proceeding, the gospels of Matthew (26,62), Mark (14,60), and John (18,19) have the high priest (= Caiaphas; John 18,13) leading the interrogation, whereas in Luke there is no such specification. This circumstance leads Brown to suggest that the character of the high priest too has been transferred to the Stephen trial (Acts 6,9-7,1ff).[152] Luke, unlike the other

---

[145] In Stephen's speech (Acts 7,2-53), however, Luke does imply such a connection, especially when compared with Ezek 20. For a discussion on the temple, cf. below, Chapter Five.

[146] Neyrey, *Passion* 75.

[147] Neyrey, *Passion* 75.

[148] Neyrey, *Passion* 104-5.

[149] Tyson, *Death* 125.

[150] Tannehill, *Narrative* 164.

[151] Tyson, *Death* 128.

[152] Brown, *Messiah* 1; 463.

synoptics, also divides the titles in the council's accusations against Jesus, "If you are the Messiah," (22,67) and "Are you, then, the Son of God?" (22,70).[153] Brown reasons that the combined title in Mark/Matt reflects Christian awareness in the last third of the first century when "Messiah" was seen as the divine Son of God.[154] Luke shares this belief (Acts 9,20.22), but his rendition shows an historicizing touch by noting the distinction between "Messiah" as understood by the Jews and "Son of God" as comprehended by Christians.[155] This distinction is something which Luke maintains in several places in the third gospel.[156] If Jesus were to answer affirmatively to the question (v 67) his accusers would have ground to lay political charges.[157]

Jesus' response to these questions in 22,67-68 shifts him from being defendant to judge, a move which Brown believes is closer to Johannine thought, and which continues the pattern of the Lucan Jesus as one not very cooperative with hostile authorities and their questions.[158] Moreover, the rapport which Brown sees between Luke's presentation and Johannine thought is undergirded by the literary contacts this Lucan scene shares with John 10,22-39, as Boismard and Lamouille illustrate.[159]

The Lucan presentation of the questions and response are more logical than Mark's. The answer in vv 67-68 is vague and further clarification is needed in v 69, a reversal of the Marcan and Matthean order.[160] Jesus' response to the question on divine sonship, like Mark 14,62 but unlike Matt 26,64, is unambiguous. The title "Son of God" is, according to Brown, the conclusion of the previous verse where Jesus is identified as the "Son of Man".[161]

---

[153] Cf. Mark 14,61; Matt 26,63b.

[154] Brown, *Messiah* 1; 471. Not to be missed is the realized eschatology depicted in Luke 22,69 *versus* the imminent one portrayed in the other two synoptics.

[155] Brown, *Messiah* 1; 471.

[156] Cf. 3,15-16.22; 9,20.35.

[157] In the earliest stage of the gospel tradition, the question would have had a political sense, but in the last stage of formation Luke wishes to give the question a deeper, christological nuance (Fitzmyer, *Luke* 2; 1466-7).

[158] Cf. Luke 20,1-8.20-26.27-40. In addition, Luke sees Jesus' trial in relation to the trials of the Christians in Acts (cf. 7,51-53; 26,1-29); the textual variation in 22,68 ($\mu o\iota$ $\mathring{\eta}$ $\alpha\pi o\lambda\upsilon\sigma\eta\tau\varepsilon$ A D W Δ Ψ 0233 f^{13} *et al.*) increases the sense of Jesus as judge (Brown, *Messiah* 1; 487).

[159] Cf. Luke 22,67//John 10,24-25a; Luke 22,70//John 10,36; Luke 22,71//John 10,25b; in addition, n.b. the echo between Luke 22,71b and John 10,33 (M.É. Boismard, O.P. and A. Lamouille, *Synopsis Graeca Quattuor Evangeliorum* [Leuven: Peeters, 1986] 280-1).

[160] Cf. Mark 14,61b and Matt 26,63b with Luke 22,67a.70 Brown notes that in Mark the affirmative response precedes the Son of Man clarification (*Messiah* 1; 488).

That Luke has the question voiced by the whole Sanhedrin together makes the interrogation a confession and forms an inclusion with 1,32 where the angel announces to Mary that her child will be called the "Son of the Most High". Here, as Brown notes, the last words by the Sanhedrin identify Jesus as the Son of God as well; in addition, Luke begins and ends the gospel in Jerusalem, thus within the confines of Judaism.[162]

When the Sanhedrin ask in v 70a, "Are you, then, the Son of God?" they have, as Brown describes, reached the conclusion Jesus intended them to reach by his statement about the Son of Man (v 69). Hence, Jesus' response in v 70b is not enigmatic but is an affirmation.[163] Luke displays a dramatic hand by separating the question in v 67 from the one on divine sonship (v 70).[164]

The charge of blasphemy, as Brown relates, most probably arose from the early Christian period when Jews found Christian proclamation about Christ to be blasphemous; the evangelists were signaling to their readers what Jews, who did not believe in Jesus during his ministry, probably thought.[165] The Sanhedrin in v 71 does not pass a sentence of death, a departure from Mark 14,63-64 and Matt 26,65-66. Even though the Romans executed Jesus, demonstrating that the Sanhedrin condemned him on *religious* grounds was more important to Luke, and indeed to the other evangelists as well.[166] I stand with Schneider who proposes a similar understanding. With the interrogation by the Sanhedrin, Luke sketches a Christology of *Heilsgeschichte*.[167] Thus the central theme of the PN: Jesus is the Messiah and Son of God.

Jesus before Jewish and Roman political rulers; Luke 23,1-25

Brown, while stressing the overall unity of Luke 23,1-25, divides the pericope into three segments (23,1-5; 23,6-12; 23,13-25).[168] Fitzmyer sees four

---

[161] Brown, *Messiah* 1; 493. Brown also draws attention to Mark 15,39 and Matt 27,54 where the centurion affirms Jesus' divine sonship while in Luke 23,47 the reading shows the officer attesting to Jesus' innocence (*Messiah* 1; 493). With δίκαιος (Luke 23,47) the centurion is noting Jesus' innocence as well as affirming his divine sonship. Cf. below, Chapter Five.

[162] Brown, *Messiah* 1; 493.

[163] Brown, *Messiah* 1; 506. The title "Son of God" intensifies the title "Christ" (Schneider, *Verleugnung* 174).

[164] Fitzmyer notes the irony of the Sanhedrin; their question states what Jesus is implying yet they deny the truth of his reply, that he is the Son of God (*Luke* 2; 1468).

[165] Brown, *Messiah* 1; 526.

[166] Brown, *Messiah* 1; 530.

[167] Schneider, *Verleugnung* 173.

[168] Brown, *Messiah* 1; 757.

sections (23,1-5; 23,6-12; 23,13-16; 23,18-25).[169] Büchele, basing the trial on the necessity of three witnesses to effect a death sentence (Deut 17,6-7; 19,15),[170] forms an overarching tripartite structure for this chapter (23,1-25; 23,26-49; 23,50-56). Each of these sections is then divided into three with a further tripartite division of those three.[171] This theory is forced, especially since the Jewish Sanhedrin in Luke does not condemn Jesus to death; the Roman Pilate does, and he would not care about the particulars of Jewish law. In any case, for the trial, Büchele shows the same divisions as Brown (23,1-5; 23,6-12; 23,13-25). Neyrey delimits four Lucan trials (22,66-71; 23,1-5; 23,6-12; 23,13-25).[172] I hold with Brown and divide the trial into three sections (23,1-5; 23,6-12; 23,13-25) while stressing the overall unity of 23,1-25.

In the transitional first verse, Luke does not show Jesus bound.[173] I disagree with Brown who explains that the evangelist does not wish to narrate such an indignity.[174] Rather, Luke wishes to stress Christ's innocence, a point which is underscored throughout the PN and a theme which a shackled Jesus would counter.

Pilate's initial question to Jesus seems to have been directly copied from Mark into the Lucan PN (Luke 23,3; Mark 15,2),[175] "Are you the King of the Jews?"[176] Luke has amplified the scene in the preceding verse by displaying the elders, chief priests, and scribes leveling the accusation that Jesus was perverting the nation, forbidding the people to pay taxes, and calling himself a king (Luke 23,2).[177]

Two explanations exist for the Lucan elaboration. First, in addition to setting the background for the following two accusations, to say that Jesus was

---

[169] Fitzmyer, *Luke* 2; 1471.1478.1483.1486.

[170] Büchele, *Tod* 71-2.

[171] Büchele, *Tod* 73.

[172] Neyrey, *Passion* 69.98. Brown notes that the last three sections each feature Pilate who passes sentence; there is nothing to distinguish them as separate trials (*Messiah* 1; 757).

[173] Cf. Mark 15,1; Matt 27,2; but John 18,28.

[174] Brown, *Messiah* 1; 634.

[175] Although source questions are not addressed in this chapter, nb Boismard who sees two different traditions in this pericope, Matt/Mark and Luke/John; the Marcan account results from the Marcan-Lucan redactor's editing which joined the Matthean version to proto-Mark (*Marc* 222).

[176] Neyrey notes that the question-answer pattern (23,1-5) is similar to that in the Sanhedrin interrogation (22,67-70); Christ is the example of Christian witnessing (*Passion* 76-7).

[177] Cf. Mark 15,1ff; Matt 27,11ff.

perverting the nation is a self-serving statement on behalf of the accusers; they place themselves on the side of the ruling authorities. Second, with the last two charges, the accusers try to show Jesus as a rival claimant for allegiance and thus a true revolutionary bent on total rebellion against Rome. This accusation gains particular import with Pilate's threefold declaration of Jesus' innocence (23,4.13-16.22b). Taken together, charges amounting to treason and Pilate's acquittal on those same charges bespeak an apologetic dimension to this Lucan addition.[178] In all likelihood, detractors of the early Christians had the same misunderstanding about Jesus, and, by extension, leveled similar accusations against the nascent community; Luke 23,2 is the evangelist's attempt to address these same charges. The Pilate/Jesus interchange, as Brown notes, also evidences the Christian tradition concerning the issue of Jesus' identity as expressed first, with Jesus before the Jewish authorities (22,67-71) and now with Jesus before the Roman authority (Luke 23,1-5).[179]

There is one overall charge against Jesus based on the verb διαστρέφω, *make crooked, pervert, mislead someone*[180] which is divided into two specific charges.[181] The only accusation which concerns Pilate, however, is the one on kingship, a logical response by the governor of the occupying power. Though Pilate never finds Jesus guilty of this charge, it is the one which is affixed atop the cross.

Jesus before Herod; Luke 23,6-12

The interrogation by Herod (23,6-12) has no parallel in any of the other passion narratives. It is difficult to discern whether a hearing before Herod actually took place, but the Lucan treatment of Herod Antipas throughout the third gospel and Acts suggests that the description of the trial before the Tetrarch is a creation of the third evangelist even if it is possible that it had been an actual event.[182] In addition, the *Gos. Pet.* also states that Herod was involved in the

---

[178] Brown illustrates that in first century Palestine, a charge that Jesus was claiming the title "King of the Jews" could be interpreted by the Romans as an attempt to re-establish the Hasmonean dynasty (*Messiah* 1; 731).

[179] Brown, *Messiah* 1; 730. Brown also compares the charge against Jesus in 23,2 to that of *overturning the world* levelled against Paul in Acts 17,6-7 (*Messiah* 1; 738). In the four components making up Jesus' trial, Sanhedrin, Roman governor, Herod, Roman governor again, Tyson sees an inexact parallel to Paul's various trials in Acts 23-26 (Tyson, *Death* 115).

[180] BAGD 189.

[181] Luke 23,2 but cf. 23,5.14; also Brown, *Messiah* 1; 738-41.

[182] Brown draws attention to Luke 21,12 where Jesus issues the warning about facing kings and governors and suggests that here Luke is following through on the prediction (*Messiah* 1; 764), so also Neyrey (*Passion* 79-80). This argument can probably be sustained despite the fact that Herod Antipas was never a king, an historical detail to which Luke would have been sensitive. But n.b. the way Luke rearranges the particulars of secular rulers in the nativity narrative (2,1-3).

legal proceedings.[183] Although I hold that the final redaction of the *Gos. Pet.*
postdates the canonical gospels,[184] the possibility cannot be completely
discounted that the existence of the account in this apocryphal work substantiates
the historicity of the event.

Luke gives special attention to Herod. Upon hearing about Jesus, Herod
is puzzled; he had John beheaded and obviously felt that, with this course of
action, the preaching and miracles in his kingdom would cease (9,7-8). Luke
alone mentions that the Tetrarch wanted to see Jesus (9,9),[185] and Luke is the
sole synoptic not to record Herod's infamous birthday dinner.[186] Only Luke lists
the rulers, including Herod, in the narration of Jesus' baptism; this is prefaced by
a summary of John's ministry around the Jordan (3,1ff). Furthermore, only the
third evangelist shows the Pharisees warning Jesus of Herod's intention to kill
him (13,31).[187] This last point does not harmonize with anything in the other
two synoptics where the Pharisees and the Herodians are co-conspirators against
Jesus.[188] In Acts, however, Peter and John state that both Pilate and Herod had
militated against Jesus (4,27); Boismard also observes that the *Gos. Pet.* 1-3
portrays the collusion between Herod, Pilate, and the people as well,[189] thereby
suggesting a tradition common to both Luke and *Gos. Pet.*[190]

What then is Luke saying with the addition of the Herod inquiry? Three
interconnected points surface. First, it appears that Luke is trying to connect the
death of Jesus with that of John the Baptist, as he has connected their births.[191]
Second, on this basis, the trial before Herod forms a literary and thus theological
inclusio. Third, the Herod addition (23,6-12) parallels Paul's two-fold hearings
before the Roman Festus and the Jewish Herod Agrippa (Acts 25,13-26,32).[192] I
address these points in order.

---

[183] *Gospel of Peter* 1-2.

[184] Cf. below, Chapter Two.

[185] Cf. Matt 14,1-2; Mark 6,14-16.

[186] Cf. Matt 14,3-12; Mark 6,17-29.

[187] On this basis, I cannot see how Crump can say that Herod's interest in
Jesus is primarily motivated by a desire to witness some miracle (Crump, *Jesus*
29). Not to be discounted, however, is the view that the Pharisees, acting
duplicitously, concocted the warning to debilitate Jesus' mission. Cf. Tiede,
Prophecy 71ff.

[188] Cf. Matt 22,16; Mark 3,6; 12,13.

[189] Boismard, *Graeca* 378 n.

[190] But cf. below, Chapter Four, "Hypothesis".

[191] The relations between Jesus and John -- and no doubt between their
respective disciples -- were matters of concern in the early church.

[192] Brown holds that this parallel in Acts "militates against" considering the
Herod interrogation as a trial separate from Pilate's (*Messiah* 1; 757). Brown

First, having killed the Baptist, and hearing reports about Jesus, Herod also wants to see Jesus (9,7-9). This wish to see him is soon transformed into a desire to kill him (13,31ff. Luke later connects these two wishes through Peter and John's prayer (Acts 4,24-28) where the apostles blame both Herod and Pilate for Jesus' death even though in the Herod pericope (Luke 23,6-12) Herod submits Jesus only to ridicule and finds him innocent of any crime (23,15). Hence, Luke develops the idea that whatever John had undergone, so also Jesus.

Second, Jesus' hearing at Herod's court forms an *inclusio* with the beginning of his public ministry. Luke cites Herod as the Tetrarch in the area John was preaching and where Jesus was baptized (3,1.22); after John's imprisonment, Jesus begins his work in Galilee, an area controlled by Herod (4,14). Hence, Jesus' ministry comes to an end by facing that same political ruler under whom it began.

Third, the Pilate and Herod inquiries in the gospel form a double trial; this is paralleled later in the Lucan corpus (Acts 25,13-26,32) where Festus presents Paul to Agrippa.[193] With the Roman governor Festus setting Paul before King Agrippa, Luke writes a parallel account to Pilate's sending Jesus to Herod. Both examples involve a Gentile and Jewish authority. In the gospel these two authorities judge the founder of the Way; in the Acts, one of its chief proponents. In this parallel, Luke fuses two halves of the power structure, the Roman empire and the Jewish state, albeit the latter is a client of the former.[194]

That this Lucan pericope shows continuity between John and Jesus, that it forms a literary and theological *inclusio*, and that it brings together two cultures of the intertestamental world would lead to the conclusion that Luke 23,6-12 can be attributed to the creativity of the third evangelist.

There is ground, however, for considering the Herod pericope as Luke's dramatization of an historical fact. Pilate's decision to send Jesus to Herod may be based on the Roman *anakrisis* whereby Roman provincial officials delegated investigations to local authorities. It would have been in Pilate's best interest to have Herod involved in this process. Luke 13,1 notes Pilate's mingling

---

continues that Luke has used Paul's trial as the model in which to form the trial of Jesus; the Jesus trial then provides a paradigm for early Christians to follow when they stand before a Roman magistrate (Brown, *Messiah* 1; 759). Brown may be forcing the parallel. A notable difference between Jesus' and Paul's trial is that in the gospel, Jesus is sent to Herod; in Acts, the Tetrarch comes to Festus. More importantly, Paul is vociferous in his defense; Jesus is not.

[193] Brown believes that this structure of Paul's trial influenced the Lucan presentation of Jesus' trial, though historically Luke may have used a set Roman pattern on both (*Messiah* 1; 756). In a like vein, Neyrey sees parallels between Jesus' trial and that of Peter and John (Acts 4,3-22). As such, the trial in Acts is, Neyrey believes, a continuation of the trial of Jesus and thus, also that of Israel (*Passion* 89).

[194] Brown raises the point that 23,7 shows the word ἐξουσία in speaking about Herod's authority or jurisdiction, the same term used at 4,6 [temptation] and at 22,53 [arrest] (Brown, *Messiah* 1; 765). A diabolical underlay and thus a theological point cannot be discounted in this pericope.

Galileans' blood with their sacrifices; Galilee was Herodian territory, so presumably the Galileans were in Jerusalem for a feast. Pilate's deference to Herod, with the background of the Galilean sacrifice, could have been a reconciliatory, diplomatic gesture toward the Tetrarch.[195] Luke 23,12 indicates that it seems to have worked, and this was good for Pilate; the Herodian princes had good relations with the Roman imperial family.[196] Herod would benefit from Pilate's actions as well. Wanting to put Jesus to death but fearing the reaction of the people, to have Pilate dispatch Jesus for him was a finely-tuned political act.[197]

In this Herod pericope (23,11), for the taunting in the other gospels in which the Roman soldiers mock Jesus after Pilate has him scourged, but before he is led out to be crucified,[198] Luke substitutes a mocking by the Tetrarch's soldiers. Luke transposes the Roman soldiers, in an act of ridiculing Jesus, to the cross (23,36).

Brown sees this mockery as based on Jesus' prediction, "...the Son of Man...will be handed over to the Gentiles" (18,32),[199] but whether Herod and his men can strictly be considered Gentiles is a debatable point. Karris holds that there are two themes in the Herod scene, that of the innocently suffering righteous one, and that of God's justice.[200]

Crump tries to draw a parallel between Peter's confession (9,18ff) and this inquiry before Herod. Referring to Herod's desire to see Jesus (9,9), Crump posits that Peter can confess Jesus as the Christ because the apostle prays with him. Herod, on the other hand, does not pray and therefore cannot recognize Jesus' divinity. This is a plausible interpretation, but Crump's focus is too narrow. He maintains that this was Luke's only concern in writing the pericope; thus other parallels with trial scenes in Acts (e.g. 25,13-26,32) have no theological purpose other than increasing the understanding of the "structure".[201]

The inquiry before Herod is a Lucan addition which necessitated a transposition of material. On a stylistic basis, to have Roman soldiers ridicule

---

[195] Brown, *Messiah* 1; 767.

[196] Josephus, *J War* 1,20,4 (LCL 2; 186-9.398-400).

[197] Streeter, "Trial" 230. This explanation is superior to Tyson's who, viewing this solely from a narrative perspective, holds that the scene exhibits Herod's disassociating himself from the chief priests, Jesus' major opponents (*Death* 135).

[198] Cf. Mark 15,15-20a; Matt 27,26-31a; John 19,2-3.

[199] Brown, *Messiah* 1; 773.

[200] Karris, *Artist* 88.

[201] Crump, *Jesus* 30.

Jesus so close to the Herod pericope would be cumbersome. One of Luke's intentions with the interrogation by Herod is to have actions of the Roman empire paralleled by those of its Jewish client. Although the high priest had great political influence, he was a religious figure, hence the mockery which takes place in his house (22,63-65) does not fit the parallel between the Roman empire and the Herodian rulers. Luke resolved the dilemma between style and historic probability by substituting Herod's mockery (23,11) for that of Pilate's Roman soldiers (Mark 15,16-20a). Luke then transposed the historically plausible taunt by Roman soldiers to 23,36-37. Hence, Luke has three mockery scenes, one by the high priest's guards (22,63-65), a second by Herod's soldiers (23,11), and a third by the Roman soldiers at the cross (23,36-37).[202]

I disagree with Brown who sees the reconciliation between Herod and Pilate expressed at the close of this scene (23,12) as an occasion of grace which Jesus provides for the Tetrarch and Governor, and who views it as part of the forgiveness theme running through the whole PN.[203] More accurate are Tyson who reads it only as a "gratuitous" comment,[204] and Tannehill, who considers it as a Lucan way of showing that both Herod and Pilate were part of an "evil alliance".[205] The irony is not lost; these two ruthless leaders can only cement their friendship by condemning an innocent man.

The resolution of the trial; Luke 23,13-25

In the Lucan PN Pilate declares Jesus' innocence three times (23,4.13-16.22ff); there is no such statement in either Mark or Matthew.[206] What Mark offers instead is a rather nervous Roman official who shunts between Jesus and the crowd. The Marcan and Matthean Pilate wonders (15,5; 27,14), he questions (15,9ff; Matt 27,17), and he finally grants (15,15; 27,26). The Lucan presentation, on the other hand, shows Pilate as a decisive, although crafty, individual. When Jesus replies to his first question by answering, "You have said so," Pilate declares that he finds no crime in him (23,4). Thus, what in Mark and Matthew is cause for Pilate's wondering becomes in Luke a declaration of innocence. Comparing the Lucan account of the trial before Pilate with the other two synoptics, Green also calls attention to the fact that at 23,4 Luke chooses to bypass an opportunity to place the proceedings within the context of the Isaian

---

[202] Green, not seeing Luke's transposition and rewriting of material, believes that Luke omits the mockery scene after Pilate's condemnation because the evangelist wishes to accent the agency of the Jewish leaders in Jesus' execution while downplaying Roman responsibility in it (*Death* 86).

[203] Brown, *Messiah* 1; 778. So also Karris (*Artist* 85).

[204] Tyson, *Death* 135.

[205] Tannehill, *Narrative* 197 n 43.

[206] But cf. John 18,38; 19,4.6b.

Suffering Servant, "...yet he did not open his mouth" (Isa 53,7).[207] Important to note is that Pilate's two declarations of innocence (vv 4.13-16) cement the Herod pericope and the resolution of the trial into a single, literary entity.

Luke 23,16

While Mark 15,15 and Matt 27,26 state that Jesus was scourged, φραγελλόω, in the Lucan version, Pilate simply says twice (23,16.22) that he will chastise, παιδεύω, Jesus and release him. Chastisement is not the same as the flogging, as Brown also notes.[208] There is no word in Luke that such an action was actually done; Pilate eventually hands Jesus over to the will of the crowd (23,25). Brown considers the Lucan account to be close to the Johannine one in that Pilate hopes that by delivering Jesus up to the lesser punishment of flogging, he will satisfy the crowd (John 19,1-4; cf. Luke 23,16.22);[209] although, in Luke, the mob is not placated by the proposal. In addition, whereas in Mark and Matthew scourging is part of the crucifixion punishment, in Luke it is not. For the third evangelist, crucifixion is the only path to the fulfillment of Jesus' destiny.

Luke 23,17

Although Luke identifies Barabbas in 23,19, the omission of the explanation concerning the custom of releasing a prisoner, noted in both Mark and Matthew, runs counter to the Lucan tendency to rectify and clarify difficult synoptic passages. The lack of concord in the textual tradition concerning the inclusion or exclusion of 23,17 reflects scribal difficulties with this verse. Disputed is the phrase[210]

^{a}[αναγκην] δε ^{b}[ειχεν] απολυειν αυτοις κατα εορτην ενα ^{c}[ ] ℵ W Δ
Θ Ψ f^1 f^{13} 28 157 205 565 597 700 892^c 1006 1010 1071 1292 1342
1424 1505 Byz [E F G H] Lect it$^{aur,b,c,e,f,ff2,l,q,r'1}$ vg syr^{p,h}
(cop$^{bo'mss}$) arm eth geo slav Eusebian Canons Augustine

^{a}συνηθειαν N

^{b}ειχον 180 579

^{c}δεσμιον 1243

---

[207] Green, *Death* 79.

[208] Brown, *Messiah* 1; 792-3.

[209] Brown, *Messiah* 1; 827.

[210] The *UBSGNT*^{4} supplies the apparatus.

after v 19 D it^d syr^{c,s}

Text P^{75} A B L T 070 892* 1241 it^a vg^{ms} cop^{sa,bo'pt}

That Vaticanus and other Alexandrine witnesses do not show the verse is strong evidence that it is not original. Furthermore, some witnesses have transferred the disputed verse to after v 19, a short explanation about Barabbas' identity, thereby strengthening v 17 as a later interpolation. The *UBSGNT*[4] rank the omission of this verse from the text as *A*.[211] Brown believes the verse to be a gloss based on Matt 27,15 and Mark 15,6;[212] I hold with Boismard who sees it as excised by the final Lucan redactor.[213] But why would Luke, a writer sensitive to historical detail, remove an explanatory piece from the PN?

This question, no doubt, bothered many. The answer lies in Luke's overriding concern to show Jesus as innocent of any crime. A short explanation about the custom of releasing a prisoner could leave one with the impression that, somehow, Jesus and Barabbas shared the same accusation and that both were insurrectionists.[214] In addition, the absence of the verse makes the actions of both the crowd and Pontius Pilate even more capricious and thus, Jesus' crucifixion even more cruel. There is no reason for the crowd to request Barabbas, and certainly no good one for a governing official to release an insurrectionist. Hence, dispatching Jesus, in the Lucan account, is a momentary expediency.

The condemnation; Luke 23,25

After the Herod addition (23,6-12), the Lucan Pilate reiterates that Jesus is not guilty of any charges (23,14). The Herod pericope in Luke serves as a second interrogation of Jesus whereas in Mark and Matthew there is one inquiry (15,2ff; 27,11ff) after which Pilate reacts to the case presented by the priests (15,4.9.11ff; 27,13.17.20ff).

Through the threefold statements on Jesus' innocence, Luke emphasizes that officially and according to the Roman state, Jesus was guiltless of any crime, an important apologetic for the early church. In so doing, Luke also develops

---

[211] The text is certain (*UBSGNT*[4] 3*). The *UBSGNT*[3] committee, however, grade the omission as *B*; there is some degree of doubt concerning the reading selected for the text (Metzger, *Textual* xxviii).

[212] Brown, *Messiah* 788 n *.

[213] Boismard, noting the parallel in John 18,39b, also observes that John is more faithful to the source common to both Luke and John (*Synopse* 2; 412-3).

[214] Brown discusses the historical plausibility of the custom of releasing a prisoner for passover; there is no evidence in Greco-Roman or Jewish sources that such did or could occur (*Messiah* 1; 814-20). This leads Brown to conclude that a story of Barabbas with a basis in fact was dramatized to convey the truth: the conviction of Jesus was a choice for evil (*Messiah* 1; 820).

Pilate as a character in the drama. This steely Roman official is in control of the situation, and he gives sentence.[215] That he sees Jesus as innocent, makes his guilt in the crime all the greater. The tone of the Lucan presentation is reinforced by Henry Wansbrough's analysis of Pilate, his administration, and events contemporaneous with it.[216] Pilate was indeed fearful of events in Palestine which Rome might interpret as sedition. In addition, these statements of innocence bear on the centurion's declaration in 23,47.[217]

Much has been written on the Lucan use of λαός *in this passage; there is a sequence in which the "people" are favorable to Jesus (19,47-48; 20,6.19.45; 21,38; 22,2), as opposed to the "crowds" (23,4) who are not, and some would like to reconstruct this verse accordingly.[218] Brown suggests that Luke may alter the terms not only for stylistic reasons, thus making the two words synonymous, but also for narrative ones.[219] Luke wants the "people" present to hear Pilate's rejection of the charge they leveled in 23,2, that Jesus misled the people.[220] Neyrey draws attention to Luke's thematic emphasis of having the people choose. They choose Barabbas and reject Jesus (23,18), they choose (*αἰτούμενοι) that Jesus be crucified (23,23); Pilate lets their choice (αἴτημα) be granted (23,24), he releases Barabbas whom they chose (αἰτέομαι) [23,25a], and he hands Jesus over to their will (τῷ θελήματι αὐτῶν) [23,25b].[221]*

Against those who would read the Lucan PN as a pro-Roman apology at the expense of the Jews, Tiede states that placing a Roman execution within Israel is consistent with the third evangelist's intent to use the scriptural prophecies to Israel as the backdrop for interpreting Jesus' life, from birth to resurrection.[222] Karris believes the Lucan PN not only places Jesus on trial, but also the faithful

---

[215] Fitzmyer notes that the verb ἐπικρίνω (v 24) could have the technical sense of issuing an official sentence (*Luke* 2; 1492). Lagrange comments that ἐπικρίνω indicates a "positive and sovereign act" (*Luc* 583). The verb itself means *to decide, determine* (BAGD 295).

[216] In sum, Pilate served under Emperor Tiberius who was ever touchy about slights to his honor, often interpreting them as acts of treason, cf the charge in 23,2 (Henry Wansbrough, O.S.B. "Suffered Under Pontius Pilate," *Scripture* 18 [1966] 84-93). Philip F. Esler, however, considers the whole Lucan account as a "whitewashing" of Pilate's role in the condemnation with a corresponding blackening of that of the Jewish leadership (*Community and Gospel in Luke-Acts* [SNTSMS 57; Cambridge: Cambridge University Press, 1987] 202-3).

[217] Cf. below, Chapter Five.

[218] For a full discussion on varying opinions, cf. Brown, *Messiah* 1; 790-1.

[219] Brown, *Messiah* 1; 791.

[220] Brown, *Messiah* 1; 791.

[221] Neyrey, *Passion* 83.

[222] Tiede, *Prophecy* 107-8.

*God of Jesus.   Will that God remain faithful to the promises of life for his
creatures?*[223]

Simon of Cyrene and the Daughters of Jerusalem; Luke 23,26-32

The only plausible reason for the Romans' impressing Simon into service
is that they feared that Jesus, weakened by scourging, would die before being
crucified. In Luke, however, the scourging is not recorded. On this basis, some
think Luke is casting Simon in the role of disciple by having him follow behind
Jesus.[224]

*In searching for the subject of ἀπάγω, Lagrange counters those who, on
the basis of context, would consider it to be the Jews. Rationale for such would
be that Luke preferred to place the Gentile Romans, those soon to be converted,
outside the crucifixion scene.*[225] *I hold with Lagrange who proposes that it is the
Romans; Luke specifically mentions soldiers and a centurion (23,36.47).   The
Romans are also the only ones who would have the right to impress Simon into
service.*[226]

Although the daughters of Jerusalem are limited to this pericope, the
πλῆθος τοῦ λαοῦ (23,27) has a role throughout the Lucan PN.[227] In the death
account, Luke features a crowd who, after the centurion's declaration, return
beating their breasts (23,48). The presence of a crowd, then, on the way to Skull
Place (23,27-31) forms a unifying element connecting Jesus' passion with his
death. This same crowd becomes the Lucan onlookers who are separated from
the scoffing rulers in 23,35, a distinction which does not exist in the Marcan and
Matthean parallels. Furthermore, the crowd also progresses in sympathy toward
Jesus.[228] Similarly, Luke uses the acquaintances among the women disciples in
the death account (23,49) to maintain the cohesiveness of the PN; unlike Mark
and Matthew, Luke does not record the flight of the disciples (Luke 22,52-
53).[229] Hence, the women disciples are poised for the resurrection narrative;
after the burial, Luke adds a detail about their preparing spices and ointments

---

[223] Karris, *Artist* 92.

[224] Fitzmyer, *Luke* 2; 1497.

[225] Lagrange, *Luc* 584.

[226] Lagrange, *Luc* 584.

[227] Cf. below, Chapter Four.

[228] Brown, *Messiah* 2; 919.

[229] Cf. below, Chapter Five, for a discussion on the role of the disciples in the
death narrative.

before resting on the Sabbath "according to the commandment".[230]

In the ensuing dialogue with the daughters of Jerusalem,[231] Luke fashions an address which contains a thematic echo with the eschatological discourse (21,6-28); the Lord's visitation is at hand, a visitation which encompasses forgiveness, a point which connects to the theme of the rejected prophet.[232] Through the rejected prophet, God continues to offer forgiveness to those who reject his mercy,[233] and the address to the daughters of Jerusalem should be read in this light especially since it occurs within the context of the elevation of the cross and the prayer for forgiveness (vv 32-34a).[234]

Tiede observes that vv 28-31 show faithful women and their unborn children caught "in a web which is not of their own weaving".[235] This is an example where, though Luke uses the medium of Greek tragedy, the evangelist does so to amplify the story of what "God has accomplished through Jesus" rather than to show humanity standing before powers beyond its control.[236] Tiede's assessment reflects an accurate understanding of the Lucan corpus and its relationship to Greco-Roman literature. Tyson also likens the daughters of Jerusalem (v 28), the onlookers (v 35), and the repentant crowd (v 48) to a Greek chorus.[237] Especially if Luke is portraying the crowd as disciples, then in terms of the narrative, they fulfill the mediating role between the protagonist, i.e., Jesus, and the reading or listening audience.

Holding that v 31 is a reference to Ezek 17,24, Karris sees it as an act of forgiveness; Jesus will bring forgiveness even to the dry tree or the desiccated wood.[238] I am not convinced that v 31 is a reference to Ezekiel, and even if it were, the manner in which v 31 is paraphrased depicts a logic which comments

---

[230] Luke 23,56; cf. Mark 16,1.

[231] Fitzmyer notes that the term "daughters" draws upon the OT literature. Cf in plural, LXX Cant 2,7; 5,16; 8,4; in singular, LXX Isa 37,22; Zeph 3,14; Zech 9,9 (*Luke* 2; 1498).

[232] Karris, *Artist* 93. The "rejected prophet" theme has as its attributes, 1) rebellion and killing of the prophets, 2) punishment, 3) mercy through sending new prophets, 4) sin and rejection of prophets (Karris, *Artist* 19).

[233] Karris, *Artist* 93.

[234] Karris, *Artist* 93.

[235] Tiede, *Prophecy* 105.

[236] Tiede, *Prophecy* 104-5.

[237] Tyson, *Death* 36.

[238] Karris, *Artist* 94.

on the people and their actions. The theme of forgiveness expressed in v 34 can
be read as extending to this scene. A better interpretation, however, arises from
the context of the Lord's visitation: "If they do this when they have me with
them, what will they do when they do not?"[239]

As Brown notes, Simon does not take up the cross of his own accord, thus
dulling some of the overtones of discipleship.[240]   Hence, Brown thinks Simon
was an historical figure who, though unprepared and unwilling, takes the stance
of a disciple.[241]   Franz Georg Untergaßmair has a similar interpretation of the
Simon pericope.[242]   This passage creates a frame into which the crowd is
placed.[243]   Luke is trying to convey the idea that the crowd follow Simon in
taking up the cross; they too, figuratively speaking, follow behind Jesus.[244]

Less likely are the interpretations of Neyrey and Tannehill. The former
views the whole pericope as a prophetic oracle, *vaticinium ex eventu*, against
Jerusalem for rejecting God's prophets,[245] and the latter considers it as the fourth
and final part of connected passages dealing with Jerusalem's rejection of Jesus
and subsequent judgment (13,32-35; 19,41-44; 21,20-24); he also sees it as a
foreshadowing of the Jewish revolt.[246]

Crucifixion and prayer for forgiveness; Luke 23,33-34

Luke is the sole evangelist not to write *Golgotha*. Although all four are in
accord with the fact that κρανίον is the Greek name for the place of crucifixion,
the Lucan PN is the only one to read it as a definite noun. A minor difference
between Luke, the other synoptics, and John, this omission of *Golgotha* reflects
Luke's tendency to dispense with superfluous information while it also suggests
that the third gospel was written only for a Greek-speaking people.

---

[239] Important to keep in mind also is Neyrey's advice that as a popular
aphorism, the saying can be applied to a variety of situations (*Passion* 114).

[240] Brown, *Messiah* 2; 929.

[241] Brown, *Messiah* 2; 929.931. Karris translates ἐπιλαμβάνομαι as "to lay
friendly hands". For Karris, Simon then becomes the model of discipleship; the
invitation to "pick up" the cross comes unexpectedly (Karris, *Artist* 92).

[242] Franz Georg Untergaßmair, *Kreuzweg und Kreuzigung Jesu* (Paderborn:
Ferdinand Schöningh, 1980) 14-5.

[243] Untergaßmair, *Kreuzweg* 14-5. Cf. Luke 23,26.27ff. The crowd follows
Jesus to Skull Place and is present at the moment of death (23,35.48).

[244] The δέ (v 27) highlights the "followers" in relation to the "follower of the
cross" thus connecting ἀκολουθέω with φέρω ὄπισθεν (Untergaßmair, *Kreuzweg*
15). Cf. Luke 23,26.27ff.

[245] Neyrey, *Passion* 121.127.

[246] Tannehill, *Narrative* 156.198.

The many declarations of Jesus' innocence by Pilate and others underscore Luke's propensity to specify that Jesus was not guilty of any crime. The replacement of κακοῦργος (Luke 23,33) for λῃστής (Mark 15,27; Matt 27,38) in describing the two lawbreakers with whom Jesus was crucified is part of this Lucan tendency. In the scene of the arrest Jesus asks the authorities why they have come to him "as against a robber" (22,52); this phrase is identical to the one in Mark 14,48 and Matt 26,55. To state that Jesus was crucified with robbers in 23,33 could lead to the misunderstanding that he was put to death for the same crime. Luke obviates the problem with the substitution of the more ambiguous "wrongdoer".

Luke 23,34a

Luke 23,34a, the prayer of forgiveness, is omitted in part of the tradition.[247]

[[ὁ δὲ Ἰησοῦς ἔλεγεν· Πάτερ, ἄφες αὐτοῖς, οὐ γὰρ οἴδασιν τί ποιοῦσιν]]

[[*omit*]] P[75] א[1] B D* W Θ 070 579 597* 1241 it[a,d] syr[s] cop[sa,bo'pt]

Text א[*.2] A C D[2] L Δ Ψ 0250 *f*[1] *f*[13] 28 33 157 180 205 565 597[c] 700 828 892 1006 1010 1071 1243 1292 1342 1424 1505 *Byz* [F G H N] *Lect*   it[aur,b,c,e,f,ff'2,l,r'1] vg syr[c,p,h,pal] cop[bo'pt] arm eth geo slav Diatessaron Jacobus-Justus[acc. to] Hegesipp Irenaeus[lat] Hippolytus Origen[lat] Eusebius Eusebian Canons Ps-Ignatius Apostolic Constitutions Gregory-Nyssa Amphilochius Didymus[dub] Ps-Clementines Ps-Justin Chrysostom Cyril Hesychius Theodoret; Ambrosiaster Hilary Ambrose Jerome Augustine

including with asterisks E

The primary witnesses for the inclusion of 23,34a, א[*.2] and D[2] nearly match those for 22,43-44,[248] and as with 22,43-44, the *UBSGNT*[4] double-brackets this verse while considering it "certain," thus ranking its textual inclusion as *A*.[249] These facts lend a greater degree of probability to the theory

---

[247] The *UBSGNT*[4] supplies the apparatus.

[248] There is one difference of note between the textual attestations for the two citations. Here in 23,34 the second corrector of D includes the verse; in 22,43-44, it is the first hand of D. Cf. above.

[249] *UBSGNT*[4] 3*. Metzger bases this ranking on the verse's early incorporation into the Lucan text (*Textual* 2nd 155). The *UBSGNT*[3], however, hold it as *C*, there is a "considerable degree of doubt" whether it is part of the text (Metzger, *Textual* xxviii).

that both 22,43-44 and this verse may have been omitted by scribes wishing to harmonize the Lucan account with the other two synoptics despite the fact that, unlike 22,43-44, this verse contains nothing that could be interpreted as scandalous, although an anti-Jewish polemic behind its deletion cannot be entirely discounted. In addition, that neither Mark nor Matthew contains a verse similar to Luke 23,34a explains why it is omitted in part of the Lucan textual tradition; certain scribes, accustomed to the readings in the other two synoptics,[250] may not have been alerted to the verse's presence in the Lucan account. The agreement between the Alexandrine and Western traditions presses for its inclusion. Moreover, Acts 3,17 (Peter's speech) expresses the fact that the people acted from ignorance, while Acts 7,60 (Stephen's death) features a similar theme of forgiveness.

Lagrange asserts that the difficulty here is finding a cause for its omission. He doubts that it stems from an attempt at harmonization with parallel accounts, for Luke has other particular traits which are not omitted.[251] Perhaps someone thought the act of mercy toward the Jews too excessive,[252] but this opinion of Lagrange is predicated on holding that Jesus was speaking only to the Jews and not the Romans. As Lagrange remarks, however, the half-verse would not have been added had it not been part of the tradition.[253] Similarly, Brown believes that a second century scribe would have excised the verse for its pro-Jewish sentiment rather than add it.[254]

On a thematic level, Jesus' prayer in 23,34a is certainly in keeping with other events in the Lucan PN[255] and the third gospel in general (cf. 6,27-28.35-36). The sword incident at the arrest (22,49-51), shows Jesus remonstrating with his disciples for resorting to violence as he heals the wounded slave, an act of forgiveness in itself. In addition, the forgiveness theme continues with the account of the two wrongdoers (Luke 23,39-43). Luke 23,34a is a Lucan composition and thus a part of the Lucan PN.[256] According to Benedetto Prete, this prayer expresses that God has not rejected the Jews,[257] an understanding

---

[250] Cf. Matt 27,35-36; Mark 15,24-25.

[251] Lagrange, *Luc* 587-8.

[252] Lagrange, *Luc* 588.

[253] Lagrange, *Luc* 588.

[254] *Messiah* 2; 979-80.

[255] Tiede refers to Acts 3,13; 13,27 and, despite the textual problem, concludes that the word from the cross corresponds well to the judgment that the leaders and people were behaving in ignorance (*Prophecy* 111). So also Benedetto Prete, O.P., "Le Preghiere di Gesù al Monte degli Ulivi e sulla Croce" (*Atti della XXVII Settimana Biblica* [Brescia: Paideia Editrice, 1984]) 89.

[256] So also Brown (*Messiah* 2; 980). Fitzmyer, however, does not commit himself (*Luke* 2; 1500.1503).

[257] Prete, "Preghiere" 90.

which bears upon vv 27-31. Of course, God has not rejected the Romans either;[258] everyone involved in Jesus' death is forgiven, and this fact colors the whole Lucan PN.

The mocking rulers and soldiers; Luke 23,35-38

In the Lucan version, Pilate threatens scourging (23,22), but there is no record that he follows through with it. As Brown notes, historically, it seems plausible that Roman soldiers would mock a condemned man before the crucifixion even though there is no way to prove that a mockery actually took place here.[259] Although Fitzmyer is puzzled by the fact that Luke incorporates the soldiers' taunting offer of wine at 23,36-37, he observes that it probably reflects an historical incident detailed by Luke.[260]

Lagrange wonders whether the soldiers could have been motivated by the strange sight of Jews mocking their compatriot.[261] It may have been a strange spectacle, but the soldiers would have been inclined to insult the crucified anyway, as parallel accounts attest (Matt 27,27-31a; Mark 15,16-20a; John 19,2-3). These taunts by the "leaders" (v 35), "soldiers" (v 36), and "criminals" (v 39) form for Fitzmyer the "nucleus" of the Lucan crucifixion scene.[262] Neyrey compares the two groups, Jewish rulers (v 35) and Gentile soldiers (v 37); in form and content, the soldiers' remarks duplicate the mockery of the Jewish rulers.[263] Tiede sees the "chosen one's" derision on the cross as that which conveys Luke's view that the "anointed one" is also the "king of the Jews".[264]

The wrongdoers; Luke 23,39-43

Luke's account of the two wrongdoers includes a dialogue between them and Jesus as the three hang crucified (23,39-43).[265] The first criminal cannot, or

---

[258] Prete calls attention to the pronoun αὐτοῖς which is indeterminate and does not specify any group in particular, e.g., the high priests, elders, onlookers, soldiers ("Preghiere" 88 n 36).

[259] Brown, *Messiah* 1; 873-7.

[260] Fitzmyer, *Luke* 1505.

[261] Lagrange, *Luc* 589.

[262] Fitzmyer, *Luke* 2; 1501.

[263] Neyrey, *Passion* 131.

[264] Tiede, *Prophecy* 46.

[265] Cf. Mark 15,32 and Matt 27,44.

refuses to see Jesus as the anointed one. This is in contrast to the second criminal who, by correcting the former and petitioning for remembrance, shows he does comprehend. He then, of course, receives the promise of paradise. The scene portrays Jesus as forgiving right to the end, while it also continues the theme of his innocence. Pilate (23,4.14.22), Herod (23,15), now the wrongdoer, and soon the centurion (23,47) all hold Jesus as guiltless of any crime. This pericope then seems to have a two-fold apologetic purpose. First, it appears to address those who may have difficulty understanding how and why the long-awaited Messiah underwent a criminal's death, and second, it counters accusations that Jesus was an insurrectionist or a thief.

Luke often compares and contrasts two figures: Martha and Mary (10,38-42), the rich man and Lazarus (16,19-31), the pharisee and the publican (18,9-14); this is one more example.[266] The repentant criminal represents the Lucan qualities associated with salvation from Jesus: accepting Jesus as God's Christ, not being scandalized by the cross, petitioning for a blessing and receiving an answer, and both seeking and finding salvation.[267]

This pairing of two individuals is what Neyrey calls the "schism motif," introduced in Luke 2,34-35.[268] Brown extends this schism typology to include the baker and cupbearer in Genesis 40 with the suggestion that Luke is using that OT scenario as a model.[269] Looking to the rich man and Lazarus, Esler holds that Luke viewed the afterlife as the place where the rich would be punished and deprived while the poor would be rewarded with every good thing.[270] If Esler is correct, the same antithesis between the two wrongdoers exists.

The mockeries in general parallel the devil's reasoning in the desert, "If you are the Son of God..." (4,3.9). Thus, this dialogue begins with a mockery from the first wrongdoer, and by using the verb ἐπιτιμάω (v 40), the scene also parallels Jesus' *rebuke* of the devil (4,35.39.41),[271] a point worthy of further investigation.[272] Because these mockeries parallel the temptation, the diabolically associated "rebuke" seems to recall another "opportune time" for the devil (4,13) to make his reappearance.[273] What Luke effects is a two-fold

---

[266] Brown, *Messiah* 2; 1002-3.

[267] Neyrey, *Passion* 140. Tiede comments that, as in the days before the trial, even here Israel is divided; the two wrongdoers argue about Jesus and the kingdom (*Prophecy* 114).

[268] Neyrey, *Passion* 122.

[269] Brown, *Messiah* 2; 1002-3.

[270] Esler, *Community* 192.

[271] Brown, *Messiah* 2; 1003.

[272] Cf. below, Chapter Two.

negation of the temptation. Not only does Jesus refuse to come down from the cross, he also forgives, and by forgiving, he saves. Thus, with great irony, he proves he is the Son of God.

Brown cites this passage of the wrongdoers as an example of how both Romans and Jews misunderstand Jesus.[274] *Brown is too restrictive in that opinion. Karris' understanding has more to recommend it. Centering on the word "paradise," he sees a reference to the fruits present there and thus finds a food theme in the PN. Paradise is for the righteous; Jesus the righteous has the keys to the home of the righteous.*[275]

The burial;[276] Luke 23,50-56

The burial account contains the last Lucan differentiation from the Marcan/Matthean PN. The first, a comment concerning Joseph of Arimathea (23,51), is more elaborate than the simple clarification of the other synoptics or John.[277] The Lucan specification about the newness of the tomb (Luke 23,53b) seems to serve an apologetic purpose in that it offsets any accusations of body-snatching which detractors may have been circulating. To be noted is its similarity to both John 19,41 and Matt 27,60; Mark is alone among the evangelists in not mentioning the newness of the tomb.

Unlike the Marcan PN, the Lucan and Matthean PNs do not contain Pilate's sending a centurion to investigate whether Jesus is actually dead.[278] The centurion who confirms Jesus' death in Mark 15,44-45 was added to the second evangelist after the final Lucan redaction.[279]

Both Fitzmyer[280] and Brown[281] assert Joseph as an historical figure, not a product of early Christian fiction. Joseph of Arimathea went to Pilate because, as a member of the Sanhedrin,[282] he was free of any accusation of being one of

---

[273] Cf. above, the agony scene (Luke 22,43-44).

[274] Brown, *Messiah* 2; 997.

[275] Karris, *Artist* 103.

[276] The death of Jesus, Luke 23,44-49, is reserved for more detailed treatment in the following chapters; hence, the discussion here proceeds to the burial account.

[277] Mark 15,43; Matt 27,57; John 19,38.

[278] But cf John 19,31-33.

[279] Cf. below, Chapter Four.

[280] Fitzmyer, *Luke* 2; 1526.

[281] Brown, *Messiah* 2; 1240.

Jesus' disciples. Since the Sanhedrin called for his death in the first place, there would be no worry on the part of Pilate that Joseph would make Jesus a "martyr" to a revolutionary cause.

Brown maintains that the Marcan version is more accurate. Joseph was not a disciple, only a pious Jew[283] trying to fulfill the Jewish law on burial; for this reason, Pilate gave him the body.[284] In addition, the Lucan account shows that Joseph's motivation goes beyond Mark's piety; knowing the travesty of justice involved in the crucifixion, Joseph acts from respect and pity.[285] Joseph is an example that Luke does not deal with the Jewish authorities in a totally negative manner.[286] Citing Simeon and Anna (2,25.38), the two on the way to Emmaus (24,21), and the disciples themselves (Acts 1,6) in addition to Joseph of Arimathea, Tiede states that Luke appreciates the tragic character the PN has with relation to Israel. The third evangelist is thus sensitive to the compromised role that the people play; the PN was not written as a Gentile apology at Jewish expense.[287]

Luke 23,53-56

There is a consistency in the Lucan PN with the general phrase, "the women who had come with him from Galilee"; the women are not specified in 23,49 either.[288] The evangelist names the women disciples, however, in 8,2-3.[289] The note that the women rested on the Sabbath makes a good transition to the resurrection narrative.

---

[282] Squires holds that the phrase τῇ βουλῇ καὶ τῇ πράξει (v 51) is in opposition to God's will despite the reading in 22,42, μὴ τὸ θέλημά μου ἀλλὰ τὸ σὸν γινέσθω (*Plan* 171). Tiede clarifies the point by saying that opposition to God's will is never denied in L-A; the opposition is in league with the "power of darkness" [22,52-53; Acts 26,18] (*Prophecy* 110).

[283] Brown places Joseph in the same tradition as Zechariah, Elizabeth, and Simeon (*Messiah* 2; 1227-8).

[284] This also explains why the women in the synoptic accounts observe but do not help in the burial; Joseph would not let them near because they were disciples (Brown, *Messiah* 2; 1217-8).

[285] Brown, *Messiah* 2; 1255. Thus, Karris calls Joseph of Arimathea a "representative example" of the righteous person (*Artist* 114).

[286] Tiede, *Prophecy* 111.

[287] Tiede, *Prophecy* 111.

[288] Mark 15,47 and Matt 27,61.

[289] Cf. below, Chapter Four.

Conclusion

An overview of the Lucan PN reveals structural elements as well as major themes which run through it.

Structurally, there is a cohesion in the Lucan PN reflected in the narrative style:

One, the Herod inquiry (23,6-12) forms a link between Jesus and John the Baptist; hence, Jesus' presence at Herod's court becomes a literary and thus theological *inclusio*.

Two, Luke melds the two arms of political power, one of the Roman Empire and the other of the Jewish national rulers; this is done to reinforce the fact of Jesus' innocence on a legal plane, and more importantly by extension, on a moral one.

Three, Jesus' shunting between Pilate and Herod (23,6-12) also parallels Paul's trials before the Roman Festus and the Jewish Herod Agrippa (Acts 25,13-26,32). Jesus' trial then becomes the paradigm for Christians hauled off to Pagan judges; this is Brown's thesis.[290]

Four, some such as Untergaßmair,[291] also see the Simon of Cyrene pericope as a frame for the daughters of Jerusalem and the crowd on the road to Calvary.

Five, the crowd also functions as a unifying element tying the PN to the death account (23,21.27.35.48).

There are ten major themes present in the Lucan PN which resonate with differing yet complementary theologies.

One, the prophet motif, is evident in the agony (22,43-44), Feldkämper;[292] in the mockery at the arrest (22,63-65), Brown;[293] during the interrogation by the Sanhedrin (22,66-71),[294] Neyrey;[295] in the condemnation by Pilate (23,24-25), Tiede;[296] and on the road to Skull Place (23,26-33), Tannehill.[297] This prophetic theme then merges with the second motif, that of the "Suffering Just One" (23,9.11), so Büchele[298] and Schneider, with a slight variation.[299]

---

290 Brown, *Messiah* 1; 759.

291 Untergaßmair, *Kreuzweg* 14-5.

292 Feldkämper, *Heilsmittler* 243-4.

293 Brown, *Messiah* 1; 584-5.

294 The prophet theme is more pronounced in the non-passion material, cf. Luke 6,22-23; 11,47-51; 13,33-34, and continues in Acts (7,51-53).

295 Neyrey, *Passion* 70.

296 Tiede, *Prophecy* 107-8.

297 Tannehill, *Narrative* 156.

298 Büchele, *Tod* 93-4.

Third, there is the confessional theme, Jesus as Messiah and Son of God (22,67-71), Brown[300] and Schneider.[301]

Four, the disciple motif first occurs at the agony scene (22,40.46) but gains prominence in the pericope of the road to Skull Place (23,27-31). This is the understanding of Fitzmyer,[302] Karris,[303] Untergaßmair,[304] Neyrey,[305] Schneider,[306] and to a lesser extent, Brown.[307]

Five, the innocence motif, existing in statements about Jesus' guiltlessness, arises in the pronouncements of Pilate (23,4.14.22), Herod (23,15), and the wrongdoer (23,41). Innocence is sharpened into "just" with the centurion (23,47).

Six, the interceding and praying Jesus motif throughout the PN is posited by Crump,[308] Feldkämper,[309] and Prete.[310]

Seven, Jesus as martyr is evident in the agony (22,43-44) as well as in the mockery at the arrest (22,63-65), Brown.[311]

Eight, Jesus who, as servant of the Lord, must suffer, Green[312] and Karris.[313]

Nine, the theme of forgiveness is expressed in 22,51; 23,34.43.

Ten, the Satan motif is voiced in Jesus' prayer to Simon (22,31-32). This

---

[299] Schneider, *Verleugnung* 171-2.

[300] Brown, *vis-à-vis* Matt/Mark, underlines the Lucan distinction between "Messiah" as understood by the Jews and "Son of God" as comprehended by Christians (*Messiah* 1; 471).

[301] This is the basis of *Heilsgeschichte* (Schneider, *Verleugnung* 173).

[302] Fitzmyer, *Luke* 2; 1497.

[303] Karris, *Artist* 92.

[304] Untergaßmair, *Kreuzweg* 14-5.

[305] Neyrey, *Passion* 121.

[306] Schneider, *Passion* 164.

[307] Brown, *Messiah* 2; 931.

[308] Crump, *Jesus*.

[309] Feldkämper, *Heilsmittler*.

[310] Prete, "Preghiere".

[311] Brown, *Messiah* 1; 187-90.584.

[312] Green, "Jesus" 42.

[313] Karris, *Artist* 89.

theme recurs at the agony on the Mount of Olives (22,39-46), at the arrest (22,52-53), at the trial before Pilate [διαστρέφω] (23,1-5), the inquiry before Herod (23,6-12), the taunting on the cross (23,35-37), and the death itself (23,44-45).[314]

On the whole, none of these themes nullifies or contradicts the other. That such is the case underscores the polyvalent nature of the gospel. That all exist in the Lucan corpus, however, does not mean that all are of equal value. The one current which has not been studied sufficiently is the last. The references to Satan, the devil, and the "hour of the power of darkness" (22,53) are an important part of the picture that Luke is clearly depicting. It is a theme which informs many of the eschatological passages, it is a theme which cannot be explained along the lines of the 2DH or the GH, and it is the theme to which this study now turns.

---

[314] Cf. also Neyrey (*Passion* 31-2). N.b. references in John 13,27-30 where night provides the background for sinister action; in addition, cf. below, Chapter Two.

Chapter Two

Diabolical Force and Ministering Angel Traditions

Among the many themes discussed in the Lucan PN, one seems to deserve greater attention than it normally receives, namely that of Jesus in conflict with the forces of evil. This theme, running through the whole Lucan corpus, is most manifest in the PN, specifically the death account, but often seems to go unnoticed. Although Tannehill sees that Satan has power to expose the faithlessness of the apostles,[1] Tyson simply states that Satan reenters the narrative at 22,3.[2] Even Graham H. Twelftree, who studies in depth Jesus as an exorcist, does not include the passion and death narratives in his treatment.[3] Tiede concludes that Satan's agency in Luke 22,31 indicates "that the struggle transcends mere choice,"[4] while Squires observes that Luke 22,3.31 increases the "tension between God and Satan which has been present throughout the ministry of Jesus".[5] Robert F. O'Toole mentions that Luke views the "whole world" as "divided into two camps, that of God and that of Satan".[6]

Neyrey, however, notes the role of Satan in the third gospel and outlines the Lucan presentation in six points: a) the framing of the narrative by reference to Satanic attacks on Christ and the disciples, b) the portrayal of Satan as the enemy of faith, c) the depiction of two kingdoms at war, God's and Satan's, d) the demonstration of Jesus' mastery over Satan, e) the proclamation of Satan's ruin (10,18), f) the representation of Jesus' mission as a rescue of those under Satan's power.[7] This view forms part of the basis for Neyrey's conclusions on Lucan soteriology.[8]

A close investigation of Luke 22,3; 22,31; 22,43 and 22,53b brings to light not only key elements in L-A but also clarifies Luke's theology while increasing the dramatic tension of the narrative. The study involves an explanation of key Lucan words and phrases both in their use proper to the third gospel as well as, where applicable, in their employment by the other evangelists.

The research shows that Luke drew upon two traditions present in the OT

---

[1] Tannehill, *Narrative* 264.

[2] Tyson, *Death* 37.

[3] Graham H. Twelftree, *Jesus the Exorcist* (WUNT 2/54; Tübingen: J.C.B. Mohr [Paul Siebeck], 1993).

[4] Tiede, *Prophecy* 107.

[5] Squires, *Plan* 56.

[6] Robert F. O'Toole, S.J., *The Unity of Luke's Theology* (Wilmington, Delaware: Michael Glazier, 1984) 110.

[7] Neyrey, *Passion* 31-2.

[8] Neyrey holds that Luke has developed an Adam-Jesus model of soteriology (*Passion* 190-2).

and pseudepigraphic literature, the *diabolical force* on the one hand and the *ministering angel* on the other, which he reshaped and reinterpreted through the lens of Christ's own passion, death, and resurrection. The basis of this development is a traditioning process that relied on "fixed points" which an evangelist, in this case Luke, would shape according to a respective theology by combining the "fixed point" with other pieces of information.[9]

"Then Satan entered into Judas called Iscariot" (Luke 22,3a)

Luke uses the name Satan more often than any of the other evangelists, and this verse is one of the very few mentioning Satan which has a parallel (John 13,27). To be sure, although all four gospels show occurrences of Satan, and the devil, only Luke and John tie these titles to Judas, and John does so more than Luke.[10] In addition, these readings from Luke 22,3 and John 13,27 are nearly identical. Boismard attributes this coincidence to Lucan influence on the fourth gospel, as he does for the equivalent reading, but with διάβολος, at John 13,2.[11] Fitzmyer, on the other hand, believes that though the whole episode of the betrayal is derived from Mark 14,10-11, this verse originates from "L".[12]

In Luke, maintains Lagrange, Satan is an instigator, a concept which approximates the role the devil and Satan play in John 13,2.27.[13] Lagrange also

---

[9] A "fixed point" is borrowed from James D.G. Dunn's article "John and the Oral Gospel Tradition," (*Jesus and the Oral Gospel Tradition* [ed. Henry Wansbrough, Sheffield: Academic Press, 1991 (= JSNTSup 64)] 351-79). Dunn applies the term only in reference to the fourth gospel which he feels is "*an example* of how elaboration of the Jesus tradition did (and might) happen" (379). Because the phrase represents how I view the formation of the gospel tradition, I utilize it here. By no means do I intend this employment to be a critique of Dunn's work.
This theory views "fixed points" as the earliest forms of the various traditions which tradition-bearers would directly rely on and retell with their own respective emphases (378). Added to the fixed points in the oral tradition process would be a story or teaching (378). A considerable degree of freedom existed for the story-tellers or teachers under the restraints of the fixed points of the earlier tradition and those of the gospel itself (378-9).

[10] Cf. also John 6,70-71.

[11] Boismard, *Synopse* 2; 374. In addition, Bailey maintains that John 13,27 derives from Luke (*Traditions* 30).

[12] Fitzmyer, *Luke* 2; 1373. "L," as Fitzmyer explains, is Luke's "private source, written or oral" (*Luke* 1; vii). So also Taylor, but who believes the reference to Satan, in reflecting Johannine tradition, may be Luke's attempt to "reconcile two different views" (*Passion* 44).

[13] Lagrange, *Luc* 539.

observes that, although the verb εἰσέρχομαι often refers to diabolical possession,[14] the context here indicates that such is not the case with Judas.[15] Judas does not exhibit a double personality; rather, Satan provides an evil suggestion.[16] Furthermore, this verse describes Satan's return at the "opportune time" anticipated at the temptation (Luke 4,13).[17]

The similarities between Luke and John notwithstanding, in John, Satan and the devil are almost exclusively limited to the fallen apostle; in Luke, however, Judas certainly becomes the agent for Satan, but references to Satan and the devil do not center solely on him. Luke's purpose, it seems, is to shape and form Satan or the devil, with all his underlings, into a *diabolical force* which is contrary to Jesus, which Jesus must battle, and which he must overcome.

Diabolical Force

The Beelzebul controversy[18] in all three synoptics substantiates that, when compared to σατανᾶς, a δαιμόνιον is treated as a lesser being, and although evil and unclean spirits do not occur in this pericope, they are synonymous with δαιμόνιον. It seems that Luke is utilizing the term *demon* for a specific purpose. The word, *demon*, functions as a *leitmotif* which, like a steady drum beat, tells all hearers and readers that those who are sick or possessed are not merely suffering from some misfortune, rather, they are under the influence of a divinity,[19] itself subject to Satan. As H. A. Kelly observes, the activity of the demons and unclean spirits is limited to physical disturbances;[20] unlike Satan or the devil, these beings do not incite to moral evil.

Several examples support this assumption and develop the *diabolical force* tradition. To the Pharisees who warn him about Herod Jesus replies, "Listen, I am casting out demons and performing cures today and tomorrow, and on the third day I finish my work" (Luke 13,32). Luke makes very little distinction between an exorcism and a cure;[21] in fact, in some cases, the malady is attributed to Satan.[22] This situation is certainly true for the healing of the crippled woman (13,10-17) immediately before the Pharisees' warning to Jesus.

---

[14] Cf. Luke 8,30.33; 11,26.

[15] Lagrange, *Luc* 539.

[16] Lagrange, *Luc* 539.

[17] Lagrange, *Luc* 539.

[18] Matt 12,22-30; Mark 3,22-27; Luke 11,14-23.

[19] The very meaning of δαιμόνιον (BAGD 169).

[20] H. A. Kelly, S.J., "The Devil in the Desert," *CBQ* 26 (1964) 195.

[21] N.b. the boy with an unclean spirit (Luke 9,37-43), Jesus *rebukes* the spirit and *heals* the boy (v 42).

[22] N.b. Acts 10,38 where it is implied that no difference exists between

Both these pericopes are Lucan material with no parallel in the other gospels.[23] They represent the confluence of two streams. The healing of the crippled woman flows into Jesus' statement at 13,32. Verse 13,32 also continues the Herod theme which had made its debut with the arrest of John the Baptist (3,18-20).[24] Jesus' reply to the Pharisees (13,32) says nothing about preaching or exciting the social consciousness of the people, a threat to any political ruler. Instead his answer is that he will continue exorcizing and curing, an action which attacks only Satan.

This point is confirmed by the use of ὥρα (13,31) which occurs at other locations thereby underscoring the struggle against Satan.[25] In one such instance Jesus rejoices at the return of the seventy-two and the success of their mission (10,21). Their ministry consists of subjugating the demons (10,17), treading upon scorpions and serpents, and overpowering the enemy (10,19). In the midst of this activity, the text reads εἶπεν δὲ αὐτοῖς· ἐθεώρουν τὸν σατανᾶν ὡς ἀστραπὴν ἐκ τοῦ οὐρανοῦ πεσόντα (10,18). This scene in Luke 10,18 echoes both 2 Enoch 29,4-5, where God casts the rebellious Satanail and his minions into a perpetual fall after he presumed to place his throne on a level equal to the Lord God's,[26] and Rev 12,9, where Satan and his angels are cast down to earth during the battle with Michael.

Julian V. Hills presents a strong argument for allowing ἐθεώρουν to be read as a "third person plural verb with the neuter plural noun, 'demons'" as subject in v 17.[27] In this case, Jesus explains the success of the disciples' mission: the demons saw Satan's fall, therefore they submitted.[28] Above all, Satan's fall is through Jesus' agency, i.e., his ἐξουσία (10,19)[29] and his name (10,17b); this is a skirmish before the battle, a battle which takes place at the crucifixion. Furthermore, the instance of hour at Luke 12,12 is within the context of confessing Christ before others. To do so will not be without its

───────────────────────────────────

sickness and diabolical oppression.

[23] While viewing vv 15-17 to be the work either of proto-Luke or the final redactor, Boismard leaves open the possibility that the pericope could have had its origin in Q despite its absence in Matthew (Synopse 2; 287). Boismard holds the pericope of the Pharisees' warning to be an episode proper to Luke and intimates that 13,32 could have been an actual logion of Jesus (Synopse 2; 289).

[24] Cf. Luke 23,6-12 and above, Chapter One.

[25] Cf. Luke 12,12; 20,19; 22,53. Boismard notes this as a sign of the Lucan redaction (Synopse 2; 289). Cf. also Luke 12,39.40.46. Unfortunately this sense of ὥρα is often lost when it is rendered as time in many translations.

[26] OTPseud 1; 148. The reading exists in the [J] or longer recension.

[27] Julian V. Hills, "Luke 10.18 -- Who Saw Satan Fall," JSNT 46 (1992) 39.

[28] Hills, "Saw" 39.

[29] Hills, "Saw" 34.

tortures (12,4), but the real enemy is not a human one but those who have power to cast into Gehenna (12,5). When the *hour* of such trials arrives, one can rely on the Holy Spirit to counter the diabolical nemesis.

Appealing to the Lucan use of ὥρα at 12,12 and 13,31, it is not far-fetched to ascribe a similar understanding to *hour* at 20,19. Luke is trying to portray the idea that the scribes' and chief priests' attempt to arrest Jesus is premature; it is not yet time for Jesus' *hour*, i.e., rendezvous with Satan.

But what of Satan's entering Judas at 22,3? Luke's use of the verb εἰσέρχομαι to describe the betrayer's corruption is a key for interpreting this verse. At the prayer on the Mount of Olives (Luke 22,39-46), Jesus tells the apostles twice to pray that they may not *enter* into temptation (vv 40.46b). If the narrative displays a constant internal logic, the message is that Judas had entered into temptation, therefore, the remaining apostles should keep from doing likewise. This argument, however, is weak on the ground that Judas is the object of the verb in 22,3, and in 22,40.46b, the apostles are the subject.

The context for Satan's entering Judas can be found in the Beelzebul controversy and in the following pericope of the return of the evil spirit. First, the name *Satan*, which Luke uses sparingly, occurs at 11,18. Second, the imagery employed entails concepts of dominion and ownership: "kingdom" (11,18), "his castle," "his property" (11,21), "my house" (11,24). Third, the return of the evil spirit displays variations of the verb ἔρχομαι.[30] Fourth, the nature of the argument between Jesus and the Pharisees centers around conflicting claims of allegiance; is Jesus casting out demons on behalf of the prince of demons (11,15) or on behalf of God (11,20)?

The Beelzebul controversy

Some version of the Beelzebul controversy is present in all four gospels. Although Jesus' reply to those accusing him of collusion with Beelzebul is nearly the same among all three synoptics,[31] Matthew and Luke both continue with a reprimand,[32] and with Q material on the arrival of the kingdom of God,[33] before rejoining the Marcan parallel with the strong man parable.[34] Matthew and Luke then conclude with a Q saying.[35] It is difficult to extract a Johannine parallel to

---

[30] Luke 11,24.25.26.

[31] Matt 12,25-26; Mark 3,23-26; Luke 11,17-18a.

[32] Matt 12,27-28; Luke 11,18b-20.

[33] Matt 12,28; Luke 11,20 (Ivan Havener, O.S.B., *Q, The Sayings of Jesus* [Wilmington, Delaware: Michael Glazier, 1987] 133).

[34] Matt 12,29; Mark 3,27; Luke 11,21-22. This is a Mark-Q overlap (Havener, *Q* 156).

[35] Matt 12,30; Luke 11,23 (Havener, *Q* 133). Boismard explains that these Marcan-Q overlaps in the second gospel (Havener, *Q* 155-6) resulted when the Marcan-Lucan redactor, who was influenced by the Matthean-Lucan tradition, itself dependent on Q, added them to proto-Mark (*Marc* 92).

the synoptic accounts of the Beelzebul controversy, but accusations in John 7,20; 8,48.49.52; 10,20.21 certainly echo the synoptic Beelzebul pericopes. That people in all four gospels either state or imply that Jesus is possessed by demons leads to the conclusion that such was a frequent charge directed against him during his lifetime. It seems that Luke, however, uses the episode as one of the defining moments in the gospel narrative.

When Jesus is accused of being in league with Satan, the insinuation reflects back to the Pharisees themselves; they cannot conceive of a force or person more powerful in creation than Beelzebul. Jesus' actions and subsequent admonition challenge this assumption. The metaphor of the strong man, immediately following the Beelzebul controversy, describes Jesus' role in the world.

The parable of the strong man

When compared to the Matthean and Marcan accounts, the Lucan version of the strong man displays a notable change. The passage itself is a Marcan-Q overlap[36] with the last phrase "Whoever is not with me is against me, and whoever does not gather with me scatters" (Luke 11,23) standing as Q material.[37] The Lucan redaction is evident in v 22 with the verb νικάω; both Matt 12,29 and Mark 3,27 show the verb δέω.[38] The Lucan exemplar of the "stronger one" does not merely "bind" or "tie up" the strong man, but "overcomes" him, or even better, is victorious over him. The preceding Beelzebul controversy clarifies Jesus as the "one stronger" who attacks and overpowers the "strong man," i.e., Satan (11,21-22). It is to be recalled that only Luke includes mention of Satan falling from heaven (10,18), and the healing of the crippled woman whom "Satan bound" (13,16).

Luke qualifies this attack on Satan with the pericope of the return of the evil spirit (11,24-26), a Q saying[39] which Matthew places further on in the gospel. The evil spirit returns, with seven others, to the person from whom it has been discharged. Following, as it does, the pericope of the attack upon the strong man, it appears that Luke is conveying that Satan and his associated demons still exercise some power in the world. To be noted is that the house which they re-enter had been inhabited by an evil spirit at a previous time. Furthermore, in terms of a *diabolical force* tradition, Christ's instruction to the returning seventy-two (Luke 10,17-20) and the parable of the binding of the strong man (Luke 11,21-22) resonate with material from the *T. Levi* 18,12, "And Beliar shall be bound by him. / And he shall grant to his children the authority to trample on wicked spirits".[40]

---

[36] Havener, *Q* 156.

[37] Havener, *Q* 133.

[38] Havener indicates that νικάω is from Q whereas δέω reflects a Marcan redaction (*Q* 133 and 156).

[39] Havener, *Q* 133.

[40] *OTPseud* 1; 795. Cf. also *APOT* 2; 315 n 12.

When Satan's entering into Judas (22,3) is placed within this background, then it is possible to presume that one, Jesus had claimed Judas for himself else he would not have been an apostle, and two, Judas being unreceptive to this claim, allows Satan to enter. If Satan's underling (unclean spirit) has free rein, so does its master; hence, Satan *enters* Judas.

A study by John J. Kilgallen, however, adds a nuance to this conclusion.[41] Not only does the parable of the unclean spirit (11,24-26) refute the accusation that Jesus is in league with Beelzebul, but it also serves to show the true natures of both Jesus and the unclean spirit.[42] Thus, Jesus' description of the wandering spirit presents a circumstance in which the work done by Jesus induces not only repossession by one demon but the "imposition of a condition which totally obliterates" what he has already accomplished.[43] True, there is no account depicting Jesus at any time exorcising a demon from Judas; however, insofar as Jesus goes about releasing human beings from Satan's clutches, Satan's entering Judas can be understood as Satan's own redoubling of his efforts to wreak worse havoc on creation through a person whom Jesus had claimed as one of his own.

The tradition of the diabolical force

It appears that the concept of Satan wandering the world and entering certain individuals is one developed from OT and intertestamental material. Fitzmyer, besides suggesting that the understanding of Satan's ability to "enter" people or animals is also reflected in the pericope of the Gerasene demoniac (Luke 8,30-32),[44] also notes that *Mart. Isa.* 3,11 reads, "But Beliar dwelt in the heart of Manasseh and in the heart of the princes of Judah and Benjamin and of the eunuchs and of the king's counselors".[45] In addition, John 13,27 is nearly equal to Luke 22,3; there is little doubt that such a saying existed in the gospel tradition.[46] Those works with the most observable similarity to the *diabolical force* evident in the gospels, however, are in Job, Zechariah, and *1 Enoch*.

In Job 1,12 the Lord gives Satan (= LXX διάβολος) charge over Job's possessions in order that Satan may tempt Job to forsake his devotion to the Lord

---

[41] John J. Kilgallen, S.J., "The Return of the Unclean Spirit (Luke 11,24-26)" *Bib* 74 (1993) 45-59.

[42] Kilgallen, "Return" 57-8.

[43] Kilgallen, "Return" 56.

[44] Cf. also Mark 5,12-13 and Matt 8,31-32.

[45] Fitzmyer, *Luke* 2; 1374. Cf. also *OTPseud* 2; 160.

[46] Cf. below. N.b. also the account of Cain's taking his brother Abel into the field in order to slay him (Gen 4,8) with its echo in John 8,40-44 where the intent to murder is associated with being a child of the devil.

and allows him to inflict Job with a loathsome disease. Zech 3,1-2 portrays the Lord rebuking Satan (= LXX διάβολος). In each of these accounts, Satan is not so much depicted as the embodiment of evil; rather, this devil is cast in the role of tester or adversary, indeed, the very meaning of *Satan* in Hebrew.[47] Kelly cautions against viewing Satan as a "fallen angel" in these OT descriptions, for the concept of sinful angels is an intertestamental one.[48] As such, the elaboration in *1 Enoch* of the account in Gen 6,2ff furnishes the myth. Angels in heaven lusted after the beautiful "daughters of man" (*1 Enoch* 6,1-8), though Satan is not among those listed (*1 Enoch* 6,7-8).[49]

Kelly distinguishes between two types of metaphorical falls: a) the moral lapse and b) the fall from "authority or dignity or power" as a result of weakness, physical struggle, or punishment by a superior power.[50] Establishing a chronological order in which one can observe the formation of the concept of Satan as a disgraced angel is hampered by the fact that both moral lapse and the fall from dignity have been operative at various times.[51] What developed was a "gradual denigration of the satan's character" where ill will toward humankind became affixed to Satan's reputation to the point that, as specified in Wis 2,24, the envy of the διάβολος brought death into the world; Kelly sees this verse (Wis 2,24) as a reference to Satan as the Angel of Death.[52] Above all, Satan became considered as responsible and thus punishable for both the primordial fall and for wicked deeds.[53] In the NT, as in other contemporaneous messianic writings, Satan is portrayed as opposing the messianic kingdom in which the victory of the Messiah implies Satan's downfall.[54]

On this basis, it is possible to trace the influence of the demonology in *1 Enoch* upon the NT.[55] If the offspring from the union between the fallen angels

---

[47] BDB 966.

[48] Kelly, "Devil" 203.

[49] *OTPseud* 1; 15-6.

[50] Kelly, "Devil" 203. Cf. also Isa 14,12-21.

[51] Kelly, "Devil" 203. For a brief survey of this tradition, cf. Kelly ("Devil" 203-6).

[52] Kelly, "Devil" 206-7.

[53] Kelly, "Devil" 208. Cf. the Book of *Jub.* 10,8-9 where Mastema requests from God and is allowed to retain, a tenth of the spirits to corrupt and to lead astray humanity until the final judgment (*OTPseud* 2; 76).

[54] Kelly, "Devil" 209.

[55] Although speaking specifically about *1 Enoch* 92-105, the 1978 Pseudepigrapha Seminar makes the general statement, "Examining the parallels between 1 (Ethiopic) Enoch and Luke is a significant means towards a better understanding of the latter, its theology and its sources" (James H. Charlesworth, *The Old Testament Pseudepigrapha and the New Testament* [SNTSMS 54; New York: Cambridge University Press, 1987] 110).

and the human daughters are disembodied, evil spirits which "corrupt, fall" and "cause sorrow" (*1 Enoch* 15,11) until the "great age is consummated" (*1 Enoch* 16,1),[56] then, as R. H. Charles indicates, this representation in *Enoch* is tied to Matt 12,43-45 and Luke 11,24-26 where the unclean spirit walks the waterless places seeking rest.[57]

Interpretation of the sower and the seed

        The image of the wandering, unclean spirit furnishes the background for the interpretation of the sower and the seed,[58] particularly the Lucan account. Although both Matt 13,19 and Luke 8,12 read that the devil comes and takes away the word from the hearers' hearts,[59] Luke clarifies that the διάβολος [= ὁ πονηρὸς Matt] does this so that "they may not believe and be saved"; this purpose clause is uniquely Lucan which supplies a clarification for Judas' deed in the PN. Judas stands among those from whose heart the devil has taken the word. With the heart thus empty, Satan enters it (Luke 22,3).
        Although the *diabolical force* tradition is evident throughout all the gospels and nearly the whole NT, the Lucan redaction with its special material reflects a different way of employing it. This Lucan reworking is evident in the explanation of the sower and the seed (8,11-15), the return of the seventy-two (10,17-20), the Beelzebul controversy (11,14-23; n.b. vv 21-22), the return of the evil spirit (11,24-26), the healing of the crippled woman (13,10-17), and the reply to the Pharisees (13,31-33). These pericopes provide the overarching context for Satan's entering Judas (Luke 22,3) as well as the other references to Satan in the PN.

Luke 22,3

        Luke 22,3 marks a turning point for the *diabolical force* tradition in the third gospel. Whereas in the Lucan account diabolical activity is limited to the world of Jesus' ministry in which Jesus' inner circle of disciples is not touched,[60] the situation changes at Luke 22,3 with Satan's entry into Judas. This verse in turn directs attention onto the next occurrence of Satan at 22,31.

---

[56] *OTPseud* 1; 22.

[57] *APOT* 2; 185.

[58] Matt 13,18-23; Mark 4,13-20; Luke 8,11-15.

[59] Boismard holds that Mark 4,13-20 was introduced into proto-Mark by the Marco-Lucan redactor who was influenced by the Matthean parallel (*Marc* 96).

[60] The case can be made that in the temptation (Luke 4,1-13) the devil impinges upon Jesus himself. It must be borne in mind, however, that Jesus never succumbs to temptation and the devil finally departs until an "opportune time" (4,13).

Précis

The OT and the pseudepigraphic literature provide "fixed points" for the Lucan development of the *diabolical force* and *ministering angel* traditions which are visible in the whole of Luke's gospel, but which are refined in the PN. These traditions have echoes in John which the evangelist utilizes for purposes proper to the fourth gospel.

In Luke 22,3 Judas is the agent of Satan while in the parallel in John (13,27), Judas is identified with the devil, an interpretation based on other readings in John (6,70-71; 13,2).

The Beelzebul controversy (Luke 11,14-23) serves three functions in the third gospel. First, it demonstrates that a) demons, evil and unclean spirits are synonymous terms and b) are underlings of Satan who is also called the devil. Second, its meaning as well as the significance of Jesus' ministry are clarified in succeeding sayings and pericopes, especially the parable of the strong man (11,21-22). Third, it highlights the term *demon* in order to underscore the point that sickness and misfortune result from Satanic influence.

It appears that the Beelzebul pericope has its roots in the canonical and pseudepigraphic OT. These works themselves are part of a *diabolical force* tradition which Luke both utilizes and reshapes in the explanation of the sower and the seed (8,11-15), in the healing of the crippled woman (13,10-17), and in the reply to the Pharisees (13,31-33). With this background in the Lucan gospel, Satan's entering Judas in 22,3 is a result of Satan's own attempt to destroy any good which Jesus has accomplished in his ministry.

"Then the Lord said, 'Simon, Simon, listen! Satan has demanded to sift all of you like wheat'"[61] *(Luke 22,31)*

To be sure, a prediction of Peter's denial exists in all four gospels,[62] but Luke is the only evangelist to include this admonition to Peter; indeed, this verse witnesses the only NT occurrences of ἐξαιτέομαι and σινιάζω,[63] verbs which do not occur in the LXX.

Logion

In some witnesses this verse is prefaced by ειπεν δε ο κυριος[64]

---

[61] The Greek reads ὑμᾶς in v 31 but σοῦ in v 32. The translation of this verse follows the *NRSV* which I believe captures the sense of the Greek.

[62] Matt 26,34; Mark 14,30; Luke 22,34; John 13,38.

[63] *VKGNT* 1/1; 416 and 1/2; 1204.

[64] The *UBSGNT*[4] supplies the apparatus.

א A D W Δ Θ Ψ f^1 f^{13} 157 180 205 565 579 597 700 892 1006 1010
1071 1243 1292 1342 1424 1505 Byz [E F G H N Q] Lect
it(a),aur,b,c,d,(e),f,(ff²),(i),(l),q,(r'1) vg syr(c),(p),h,(pal) (copbo'mss) arm (eth) slav
Basil1/2 (Cyrillem); Tertullianvid Cyprianvid Augustine

Text P75 B L T 1241 syrs copsa,bo geo Basil1/2

The committee for the *UBSGNT*⁴ rate the text as *B*, "almost certain".[65]
Likewise, Fitzmyer does not see an interruption in the narrative which would
necessitate the phrase ειπεν δε ο κυριος; thus, he opts for the shorter reading,
lectio brevior potior.[66] Boismard, however, considers ειπεν δε ο κυριος original;
the Alexandrine tradition, considering the phrase superfluous, omitted it.[67]
Boismard also notes that the style is Lucan,[68] and that the title, "the Lord," is a
typical reference to Jesus outside the apparition narratives. Hence, this verse,
(22,31) is an isolated logion from the tradition.   Furthermore, Boismard
demonstrates that this verse as well as John 13,36-38 arises from a common
source, Document C.[69]
    Günter Klein also sees this Lucan verse (22,31) as a post-Easter logion
which arose within the tradition of the denial.[70] Although at first an anti-Petrine
polemic, this logion later became crystallized into a saying for the edification of
the early church.[71] In addition, Fitzmyer considers the name *Simon* as part of a
pre-Lucan tradition and sees in it a similarity of form with the lament over
Jerusalem (13,34-35),[72] a passage immediately following the Pharisees' warning
to Jesus (13,31-33). As such, its occurrence here signals Luke's intensification
of the *diabolical force*; Herod seeks to kill, but Jesus is resolved, nonetheless, to
continue on his way to Jerusalem, a place of death. These findings all reflect a
gradual development of the tradition, hence, I hold with Boismard that ειπεν δε ο
κυριος is original and introduces an isolated logion.
    Luke's reworking of this tradition is made more keen by the third
evangelist's use of the Hebrew term σατανας which, as Benedetto Prete notes,

---

[65] *UBSGNT*⁴ 3*.

[66] Fitzmyer 2; 1424.

[67] Boismard, private communication.

[68] Cf. 11,39; 17,9; 18,6.

[69] Boismard, *Synopse* 2; 388.

[70] Günter Klein, "Die Berufung des Petrus," *ZNW* 58 (1967) 44. Cf. also
Klein, *Rekonstruktion und Interpretation* (BEvT 50; München: Chr. Kaiser
Verlag, 1969) 49-98.

[71] Klein, "Berufung" 44. Cf. Bailey who posits that John 13,36-38 depends
on Luke 22,31 (*Traditions* 37-9), a point corraborated by Taylor who concludes
that Luke 22,31-33 is of non-Marcan origin (*Passion* 66).

[72] Fitzmyer, *Luke* 2; 1424.

results from Luke's preference for specifying the religious enemy of the apostles, a nuance which the Greek διάβολος lacks.[73] Moreover, this verse witnesses the qualities of a literary seam, a point substantiated by the textual tradition as well as by Klein's own study.

Referent

Fitzmyer suggests that, despite a formulation different from the LXX, the thought content of this verse is similar to Amos 9,9,[74] and thus this verse may be an allusion to the prophecy, "For lo, I will command, and shake the house of Israel among all the nations as one shakes with a sieve". If this verse is a logion, however, its origin would lie closer to the MT. Can a literary connection between this verse and MT Amos 9,9 be maintained? The answer is negative.

MT Amos 9,9

"For lo,I will command, and shake the house of Israel among the nations as one shakes with a sieve, but no pebble shall fall to the ground" (Amos 9,9)

There are several problems with the MT version of Amos 9,9 which preclude this verse as the referent for the logion in Luke 22,31.
Amos 9,9 uses the verb "command" (צָוָה) and not "demand" or "ask" (שָׁאַל). In addition, the term, "sieve" (כְּבָרָה) is a hapaxlegomenon,[75] and (צְרוֹר), whose primary meaning is "bundle, parcel, pouch, bag,"[76] occurs only here and 2 Sam 17,13 as "pebble".[77] Furthermore, there is no Hebrew verb for "sift". In Luke 22,31, Satan is the grammatical subject of the verb "demand"; while in Amos 9,9, the grammatical subject for the verb "command" is God. Luke 22,31 uses the term, "sift," whereas Amos 9,9 employs the phrase "shake...with a sieve".
Some view the Book of Job as the referent for the logion,[78] but neither is this a good solution. True, Job features Satan contesting with God about the protagonist's fidelity, but the piece does not employ the Hebrew verbs discussed above.[79] Furthermore, a major question, surfacing at Luke 22,31, does not apply to either Amos or Job: From whom is Satan making the demand?

---

[73] Benedetto Prete, O.P., *Il Primato e la Missione di Pietro* (Brescia: Paideia Editrice, 1969) 79-80.

[74] Fitzmyer, *Luke* 2; 1424.

[75] BDB 460.

[76] BDB 865.

[77] KB 816.

[78] Cf. Fitzmyer, *Luke* 2; 1424; Lagrange, *Luc* 553; Prete, *Primato* 80.

[79] Cf. Job 1,7.11-12; 2,2.

The difficulties present in linking the logion (Luke 22,31) with either the prophecy in MT Amos 9,9 or Satan's dialogue in Job recommend that there is no connection between the OT texts and the Lucan verse. Has Luke taken Christ's Aramaic logion, and relying on the Amos and Job readings in the LXX, translated the logion into Greek? This solution, too, has difficulties.

LXX Amos 9,9

There are two problems with explaining the logion in Luke 22,31 through LXX Amos 9,9, problems similar to those found in citing MT Amos 9,9 as the referent for this Lucan verse. The first lies with both the grammatical subject and the verb in each respective verse. In Amos, the Lord God commands;[80] in Luke 22,31, Satan demands (ἐξαιτέομαι). The second difficulty surfaces with the different verbs employed by LXX Amos and Luke, λικμάω (crush)[81] and σινιάζω (shake in a sieve)[82] respectively. Because Luke utilizes λικμάω at 20,18 in a non-agricultural vein to express specifically the notion of crush, drawing a parallel between LXX Amos 9,9 and Luke 22,31 is less than accurate.[83]

σινιάζω

The image painted by the use of σινιάζω is clear. To be shaken in a sieve is to be separated and sorted out, and in this Lucan verse, the intent is to describe Satan's desire to separate all the disciples from Christ[84] even though Simon is the one addressed; this is the reason for the use of the plural, ὑμᾶς. In no way does this reading negate Jesus' prayer for Peter's steadfastness in v 32.[85] The term σῖτος, also used in a similar image of separating at Luke 3,17, undergirds the concept of sorting which 22,31 conveys.[86]

---

[80] Cf. MT Amos 9,9: צִוָּה, and LXX Amos 9,9 ἐντέλλομαι.

[81] BAGD 474-5.

[82] BAGD 751.

[83] Prete argues this point as well (Primato 81-3).

[84] Boismard believes that the use of σῖτος here is an echo of John 12,24 which itself is tied to 12,26, a literary contact with 2 Sam 15,21. On the whole, this Johannine verse could have had some contact with the Last Supper (Synopse 2; 388). The context of the Last Supper and discipleship noted by Boismard is plausible, but the emphasis in Luke, I believe, is not on the grain per se but on the action of shaking out for separation.

[85] F. J. Botha's explanation is similar ("'Umâs in Luke xxii. 31," ExpTim 64 [1952-53] 125).

[86] The important difference is that at Luke 3,17 the central image is judgment whereas at 22,31, it is temptation.

ἐξαιτέομαι

A more difficult problem rests with the verb, *ἐξαιτέομαι*. In middle voice, Satan can make the demand only for himself.[87] In addition, as with the MT, the context cannot support the assumption[88] that this verse is a reference to Job[89] because in Job, Satan does not make any demands. In the Lucan context, it does not make sense for Jesus to pray for Peter (v 32) if the Lord had granted Satan permission to *sift* the disciples like wheat. Furthermore, that the verb *ἐξαιτέομαι* does not appear in the LXX and is a hapaxlegomenon in the NT[90] renders weak any appeal to the septuagintal OT, specifically Job, as that which supplies the background to this verse.

To be sure, there are texts supporting the understanding that Satan demands permission from the Lord. *Jub* 10,8-9 has Mastema ask the Lord for control over a portion of the condemned spirits in order to exercise authority over humans for evil until his judgment, to which the Lord responds, "Let a tenth of them remain before him..."[91] Further on, Mastema is the one who suggests to the Lord that Abraham should be tested by directive to sacrifice Isaac (*Jub.* 17,16).[92] The *T. Benj.* reads, "Even if the spirits of Beliar seek to derange you with all sorts of wicked oppression, they will not dominate you, any more than they dominated Joseph, my brother" (3,3).[93] These three pseudepigraphic accounts present Satan in a manner similar to Job 1,1,11-12.

Reliance on Job, *Jub.*, or the *T. Benj.* as the basis of interpretation for Luke 22,31 is not without its problems, despite Lucan dependence on the *diabolical force* tradition as a whole. Kee's choice of the verb *seek* for his translation in *T. Benj.* 3,3 belies the problems in the manuscript tradition of the text.[94] Fitzmyer renders *ἐξαιτέομαι* in Luke 22,31 as *seek out*,[95] and he defends

---

[87] In active voice, *ἐξαιτέομαι* signifies *ask for, from another*; in middle, *ask for oneself, demand* (LS 582). In the NT and early Christian literature, it appears only in middle voice (BAGD 272).

[88] Cf. Fitzmyer, *Luke* 2; 1424; Lagrange, *Luc* 553; Prete, *Primato* 80.

[89] Especially Job 1,7.11-12; 2,2.

[90] *VKGNT* 1/1; 416.

[91] *OTPseud* 2; 76.

[92] *OTPseud* 2; 90.

[93] *OTPseud* 1; 825.

[94] Manuscripts *c* and *S* show *ἐξίστημι* while *β* and *S*[1] read *ἐξαιτέομαι* (*Greek Versions of the Testaments of the Twelve Patriarchs*, ed. R.H. Charles [Oxford: Clarendon Press, 1908] 217 n 14).

[95] Fitzmyer, *Luke* 2; 1424.

his reading by stating that this verse may be an allusion to Satan's roaming upon the earth in Job 1,7 and 2,2. Fitzmyer's translation may be convenient, but it is weakened by the fact that ἐξαιτέομαι never signifies *seek out* nor is there a variant in the text to suggest that it could. Lagrange clarifies that ἐξαιτέομαι means *to demand,* especially for the delivering over of another; thus, it has the sense of *to obtain.*[96]

To whom Satan makes the demand, to Jesus or the disciples, can be answered by observing the role Satan plays in this period. Does Luke view Satan as a prosecuting attorney as in the early OT literature, or as a slanderous, fallen angel as in the later works?[97] Judging by Luke's treatment of Satan throughout L-A -- Satan is never depicted in a position remotely similar to a member of the Council of the Lord as in Job[98] -- it seems that the latter is correct. On this basis, it is possible that Satan makes the demand of the disciples themselves.

The meaning of ἐξαιτέομαι in three secular works makes this interpretation most plausible. The verb ἐξαιτέομαι can mean *demand the surrender of a person;*[99] both Herodotus[100] and Josephus[101] employ it accordingly. Although it is sometimes specified that, when utilized in this manner, the demand is for the surrender of a criminal,[102] there is no reason why it could not refer to the surrender of an enemy; enemies are often criminalized by those for whom they are enemies and indeed, the occurrences in Herodotus and Josephus suggest as much.[103] Combining the understanding of ἐξαιτέομαι present in Herodotus and Josephus with that of Plutarch, a greater precision results. In the *Moralia,* ἐξαιτέομαι appears where "impetuous divinities" (δαίμονες) demand an incarnate human soul in order to work their malice.[104] In all three cases, ἐξαιτέομαι expresses the meaning inherent in the middle voice of *asking or demanding for oneself.*

---

[96] Lagrange, *Luc* 553.

[97] For a discussion of this issue, cf. above and Kelly (*Devil* 202-13).

[98] *Pace* Fitzmyer, Lagrange, and Prete.

[99] LS 582.

[100] Herodotus, *Book* 1,74 (trans. A. D. Godley, Cambridge: Harvard University Press, 1975) LCL 1; 90.

[101] Josephus, *J Ant* 5,2,9 (LCL 5; 70.152).

[102] LS 582.

[103] Herodotus employs it in a description of events leading up to a war between the Lydians and Medes (*Book* 1,73-74 [LCL 1; 88-92]), and Josephus does likewise in relaying the story about the slaughter of the Benjaminites at the hands of the other Israelites (*J Ant* 5,2,8-11 [LCL 5; 62-74.136-65]).

[104] Plutarch, *Moralia V: Obsolescence of Oracles* 417 D (trans. Frank Cole Babbitt, Cambridge: Harvard University Press, 1969) LCL 5; 392.

On this ground, it is most probable that Satan demands of the disciples themselves that they surrender to his temptations, for the followers, like the master, are his enemies. Jesus, who is familiar with temptation, knows full well Satan's designs and his power to accomplish them; hence the notification about the prayer in v 32. That Judas later betrays Jesus (22,47-48) and Peter denies him (22,57.58.60) demonstrate the force of Satan's demand of the disciples to capitulate in order to be *sifted* away and separated from Christ.

Diabolical force tradition

Boismard sees Luke 22,31-34 and John 13,36-38 as a distinct line of tradition.[105] In fact, the whole announcement of the denial in the third gospel, according to Boismard, stands as a definite switch from a Lucan copying of proto-Mark to following a very different tradition known also to John.[106] The major difference here, of course, is the ongoing development of Satan in the Lucan version where neither *Satan* nor the *devil* is limited to Judas as they are in John.[107]

There are several theories accounting for these similarities and differences between Luke and John. Bailey draws a parallel between Luke 22,31 and John 17,15, the only instance in John where it is unclear whether *evil* or the *evil one* is intended.[108] Although Bailey attributes the reading in John 17,15 to Johannine dependence on Luke 22,31,[109] I feel that a preferable explanation can be found in the *diabolical force* tradition, a "fixed point" in both the Lucan and Johannine accounts; the redactors of the third and fourth gospels utilized this tradition to suit their theological purposes. In Luke's case, Satan has already wrested control of the apostle Judas (22,3) and now in 22,31 seeks to continue infiltrating the innermost circle, even to Christ himself.

Précis

The phrase ειπεν δε ο κυριος at Luke 22,31 is original to the text. It is highly probable that this Lucan verse existed as an isolated logion from another context. Analysis of the logion's vocabulary and grammar demonstrates that

---

[105] Boismard, *Marc* 202. So also Schniewind who underlines the similarity of Peter's protest in Luke 22,33 and John 13,37 (*Parallelperikopen* 28). In addition, Boismard demonstrates that Luke and John create a parallel with David's flight from Absalom (*Synopse* 2; 387). Cf. M.-É. Boismard, O.P. and A. Lamouille, *Synopse des Quatre Évangiles: L'Évangile de Jean* [3; Paris: Les Éditions du Cerf, 1977] 347), a point which he later reiterates (*Marc* 204 n 2).

[106] Boismard, *Marc* 204.

[107] John 6,70.71; 13,2.27.

[108] The confusion arises from the use of του πονηρου. Is it the genitive of the masculine ὁ πονηρός or of the neuter τὸ πονηρόν?

[109] Bailey, *Traditions* 40.

linking its context to either MT or LXX Amos 9,9 or Job is baseless. No matter how it existed as an isolated logion, Luke, especially through the verb, ἐξαιτέομαι, reinterprets it according to battle imagery.

Luke's use of σινιάζω stresses the idea that Satan wishes to separate the disciples from Christ. Since by the date of the compilation of the gospel, Satan is no longer portrayed as an adversarial member of the Council of the Lord, and particularly since in the Lucan corpus he is not depicted as one, seeing Luke 22,31 as a thematic echo of *Jub.* 10,8-9; 17,16 and *T. Benj.* 3,3 is unsustainable. Rather, the middle voice of the verb ἐξαιτέομαι specifies that Satan enjoins the disciples to capitulate and to surrender themselves to him so that he can *sift* and *separate* them from Christ. Such an understanding is based on the Lucan context as well as the use of ἐξαιτέομαι in Herodotus, Plutarch, and Josephus.

The similarities between Luke and John can best be explained by their common reliance on the *diabolical force* tradition evident in the canonical and pseudepigraphic OT; Luke borrows from this tradition and develops it into a major theme.

"Then an angel from heaven appeared to him, strengthening him" [110] *(Luke 22,43)*[111]

The Lucan agony scene (22,39-46) is tied to the *diabolical force* tradition by the word πειρασμός which both opens (v 40) and closes (v 46) Jesus' prayer on the Mount of Olives.[112] This scene also reflects the *ministering angel* tradition proposed by Brown;[113] the two traditions, *diabolical force* and *ministering angel* often merge, as, for example, in the synoptic temptation scene.[114] Not only does the *ministering angel* tradition appear among the synoptics, but it also surfaces at John 12,28-29.[115] Common to all four evangelists, then, are those cases where an angel either comes to Jesus' aid[116] or is mentioned as doing so.[117]

---

[110] Translation mine.

[111] For the discussion on the textual tradition of both this verse and v 44 along with the opinions of various scholars, cf. above, Chapter One.

[112] Cf. the temptation scene Matt 4,1 [πειρασθῆναι] (// Mark 1,13 [πειραζόμενος]; Luke 4,2 [πειραζόμενος]).

[113] Brown bases this tradition on Matt 4,11 and Mark 1,13 though he holds that Luke echoes LXX Deut 32,43 (*Messiah* 1; 186-7).

[114] Matt 4,1-11; Mark 1,12-13; Luke 4,1-13.

[115] So also Boismard, *Marc* 206 n 3.

[116] Matt 4,11; Mark 1,13; Luke 22,43.

[117] Matt 4,6; 26,53; Luke 4,10; John 12,28-29.

Boismard champions both a Matthean-Marcan and a Lucan tradition for the formation of the agony scene.[118] In addition, Boismard notes that because neither Luke 22,40 nor John 18,1-2 mentions the name Gethsemane,[119] the Lucan tradition has contact with John.[120] The similarity between John and Luke notwithstanding,[121] the Johannine reading does not digress much from its Matthean and Marcan parallels;[122] only Luke, however, has a ministering angel.

In studying the temptation scene Boismard explains that the *ministering angel* tradition, present only in Matthew and Mark, results from proto-Mark's influence over the final Matthean redaction;[123] he does not analyze the presence of the *ministering angel* in Luke and John.[124] Combining Boismard's research with Dunn's, it is most likely that the *ministering angel* existed in the tradition as a "fixed point". The Matthean-Marcan version placed the "fixed point" at the temptation while the Lucan-Johannine set it at events surrounding the PN. By the final Lucan redaction, it became the strengthening angel of 22,43. This *ministering angel* tradition has a varied background necessitating investigation.

Canonical Old Testament

Angels permeate the OT with over 200 references to an angel or angels in the MT and LXX.[125] This count is based on Greek, ἄγγελος and Hebrew, מַלְאָךְ where "angel" refers either to a messenger of God or to a theophanic angel; in either case, angels can be both personal or communal. When a ministering angel is personal, it rescues an individual or carries a divine message: Gen 19,1-15 (Lot's rescue); 21,17-19 (intercession on behalf of Hagar); 28,12 and 31,11-13 (Jacob's dream); Judg 6,11-22 (announcement to Gideon); 1 Kgs 19,5-7 [LXX 3

---

[118] Boismard, *Marc* 206.

[119] Cf. Matt 26,36; Mark 14,32.

[120] Boismard, *Marc* 206. Cf. also Anton Dauer (*Die Passionsgeschichte im Johannesevangelium* [München: Kösel-Verlag, 1972] 22). Bailey sees a connection between Luke 22,40 and John 18,2 in that both evangelists use τόπος to describe the place of the agony (*Traditions* 47 n 4).

[121] Boismard calls attention to the foretelling of the arrest by Jesus [John 18,4] and the disciples [Luke 22,49] (Boismard, *Marc* 208) as does Bailey (*Traditions* 47-8 n 4).

[122] Boismard, *Marc* 208.

[123] Boismard, *Marc* 57.

[124] Boismard notes, however, the parallel between Luke 22,43 and John 12,27-29 (*Graeca* 363).

[125] HR 7-9. Selected for discussion are those examples considered most representative of the *ministering angel* tradition.

Kgs 19,5-7 (τις)] (aid to Elijah); Dan 3,28 (Daniel's rescue).[126]   When ministering angels are communal, they are often tied to material describing battles against enemies of God's people. Sometimes later literature borrows from earlier works; e.g., the *angel of the Lord* who strikes the camp of the Assyrians (2 Kgs 19,35 (LXX 4 Kgs 19,35) inspires Maccabaeus' prayer for deliverance (2 Macc 15,22-23).[127] LXX Deut 32,43 and Psalm 91,11-13 (LXX 90,11-13), by virtue of the manner in which they are used in the NT, have a prophetic nuance.

All four evangelists utilize angels to greater or lesser degrees, but L-A contains the greatest number of instances.[128] Although the canonical writings of the OT provide the basis for many of the angel passages in the gospels, these same accounts acquired traces of other material, making the determination of traditions influencing a particular gospel, in this case Luke, difficult.

Gnostic literature

That Syria and Asia Minor were main centers of the Gnostic movement in the first century AD[129] makes Gnostic works one of the literary streams present at the time of the formation of the NT. In addition to the Iranian and Hellenistic elements influencing Gnosticism,[130] Jewish sapiential and apocalyptic traditions also exist in Gnostic works, resulting in a highly syncretic literature. The Jewish apocryphal and pseudepigraphic writings furnish most of the material for both Jewish[131] and thus Christian apocalyptic works.

The *Gos. Pet.* provides one example of Gnostic literature which draws close to Luke, but it contains no material related to the *diabolical force* or *ministering angel* traditions.[132]   Likewise, the *Gos. Thom.* features nothing reflecting the semantic field of the diabolical. On the other hand, this gospel contains two occurrences of ἄγγελος. In reply to Jesus' directive, Peter answers that Jesus is like a "righteous angel".[133] In another saying, Jesus states, "The angels and the prophets will come to you and they will give you what is yours".[134]   These two brief logia are unremarkable, stand well within the

---

[126] Cf. also Dan 10,5-12,13.

[127] Cf. also 2 Macc 11,6 and 4 Macc 4,10.

[128] ἄγγελος: 20 occurrences in Matt, 6 in Mark, 46 in L-A, 2 in John (*VKGNT* 1/1; 6-7).

[129] Kurt Rudolph, "Gnosticism," *Anchor Bible Dictionary* (ed. David Noel Freedman, 2; New York: Doubleday, 1992) 1037.

[130] Rudolph, "Gnosticism" 2; 1036.

[131] Rudolph, "Gnosticism" 2; 1036.

[132] For a discussion dating the *Gospel of Peter* later than the canonical gospels, cf. below, Chapter Four.

[133] *Gos. Thom.* 82,34, Log. 9-11 (Brill; 9).

tradition of the *ministering angel*, and as such, are no different from like passages in the canonical and apocryphal Old and New Testaments.

These facts suggest that both the early Church and the Gnostic movement drew from the same Jewish sources. Indeed, Gnostics were eclectic and incorporated in their beliefs whatever they considered useful.[135] Since the gospel writings often echo and sometimes even parallel Jewish pseudepigraphic writings, as do some Gnostic pieces,[136] it seems most probable that, at least in light of the *diabolical force* and *ministering angel* traditions, the Gnostic influence on the gospels is minimal.[137]

Qumran

The manuscripts from the Judean Desert contain a range of writings from "very different periods, varying widely in content and origin".[138] Some of these works offer another literary deposit evidencing imagery of the diabolical and angelic.[139] These depictions are most noticeable in the literature with eschatological content, namely, the *War Scroll*,[140] the *Rule of the Community*,[141]

---

[134] *Gos. Thom.* 96,7-9, Log. 86-91 (Brill; 47).

[135] Bernard McGinn, *The Foundations of Mysticism* (1; New York: Crossroad, 1992) 90.

[136] For example, cf. the journeys of Enoch and Paul in *Apoc. Paul* 22,12-23,30 (*Apoc. Paul*, trans. William R. Murdock and George W. MacRae in *Nag Hammadi Codices* [ed. Douglas M. Parrott, NHS 11; Leiden: E.J. Brill, 1979; 58-61] and *1 Enoch* 46-47 (*OTPseud* 1; 34-5).

[137] On the whole, any Gnostic influence on Christianity would have to enter at a much later date under the influence of Marcionism and Valentianism (AD 2nd cent), as patristic literature testifies. McGinn offers a fine outline of the relationship between Gnosticism and Christianity (*Foundations* 1; 89-99).

[138] Florentino García Martínez, *The Dead Sea Scrolls Translated*, 2nd edition (Leiden: E.J. Brill, 1996) xxiv.

[139] If the Essenes were a Jewish group returning from Babylon to Palestine, as Jerome Murphy-O'Connor, O.P. demonstrates ("The Essenes and Their History," *RB* 81 [1974] esp. 224-9), then the influence of Babylonian literature and imagery in their writings cannot be ruled out.

[140] Cf. references to "Sons of Light" contrasted with "Sons of Darkness" 1QM I,1.11 (Martínez, *Scrolls* 95),
  "Belial" 1QM I,13.15 (Martínez, *Scrolls* 95), 1QM IV,2 (Martínez, *Scrolls* 97), 1QM X,8 (Martínez, *Scrolls* 104), 1QM XIII,2.4.10-12 (Martínez, *Scrolls* 107-8)
  "Princes of God" and "Rule of God" 1QM III,3 (Martínez, *Scrolls* 97)
  "Angels" 1QM IX,15-X,11 (Martínez, *Scrolls* 102-3), 1QM XII,4.8 (Martínez, *Scrolls* 105-6).
  Contrast between salvation and destruction 4papQM^f 4-5 (Martínez, *Scrolls*

the *Visions of Amram*,[142] and the *Damascus Document*,[143] although various other works often make similar allusions.[144]

Martínez maintains that both the "chronological outline" and the "resulting profile" precludes identifying Qumran with either members of an early Christian or Jewish community at the turn of the era,[145] a point substantiated by Jerome Murphy-O'Connor who asserts, "The palaeographical evidence makes it difficult to date any of the events mentioned in the manuscripts later than the middle of the 1st cent. B.C."[146] Furthermore, the manuscripts themselves, in their constant reference to the decisive split between the community and the rest of society, utilize the term "Teacher of Righteousness" for the "senior member of the Sadokite dynasty,"[147] and for the rival Jonathan Maccabaeus, "Wicked Priest".[148] With these two titles, the Judean Desert literature assumes the tone of both the *diabolical force* and *ministering angel* traditions. For present purposes, namely defining the *diabolical force* and *ministering angel* traditions, it is necessary to focus on two issues.

---

121).

[141] Cf. references to "lot of Belial" 1QS II,5 (Martínez, *Scrolls* 4), 5QS I,2 (Martínez, *Scrolls* 32); "Belial" 1QS X,21 (Martínez, *Scrolls* 17), 4QS^f V,2 (Martínez, *Scrolls* 30)
"Prince of Lights," "Angel of Darkness" 1QS III, 20ff (Martínez, *Scrolls* 6).

[142] Émile Puech, following Milik, supplies a reading in 4QVisAmr^{b}2,3 and in 4QVisAmr^{b}3,2 which includes both diabolical and angelic names: Belial, Prince of Darkness, and Melki-resha, Michael, Prince of Light, and Melki-sedek, (*La croyance des Esséniens en la vie future: immortalité, résurrection, vie éternelle? Histoire d'une croyance dans le judaïsme ancien* [EBib 22; Paris: J. Gabalda et Cie, 1993] 535-36).

[143] Cf. references appealing to the "angels of destruction" to visit those who turn aside from the "path" CD II,6 (Martínez, *Scrolls* 34)
"Prince of Lights" contrasted with Belial CD V,18 (Martínez, *Scrolls* 36) [= 4QD^b II,14 (Martínez, *Scrolls* 50), 4QD^d Frag. 2,1 (Martínez, *Scrolls* 60), 6QD Frag. 3,1 (Martínez, *Scrolls* 71)]
"Belial" CD, VIII,2 (Martínez, *Scrolls* 38), CD, XII,2 (Martínez, *Scrolls* 42) [= 4QD^c Frag. 3,18 (Martínez, *Scrolls* 59)]
"Angel Mastema" CD, XVI, 5 (Martínez, *Scrolls* 39)
"Sons of Light" 4QD^a Frag. 1,1 (Martínez, *Scrolls* 48).

[144] Cf. also 4QFlor I,8; (Martínez, *Scrolls* 136); 4QPs^f X,10-12 (Martínez, *Scrolls* 304); 1QH XI, 28-32 (Martínez, *Scrolls* 333).

[145] Martínez, *Scrolls* lii.

[146] Murphy-O'Connor, "Essenes" 216.

[147] Murphy-O'Connor, "Essenes" 230.

[148] Murphy-O'Connor, "Essenes" 229.

First, the dating of the extra-canonical OT, particularly *1* and *2 Enoch*, *Jubilees*, and the *Testaments of the 12 Patriarchs* is almost identical to that of the Qumran scrolls.   The Essenes were a sect of Judaism, and the Qumran community was a sect of the Essenes;[149] this fact is reflected in their restricted ideology, specifically, a dispute about temple worship[150] and fear of contamination from the greater society.[151] Hence, it is plausible to state that, for their writings, they borrowed from the OT and its pseudepigrapha instead of *vice-versa*.

Second, since an apocalyptic tone is a characteristic of the Essene community in general, the Qumran community reinterpreted the genre according to their own ideology. Because they were pious Jews, in forming their writings they drew upon the apocalyptic material of the canonical and extra-canonical OT. This would explain the existence of a great number of biblical books among the Dead Sea Scrolls.

While the manuscripts from the Judean Desert may not have influenced the formation of the *diabolical force* and *ministering angel* traditions within the canonical and extra-canonical OT, the Judean Desert writings are representative of a group that drew upon material to which other groups also had access. One of these groups was the early Christian community. As Martínez notes, the retrieval of the extra-canonical books on the "periphery" of the Bible, no matter how fragmentary, "allows us to envisage the breadth of para-biblical literature in circulation".[152] Though it is more likely that the canonical and extra-canonical OT are the wellspring of the *diabolical force* and *ministering angel* traditions, the Judean Desert writings represent a development, or at least a branch, of these two traditions.

Visions of Amram

An example of the Judean Desert influence can be seen in the *Visions of Amram*, especially in the interplay between light and darkness; the former is always associated with the good, and the latter, with the bad. A pre-Qumranic work,[153] the *Visions of Amram*, arises from a sect which, in the words of Émile Puech, shows a "...dualism to the degree never before seen in Jewish literature".[154] Furthermore, Puech, along with Milik, believes that the work

---

[149] Murphy-O'Connor explains that the "Teacher of Righteousness" and his followers moved to Qumran after having split from the main group of Essenes. At this point, those at Qumran referred to the larger body of Essenes as followers of the "Man of Lies" ("Essenes" 238).

[150] Martínez, *Scrolls* liii-liv.

[151] Murphy-O'Connor, "Essenes" 238.

[152] Martínez, *Scrolls* 218.

[153] *Pre-Qumranic* means copied but not composed at Qumran.

[154] Puech, *Croyance* 532.

dates from at least the Second Century BC.[155] The *Visions*, stemming from five (maybe six) Aramaic manuscripts, pits an evil force against the good. The evil force has three names: Belial, Prince of Darkness, and Melki-resha.[156] Likewise, the good force has three names as well: Michael, Prince of Light, and Melki-sedek.[157]

War Scroll

Judean Desert influence on the *diabolical force* and *minstering angel* traditions is even more pronounced in the *War Scroll*. In this work, Puech delineates an evolution of eschatology.[158] Here, the "angel of darkness" and the "sons of darkness" encounter the "prince of light" (Michael) and the "sons of justice" in the eschatological battle.[159] Michael is on the side of the eternal light, but he is only the personification of Yahweh's earthly interventions.[160] Puech notes that in 1QM XII 4, XIII 10,15, or Dan 10,13.21, Michael is the prince of gods.[161] Such phraseology, holds Puech, is directly from Dan 12,1.[162]

As Puech observes, in 1QM XIII, the theme of light occupies a central position.[163] The great battle is fixed by God and confided to his prince of light, Michael, who will lead the faithful.[164] Michael will illuminate the faithful while exterminating the guilty and binding Belial forever.[165]

The *War Scroll*, specifically column 14, shows the lot of these conquerors. Puech notes the phrase "...great is your design of glory, and the secrets of your marvels are so exalted as to elevate the dust to You while debasing the gods"(1QM XIV 14ff).[166] Whether this is a direct or indirect

---

[155] Puech, *Croyance* 532.

[156] 4QVisAmr^b2,3 (Puech, *Croyance* 535).

[157] 4QVisAmr^b3,2 (Puech, *Croyance* 536).

[158] Puech dates the scroll from Cave 1 from the beginning to the middle of the First Century BC (*Croyance* 447).

[159] Puech, *Croyance* 461.

[160] Puech, *Croyance* 461.

[161] Puech states that this is in contrast to the *Hymns* (1QH XVIII 10 (=X 8) where God is the prince of gods (*Croyance* 461).

[162] Puech, *Croyance* 461.

[163] Puech, *Croyance* 463.

[164] Puech, *Croyance* 466.

[165] N.b. the similarity to the synoptic parable of the strong man (Mark 3,27; Matt 12,29; Luke 11,22).

allusion to the resurrection, Puech sees it as a reference to a transformation of the Just One, a creature of dust and ashes, who, in light and in the company of angels, is called to participate in the eternal inheritance and to celebrate God, the Creator and Savior.[167] Moreover, Puech affirms that such an idea is similar to 1QH XI (=III), XIV (=VI), and even Tobit 4,19; 13,2 thus showing the similarity with contemporaneous texts treating the same subject.[168]

The Pseudepigraphic Old Testament

The pseudepigraphic OT is rife with accounts of good and fallen angels, the battles between them, and their corresponding rewards and punishments; much of the literature is exceedingly repetitious. The whole notion of the angels' fall from grace is predicated on the understanding that good angels existed before some of them sinned or rebelled. Although this concept is implied in the canonical OT, it is elaborated in the pseudepigraphic works, especially *1 Enoch*[169], *2 Enoch*[170], selected books in the *T. 12 Patr.*,[171] and the *Jub.*[172] The *Mart. Isa.*,[173] while it does not recount an angel, is also part of the tradition. For the purpose of studying the development of the *diabolical force* and *ministering angel* traditions then, these five works furnish the most pertinent material.

---

[166] Puech, *Croyance* 479.

[167] Puech, *Croyance* 479.

[168] Puech, *Croyance* 479.

[169] *OTPseud* 1; 13-89. *1 Enoch* is a composite piece with the dates of individual works ranging from the early 3rd cent. BC to the end of AD 1st cent. (*OTPseud* 1; 7). Charles notes that the entire myth of angels in Enoch is based on Gen 6,1-4 (*APOT* 2; 191 n VI.2).

[170] *OTPseud* 1; 102-213. The Book of the Secrets of Enoch (*2 Enoch*) is known only from manuscripts in Old Slavonic whose linguistic features betray Greek "words and expressions" (*OTPseud* 1; 94). Andersen, noting both its early and late sections, is inclined to place at least the original nucleus as the work of an early Jewish group which held marginal if not deviant beliefs (*OTPseud* 1; 97).

[171] *OTPseud* 1; 782-828. Kee dates the *T. 12 Patr.* ca. 150 BC (*OTPseud* 1; 778).

[172] *OTPseud* 2; 52-142. Wintermute dates this work to between 161-140 BC (*OTPseud* 2; 44).

[173] *OTPseud* 2; 156-64. Although the final redaction of the *Mart. Isa.* dates to the first century AD, the basic material of the *Martyrdom* itself (1,1-3,12 and 5,1-16) is the oldest element and is of Jewish origin (Knibb, "Martyrdom" *OTPseud* 2; 143 and 149). Kelly dates this to the second half of the first century BC (Kelly, "Devil" 210 n 55).

Martyrdom of Isaiah

According to Kelly, the *Mart. Isa.*[174] evidences a thematic structure similar to Jesus' temptation in the desert.[175]   Because under Manasseh the worship of Satan arose in Jerusalem, Isaiah withdraws from there to Bethlehem, and thence to a "mountain in a desert place" (*Mart. Isa.* 2,7-8).[176]   It is because Beliar dwelt in the hearts of Manasseh, the princes of Judah and Benjamin, the eunuchs, and king's counselors (n.b. Luke 22,3) that Isaiah is seized and sawn in two (*Mart. Isa.* 3,11-12; 5,11).   With the lure that Manasseh and the princes will worship Isaiah, Belkira/Beliar demands that the prophet apostasize (*Mart. Isa.* 5,2-8).

Discernible in the *Mart. Isa.* is a counterpart to both Jesus' desert temptation and to his agony on the Mount of Olives.   As in the *Martyrdom*, the devil's testing of Jesus features the temptation to self-glorification.[177]   Isaiah refuses (*Mart. Isa.* 5,9-10); equally so, Jesus (Luke 4,8).   Isaiah's steadfastness leads to his death but not before he tells his sympathetic prophets, "Go to the district of Tyre and Sidon, because for me alone the Lord has mixed the cup" (*Mart. Isa.* 5,13).[178]   Of course, Jesus speaks of the cup during the agony;[179] thus, this apocryphal piece combines the notions of temptation, death, and cup which, in the gospels, are divided between the desert temptation and the agony on the Mount of Olives.

The points of contact between *Mart. Isa.* and the Lucan temptation and agony scenes bring to relief three pertinent points.   First, Beliar/devil is the tempter; second, the cup which God offers leads to death; third, there is no ministering angel.   The dating of the *Mart. Isa.* along with the thematic parallels between it and the temptation and agony pericopes among the three synoptics strongly suggest that this piece represented a prototypical *diabolical force* in the formation of the gospel tradition.   Although there is no *ministering angel* in the *Mart. Isa.*, in terms of the development of the four gospels, all appearances suggest that a Matthean-Marcan tradition combined a *ministering angel* with the temptation scene while a Lucan-Johannine one set it in the PN.   The existence of such a tradition alongside the *diabolical force* has its precedents in the pseudepigraphic literature.

---

[174] Kelly, "Devil" 210 n 55.

[175] Kelly, "Devil" 210-1.

[176] Of course, Exod 16,2ff and Deut 8,2-3a form the prototype for the desert scene in *Mart. Isa.* as well as for the gospel accounts of the temptation.

[177] Luke 4,6-7a (// Matt 4,9).

[178] *OTPseud* 2; 164.

[179] Luke 22,42 (// Matt 26,39b; Mark 14,36).

Summary

The development of the *ministering angel* and the *diabolical force* is traceable in both the canonical OT and the intertestamental books.

The concept of the *ministering angel* exists in the OT which can be both personal (Gen 19,1-15; 21,17-19; 28,12 and 31,11-13; Judg 6,12-22; 1 Kgs 19,5-7 [LXX 3 Kgs 19,5-7]; Dan 3,28) and communal (2 Kgs 19,35 [LXX 4 Kgs 19,35]; 2 Macc 15,22-23).[180] Included as well but outside these categories are two other citations (Ps 91,11-13 [LXX 90,11-13] and LXX Deut 32,43). This *ministering angel* theme is greatly elaborated in certain pseudepigraphic works alongside that of the *diabolical force*. The *Mart. Isa.* features traces of the latter, and in terms of the gospel, offers the clearest thematic parallel. Here, the devil is portrayed as a liar and tempter, and to suffer him is depicted metaphorically as partaking of a cup (*Mart. Isa.* 5,1-14).

The extra-canonical works feature an elaboration of the *ministering angel* tradition. There is a dichotomy between good angels and bad angels (*T. Ash.* 6,1-5). The latter fell from grace either from lust by taking human daughters as wives (*T. Reub.* 5,6; *T. Naph.* 3,5; *Jub.* 4,21-22; 5,1-2), or from pride by erecting a throne equal to God's (*2 Enoch* 29,1-5). These fallen angels wreak havoc within creation (*Jub.* 10,8-9) while the good angels combat them (*1 Enoch* 9-16).

The literature speaks about the restitution of good in the end times (*1 Enoch* 1,1-5,10) after a major battle between good and fallen angels (*1 Enoch* 9-16). In addition there are angels who work on behalf of humanity (*1 Enoch* 9-11; *Jub.* 4,15; *Jub.* 10,10-12).

There is punishment for sinners (*T. Ash.* 6,1-5) and their leaders, the fallen angels (*2 Enoch* 7,1-10,1-6). Sin is simultaneously considered the heart's or soul's servitude to Beliar (*T. Dan* 5,10-11; *Jub.* 15,33-34), but the Lord will raise up a new priest who will bind him (*T. Levi* 18,2-14).

The good become identified with Israel who are protected by an angel (*T. Levi* 5,1-7; *T. Ash.* 6,5; *Jub.* 2,17-22; *T. Dan* 6,1-10), while *Jubilees* distinguishes that, whereas other nations have angels as guardians, Israel has the Lord alone (*Jub.* 15,30-32).

The pre-Qumranic and Qumranic works, the *Visions of Amram* and the *War Scroll* respectively are eschatological in content. The *Visions* (4QVisAmr^b2,3; 4QVisAmr^b3,2) shows a heightened dualism between good and bad represented by the terms *light* and *darkness* as well as by both angelic and diabolical personages. The *War Scroll* (1 QM XIV 14ff) develops this theme into an allusion of the resurrection through the transformation of the Just One.

Several episodes in these pseudepigraphic works, by virtue of their messianic overtones, are worthy of specific mention. In the conclusion to the *T. Dan*[181], the patriarch warns the children to beware of Satan while advising them to draw near to the interceding angel who stands in opposition to the kingdom of the enemy (*T. Dan* 6,1-10). The description of this angel breaks the pattern of the good angel battling the evil forces present in so many of the pseudepigraphic works. The interceding angel for the peace of Israel, described as the mediator

---

180 Cf. also 2 Macc 11,6-10 and 4 Macc 4,10.

181 *OTPseud* 1; 810.

between God and humanity, stands in opposition to the enemy (*T. Dan* 6,2-3). The enemy is ever eager to "trip up" those calling on the Lord because he knows that on the day in which Israel does so, "the enemy's kingdom will be brought to an end" (*T. Dan* 6,4). In the *T. Levi*[182] (18,2-14) the task of the interceding angel depicted in *T. Dan* is melded with that of the new priest, raised by the Lord, who will bind Beliar;[183] this concept is paralleled in *T. Sim.* 6,5-6[184] and *T. Zeb.* 9,8,[185] and it is particularly emphasized in *Jub.* 15,30-32.

Luke 22,43

Although it is nearly impossible to define an exact correlation between many of these works and the Lucan gospel, they nonetheless bear on Luke's treatment of the *ministering angel* and *diabolical force* traditions within the Lucan corpus, for they represent the OT tradition and background to this verse.

By moving the *ministering angel* from the temptation scene (4,13) to the agony on the Mount of Olives, Luke has underscored the sinister force which Christ must encounter. The presence of an angel also signals the apocalyptic nature of this encounter as well as that of the approaching death. Christ takes on the role of Israel's protecting angel, and it is at this point that Luke reinterprets the *ministering angel* tradition. Whereas the tradition depicts ministering angels helping Israel and the forces of good in the last days, in 22,43, the angel supports Christ as he prepares to battle the evil force, alone. Unlike the canonical, extra-canonical, and pseudepigraphic OT, the angel in the Lucan agony scene does not go into battle. Hence, in his prayer and acceptance of the cup, Jesus takes on the role of both Israel's ministering angel and the new priest who will overcome Beliar.[186] Furthermore, the reading from *Jub.* 15,30-32 opens the possibility of interpreting Christ as the divine intercessor for Israel. It is with this understanding that Jesus approaches his arrest in 22,53.

Précis

With the exception of the *Mart. Isa.*, the tradition of the *diabolical force* exists side by side with that of the *ministering angel*. It is evident that these two traditions, while intimated in various books of the OT, become even more pronounced in the intertestamental period.

---

[182] *OTPseud* 1; 794-5.

[183] Cf. also Isa 24,21-23.

[184] *OTPseud* 1; 787. It is not clear whether v 6, like the preceding v 5, is a Christian interpolation (cf 787 n c).

[185] *OTPseud* 1; 807.

[186] Cf. *T. Levi* 18,2-14 (*OTPseud* 1; 794-5) but Luke 11,22 (// Matt 12,29; Mark 3,27).

The research of Boismard and Dunn allows that the *ministering angel* tradition existed as a "fixed point". Matthew and Mark set the "fixed point" at the temptation while Luke and John placed it within the context of the PN. A Lucan redactor turned it into the strengthening angel of 22,43.

In the canonical OT, 2 Kgs 19,35 (LXX 4 Kgs 19,35) and 2 Macc 15,22-23[187] are passages which display a *ministering angel* on behalf of the people Israel while Gen 19,1-15; 21,17-19; 28,12 and 31,11-13; Judg 6,12-22; 1 Kgs 19,5-7 (LXX 3 Kgs 19,5-7), Dan 3,28 display this angel in a more personal frame. The citations from LXX Deut 32,43 and Psalm 91,11-13 (LXX 90,11-13), feature an angel outside these two categories.

Among the extra-canonical works, Gnostic literature has very little if any influence on the NT in general and the *ministering angel* tradition in particular. The pre-Qumranic, *Visions of Amram*, introducing "light" and "darkness" imagery, exhibit an early form of Jewish dualism. The *War Scroll* represents a further refinement of the dualism into an eschatology which includes a notion of resurrection.

The greatest development of the *ministering angel* and the *diabolical force* traditions, however, is evident in works of the pseudepigraphic OT, especially the *Mart. Isa.*, *1 and 2 Enoch*, selected books in the *T. 12 Patr.*, and *Jub.*

"But this is your time, and the dominion of darkness"[188]
(Luke 22,53b)[189]

It appears that Luke shares with John a common tradition from which this verse arises, which is visible in John 12,31 with an allusion in John 14,30 and 16,11. Boismard notes this as well[190] and also observes the Johannine tone of Luke 22,52b-53 where the presence of chief priests in v 52 is combined with Jesus' statement in v 53a about teaching in the temple. This verse seems to be influenced by the interrogation scene in John 18,20.[191] Furthermore, Boismard notes that the themes of *hour* (John 16,4) and *darkness* evoke the Johannine juxtaposition of *light* and *darkness*, and thus, the domination of the "ruler of this world".[192]

On this ground, the common *diabolical force* tradition reflected in Luke 22,53 and John 12,23.27.31 stands as a "fixed point". At a certain stage in the Lucan and Johannine redaction this tradition was adapted to suit their respective emphases. For Luke this is the dominion of darkness and by extension, Satan; for John, it is the encounter with the ruler of this world, the hour of glorification.

---

[187] Cf. also 2 Macc 11,6-10 and 4 Macc 4,10.

[188] Translation mine.

[189] For the opinions of various scholars on this verse, cf. above, Chapter One.

[190] Boismard, *Synopse* 2; 396-7.

[191] Boismard, *Synopse* 2; 396.

Power and Authority

The synoptics display near unanimity in not crediting any authority to Satan; when they employ ἐξουσία it refers either to political and religious rulers or to Jesus' authority.[193] This fact makes the only four exceptions occurring in L-A (Luke 4,6; 12,5; 22,53; Acts 26,18) important for defining the Lucan worldview. The issue is whether with the employment of ἐξουσία, Luke intends *power*, *authority*, or the *domain in which the authority is exercised*.

The manner in which the synoptics apply δύναμις helps to resolve the problem.[194] The term δύναμις, never appearing in John, is restricted to the synoptics where it has two basic meanings: in singular, *might*, *power*, or *ability*; in plural, *wonders* or *mighty works*. The two nouns, ἐξουσία and δύναμις appear together in Luke 4,36; 9,1; 10,19; in Acts 4,7 δύναμις is paired with ἐν ποίῳ ὀνόματι, a phrase whose context demands that it be read as ἐξουσία. One of the derivative definitions of ἐξουσία is *power*, the primary meaning of δύναμις.

What does ἐξουσία signify in Luke 22,53b? Luke is the only evangelist to combine ἐξουσία and δύναμις in the same verse. This style would not be necessary if Luke, who avoids needless repetition throughout L-A, felt that these two nouns were synonyms; Luke, however, is differentiating the two terms. Luke uses δύναμις to mean *power*[195] and ἐξουσία to signify *authority* or *domain in which it is exercised*.[196] Hence, ἐξουσία should be rendered as *authority*, or especially for Luke 22,53 and Acts 26,18, *reign* or *dominion*.[197]

This point is underscored in Luke 4,6 and 12,5. These verses are Q sayings[198] which in Matt 4,9 and 10,28b appear without ἐξουσία. Because Matthew lacks consistency (Matt 4,9 shows neither δύναμις nor ἐξουσία while Matt 10,28b exhibits the participle δυνάμενον), it is more plausible that the occurrence of ἐξουσία in Luke 4,6 and 12,5 is the result of a redactor's hand.[199]

---

[192] Cf. John 12,31; 14,30; 16,4.11 (Boismard, *Synopse* 2; 396-7).

[193] ἐξουσία, expresses *right to act*; *ability to do something, capability, might, power*; *authority, absolute power, warrant*; *ruling power, official power, domain in which it is exercised, bearers of authority* (BAGD 277-9).

[194] δύναμις signifies *power, might, strength, force*; *ability, capability*; *deed of power, miracle, wonder*; *the externals of power*; *power as a personal supernatural spirit or angel*; *that which gives power* (BAGD 207-8).

[195] BAGD 207.

[196] BAGD 278.

[197] Such a concept is not without its parallels. In anger against the fallen angels who take human wives, God commanded that they be "uprooted from all their dominion" (*Jub.* 5,6; *OTPseud* 2; 64). 1QM XIV,9 speaks about the "empire of Belial" (Martínez, *Scrolls* 109) which is contrasted in 1QM XVII,6 with the "dominion" of Michael (Martínez, *Scrolls* 112).

[198] Havener, *Q* 124 and 136.

[199] Boismard believes Luke added "puissance" to 4,6 (*Synopse* 2; 86) but that

Thus, an important component of the Lucan PN, indeed the whole Lucan corpus, becomes evident: Satan not only maintains power which must be neutralized; the devil also has a dominion which must be conquered.

Satan's Domain

At the Lucan temptation scene, the evangelist evinces that the devil's dominion lacks legitimacy. After showing Jesus all the kingdoms of the world, the devil states, "To you I will give their glory and all this authority; for it has been given over to me, and I give it to anyone I please" (Luke 4,5-6). These lines constitute part of a quotation from LXX Dan 4,31ff where God announces to Nebuchadnezzar that the King's authority, glory, and delight will be taken away until he recognizes that God has sovereignty over the kingdom of humankind, and he gives it to whom he wills. The devil, in tempting Jesus, tries to usurp God's authority. Jesus repudiates the devil's presumption by reminding him, "It is written, 'Worship the Lord your God, and serve only him'" (Luke 4,8). As the Lord God stood above Nebuchadnezzar, so too does he stand over the devil.

At the outset of the gospel, then, Luke establishes that, as powerful as the diabolical realm may be, it is illicit, and moreover, it is subject to the power of God. Further on in the Lucan narrative, Jesus alludes to this circumstance in the parable of the strong man (Luke 11,21-22).[200]

Where, then, does the devil's reign hold sway? It would be simple to consider the Lucan diabolical realm as this world, i.e., κόσμος, but this does not bear up under scrutiny. Nowhere do the synoptics speak of κόσμος in a way in which it could be characterized as Satan's dominion.[201] Hence, locating this reign becomes problematic, but the use of an adnominal genitive[202] with ἐξουσία in both Luke 22,53 and Acts 26,18 clarifies the matter.

In Acts 26,18 ἀπό governs σκότος and ἐξουσία, while εἰς/ἐπί rule φῶς and θεός. As such, the comparison is between ἐξουσία and θεός. Luke often prefers the genitive to an adjective,[203] thus in English the phrase could read, "...from the Satanic dominion to God." Like its counterpart in Acts 26,18, the phrase ἡ ἐξουσία τοῦ σκότους in Luke 22,53 would also translate as an adjectival phrase, "...dark dominion". Luke is speaking about a dark dominion which matches the Satanic dominion of Acts 26,18. Hence, not only does σκότος stand in the same semantic field as Satan, it is also a synonym of the forces of evil themselves: Satan, demons and unclean spirits. An investigation into the Lucan usage of σκότος and its cognates illustrates this point.

---

readings in Justin and 2 Clem 5,3-4 indicate that 12,5 ἐξουσία is Q material (*Synopse* 2; 279-80).

[200] Cf. above, Chapter Two.

[201] In all cases, Matthew, Mark, and Luke treat κόσμος as the material creation (*VKGNT* 1/1; 698-9).

[202] BDF 89 para. 162.

[203] BDF 89.

Darkness

In Luke, there is little difference between σκοτία and σκότος.[204] Although the terms denote physical darkness, their context often dictates a metaphorical meaning; the term σκοτία appearing in a Q account, Matt 10,27 and Luke 12,3,[205] represents *secrecy* in both gospels though in Luke it has a pejorative connotation.[206]   A similar negative sense exists with σκότος in the sound eye discourse (Luke 11,34-36), also a Q pericope.[207] Boismard explains that the pericope depends on the Semitic perspective which understands the eye as the organ of discernment and the body as the totality of the human person.[208] Thus, the parable describes a contrast between eye/body and light/darkness which can absorb many applications on a moral, intellectual, and even ontological plain.[209] In this case, *light* is good and *darkness* is bad. The one occurrence of σκότος which has a parallel in the other two synoptics lies in the description of the three-hour period of darkness at the crucifixion.[210]

In the material proper to Luke alone, the meaning of σκότος is further developed.   In Zechariah's canticle, the traditional *Benedictus* (Luke, 1,79), Luke has σκότος represent ignorance of salvation, a concept amplified by the phrase, "in the shadow of death".   In the Acts, σκότος occurs three times. Peter's quotation from LXX Joel 3,4 in his pentecost speech (2,20), has an apocalyptic tone. This echo of the Lucan death account (23,44), present in the phrase, "The sun shall be turned to darkness", helps to interpret the crucifixion. Jesus' death stands as part of the Lord's visitation when salvation will come to any who call upon the Lord's name (Acts 2,21).

Darkness falls upon Elymas the magician when Paul strikes him blind (Acts 13,11).   In the previous verse, Paul calls the deceitful Elymas, who perverts the straight paths of the Lord, υἱὲ διαβόλου, thus connecting darkness with the devil, a link which prepares the reader for the final Lucan use of σκότος at Acts 26,18. This verse displays the analogy, that darkness is to Satan as light is to God.

---

[204] σκοτία: Luke 12,3; no occurrence in Acts. σκότος: Luke 1,79; 11,35; 22,53; 23,44; Acts 2,20; 13,11; 26,18 (*VKGNT* 1/2; 1206-7).

[205] Havener, *Q* 136. Boismard notes that the logion in both these gospels has been so altered to fit their respective context that it is impossible to determine its sense in Q (*Synopse* 2; 278-9).

[206] Cf. also John 13,30 where the evangelist makes special mention that it was night when Judas left the table after Satan had entered him (13,27).

[207] Cf. Matt 6,22-23 and Havener, *Q* 134.

[208] Boismard, *Synopse* 2; 277.

[209] Boismard, *Synopse* 2; 277.

[210] Matt 27,45; Mark 15,33; Luke 23,44. Cf. also Chapters Three and Four below.

Hour

The use of the term ὥρα in L-A has at least two meanings.[211] On the first level it is a specific point in the day. Generally, this first level indicates a second one in which ὥρα takes on a broader meaning as the time of revelation or visitation; this is often eschatological. That this is the sense of 22,53 is clarified by two other verses.

In Luke 10,21 Jesus rejoices at the return of the seventy-two who have finished their mission in which they exorcised demons in Christ's name and who receive from him the power over the enemy. In this prayer to the Father, Jesus relates that things hidden from the wise are revealed (ἀποκαλύπτω) to babes. And what is revealed? The answer lies in the previous verse: a) that spirits submit to the disciples, and b) that the disciples' names are written in heaven. Hence, ὥρα in Luke 10,21 combines the subjection of evil spirits with the revelation of salvation.

Luke 12,12 is placed within the admonition of confessing Christ before others. When followers are brought before "synagogues, the rulers, and the authorities" (v 11), they should not worry; at that *hour*, the Holy Spirit will teach them what to say. This pericope's setting foreshadows the arrest scene in 22,53 where Jesus is about to be hauled before the Sanhedrin, an occasion in which he reveals himself as the Son of Man (22,67-70). So too with the disciples, at the hour of their arrest, there will be an inbreaking of the Holy Spirit. This hour of trial, itself a manifestation of evil, becomes then a moment of revelation. The revelatory nature of this hour is underlined by the scribes' and chief priests' aborted attempt to arrest Jesus (20,19) after his telling the parable of the vineyard and tenants (20,9-18); Jesus' hour has not yet arrived.

To be sure, the meaning of ὥρα in Luke 22,53 encapsulates the readings of 10,21 and 12,12 *vis-a-vis* evil and revelation, but in these two verses, ὥρα is restricted to the sense of *hour, moment, time*.[212] The Lucan arrest scene in 22,53 extends the concept of *moment* or *time* inherent in ὥρα to represent *period* or *duration* which, by virtue of the phrase, ἡ ἐξουσία τοῦ σκότους, also signifies the reign of the diabolical.[213] The arresting authorities are incorporated into the evil dominion and its reign by the specification ὑμῶν ἡ ὥρα.

Comparison: diabolical force in John

The Johannine writings display a treatment of the *diabolical force* which is different from the Lucan tradition, and as such, they provide a point of comparison. Many of the contacts between these two evangelists have been noted above, but one of these, John 13,2.27 and Luke 22,3 approach being parallel passages.[214] Because John uses the terms "Satan" and the "devil" as references

---

[211] The noun ὥρα occurs in Luke 1,10; 2,38; 7,21; 10,21; 12,12.39.40.46; 13,31; 14,17; 20,19; 22,14; 22,53.59; 23,44 *bis*; 24,33 and in Acts 2,15; 3,1; 5,7; 10,3.9.30; 16,18.33; 19,34; 22,13; 23,23 (*VKGNT* 1/2; 1344).

[212] BAGD 896.

[213] Cf. also Brown (*Messiah* 1; 765).

to Judas, in effect, making a human being, Satan,[215] his use of the *diabolical force* tradition differs considerably from Luke's; the third evangelist never identifies the devil with material creation, let alone a human personage.

John, however, displays another level of interpretation of the *diabolical force*. Unlike the Lucan gospel, however, in which the diabolical dominion of darkness can be sensed but not touched, John makes it tangible by referring to that same dominion as the κόσμος. In the farewell discourse promising the Holy Spirit, Jesus refers to the ruler of the world (14,30). Christ clarifies that the ἄρχων κόσμου has no power over him (literally, *"He has nothing over me"*). This reference is a thematic echo of the Lucan temptation scene where Luke underscores the illegitimacy of the devil's dominion (Luke 4,5-6).[216] Further on in the discourse, Jesus states that, even though the Advocate will come and will prove the world wrong (ἐλέγχω, fut), the "ruler of this world" has already been condemned (κρίνω, perf pass).

The Johannine diabolical force may be condemned, but it still has power. Toward the end of the discourse, Jesus prays, "I am not asking you to take them out of the world, but I ask you to protect them from the evil one (17,15).[217] Such an understanding carries over into 1 John where the writer tells the community, "I write to you, young people, because you are strong and the word of God abides in you, and you have overcome the evil one" (1 John 2,14). As in the Johannine gospel, the "evil one" in 1 John, though overcome, still has power, "We know we are God's children, and that the whole world lies under the power of the evil one" (1 John 5,19).[218]

Both Luke and John view the diabolic dominion as illegitimate, though Luke is clearer than John in expressing the devil as a usurper. Both evangelists also note that the devil or evil one has a dominion. John alone, however, refers to Judas as "Satan," thus making the devil a human personage. John also specifies that the devil's dominion is the material universe; Luke's interpretation of the dominion is less tangible. In both cases, Jesus has overcome the power of the *diabolical force* despite the fact that the effects of that power still remain.

Précis

This verse represents elements of the *diabolical force* tradition from which both Luke and John draw but use for their own respective purposes. The phrase ἡ ἐξουσία τοῦ σκότους in Luke 22,53 establishes that Satan has power and a dominion against which Christ must battle. In the desert temptation scene, Luke

---

[214] Cf. above.

[215] Nb. John 6,70-71.

[216] Cf. above.

[217] Or "evil".

[218] For a discussion on the relationship between John's gospel and and 1 John, cf. M.-É. Boismard, O.P., *Moïse ou Jésus, Essai de christologie johannique* (Leuven: University Press, 1988).

demonstrates that the devil is a usurper and his dominion has no legitimacy (Luke 4,6-8). On one level, the term *hour* signifies *moment, time, or instant,* and on another, *period* or *duration.* Both levels of interpretation are applied to the arrest when Satan marshals the forces of his evil reign to begin the final assault through the agency of the authorities. In addition, the hour of evil will also be the hour of visitation and revelation.

The evil dominion in John is attributed to the world, and Judas is called Satan. Hence, John equates a human with Satan and the created universe with the material world, something which Luke does not do. In John, the *diabolical force* is defeated by the Advocate whom Jesus will send; in Luke, it meets its judgment at the cross.

Conclusion

Part One displays an overarching analysis of the Lucan PN. A number of themes surface from this investigation, including one demanding greater attention, the *diabolical force* and *ministering angel.* This *diabolical force* hangs as a sinister cloud over the whole earthly ministry but becomes more menacing in the PN. By refashioning "fixed points", Luke constructs Satan's movements on the battlefield. Evidence of the devil's encroachment surfaces at 22,3.31.43.53 thus making these verses a key for the entire Lucan design.

It is evident that Luke draws upon references from the canonical OT and the intertestamental pseudepigrapha for the development of the *ministering angel* and *diabolical force.* But Luke does not borrow uncritically. The Lucan interpretation stands in stark contrast to the Judean desert writings, themselves nearly contemporaneous with the formation of the gospels.

The pseudepigrapha, often an elaboration of certain parts of the canonical OT, describe and forecast mythological battles between hosts of heaven and forces of evil. Despite the havoc that Satan and his minions, the fallen beings, wreak among humanity and creation, God's angels are present to protect and intervene until the final consummation. Admittedly, this statement is indeed a sweeping generalization, but it summarizes the bulk of literature which tends to be overwhelmingly repetitious.

It is this aspect of the pseudepigrapha that the Judean Desert writings, the foil for the Lucan corpus, both emphasize and reinterpret. Selections like the *War Scroll,* the *Rule of the Community,* and the *Damascus Document* identify and target actual historical personages as the "Teacher of Righteousness", the "Wicked Priest", and the "Man of Lies". The *Visions of Amram* portray a highly dualistic tension between good and evil often seen in terms of light and darkness. Hence, dichotomy and polarization between different human groups are the hallmark of these works; the mythology is concretized on a societal level, and herein lies the difference between these Judean Desert writings and Luke.

The Lucan PN, as exemplified in 22,3.31.43.53, focuses the whole earthly ministry -- Christ has been fighting Satan and his forces all along. This *diabolical force,* however, is never affixed to any human being despite the fact that an individual, such as Judas, may be an agent of the devil. Furthermore, Satan has a tangible dominion, and this dominion is darkness. Here too, Luke effects a remarkable change in the literary tradition. Darkness, like the sunlight, falls on good and bad alike; it is real, but it is not the property of any particular person or class. By concentrating on Satan as the enemy, and by attributing darkness as his dominion, Luke removes evil from the human plane. Hence, there is no justification for hatred.

The *ministering angel* tradition is also reinterpreted under Luke's pen. Unlike the angels described in the OT or the pseudepigrapha, none of the angels in L-A fight. The strengthening angel of 22,43 may support Jesus as he agonizes over his approaching arrest, but the angel does not forestall the crowd arriving to incarcerate him. Christ's approaching ordeal remains a human one.

Luke has taken the *diabolical force* and *ministering angel* traditions from the canonical OT and the pseudepigrapha and refashioned them with great skill. The *ministering angel* at the agony on the Mount of Olives (22,43), and the "dominion of darkness" at the arrest (22,53) form part of a thematic *inclusio* of the *diabolical force* which opens with the temptation scene (4,1-13). This *inclusio*, by spanning most of the gospel, performs two functions.

First, it maintains Satan and his minions as the major force of opposition to Jesus' ministry; this is evident in Lucan treatment of the sower and the seed (8,11-15), the return of the seventy-two (10,17-20), the Beelzebul controversy (11,14-23), the return of the unclean spirit (11,24-26), the healing of the crippled woman (13,10-17), the reply to the Pharisees (13,31-33), the attempt to seize Jesus (20,19), and in Satan's explicit activity at 22,3.31.

Second, Luke's use of the *ministering angel* underscores Christ's uniqueness. The *ministering angel* only sustains Christ in a moment of trial, the "opportune time" foreshadowed in the desert temptation (4,13). Unlike all the renditions of apocalyptic wars outlined in the pseudepigraphic literature, no angel fights, indeed even assists, in the battle against the "dominion of darkness" (22,53); Christ enters it alone. How Luke constructs this final battle is the topic of Part Two.

Part Two

Textual, Source, and Literary Analysis

The examination of the Lucan PN has demonstrated the interrelation this gospel has with the other three evangelists, especially in its reinterpretation of the *ministering angel* and *diabolical force* traditions. In Part Two, a textual, source, and literary investigation confirms this interconnection.

An analysis of the textual development of Luke 23,44-49 lays bare the seams of the "fixed points" which, as demonstrated above, were fundamental in the formation of the gospels. The readings in Mark 15,34.36; Matt 27,46.49.51; Luke 23,45.46.48 and John 19,25.28.29.30, form the core of the inquiry. The discussion of these twelve verses follows a changed order in which the gospels are traditionally listed. This will facilitate the progression of the argument as well as underscore the similarity between Mark and Matthew on the one side, Luke and John on the other.

The greatest textual discrepancies in each gospel arise around the last words of Christ, the moment of death, and at least in Luke and John, the description of the witnesses to the crucifixion. Each of these is a "fixed point," as the source and literary discussions testify. Furthermore, the examination reveals that in all four gospels the account of the death and the description of the witnesses had their origin in a tradition utilized by primitive versions of both Luke and John before passing on to Mark and Matthew.

Chapter Three

Textual Criticism

Mark 15,33-41

Mark, as in Matthew, shows textual problems surrounding the Greek transliteration of the Aramaic and Hebrew in 15,34 (// Matt 27,46), while the difficulties existing in v 36 center around the imperative of ἀφίημι.[1]

Mark 15,33-41
[33]Καὶ γενομένης ὥρας ἕκτης σκότος ἐγένετο ἐφ᾽ ὅλην τὴν γῆν ἕως ὥρας ἐνάτης. [34]καὶ τῇ ἐνάτῃ ὥρᾳ ἐβόησεν ὁ Ἰησοῦς φωνῇ μεγάλῃ, ελωι ελωι λεμα σαβαχθανι; ὅ ἐστιν μεθερμηνευόμενον ὁ θεός μου ὁ θεός μου, εἰς τί ἐγκατέλιπές με; [35]καί τινες τῶν παρεστηκότων ἀκούσαντες ἔλεγον, ἴδε Ἡλίαν φωνεῖ. [36]δραμὼν δέ τις καὶ γεμίσας σπόγγον ὄξους περιθεὶς καλάμῳ ἐπότιζεν αὐτὸν λέγων, ἄφετε ἴδωμεν εἰ ἔρχεται Ἡλίας καθελεῖν αὐτόν. [37]ὁ δὲ Ἰησοῦς ἀφεὶς φωνὴν μεγάλην ἐξέπνευσεν. [38]Καὶ τὸ καταπέτασμα τοῦ ναοῦ ἐσχίσθη εἰς δύο ἀπ᾽ ἄνωθεν ἕως κάτω. [39]Ἰδὼν δὲ ὁ κεντυρίων ὁ παρεστηκὼς ἐξ ἐναντίας αὐτοῦ ὅτι οὕτως ἐξέπνευσεν εἶπεν, ἀληθῶς οὗτος ὁ ἄνθρωπος υἱὸς θεοῦ ἦν. [40]Ἦσαν δὲ καὶ γυναῖκες ἀπὸ μακρόθεν θεωροῦσαι, ἐν αἷς καὶ Μαρία ἡ Μαγδαληνὴ καὶ

---

[1] The *NA*[27] supplies the apparatus and abbreviations unless otherwise noted.

Μαρία ἡ Ἰακώβου τοῦ μικροῦ καὶ Ἰωσῆτος μήτηρ καὶ Σαλώμη, ⁴¹αἳ ὅτε ἦν ἐν τῇ Γαλιλαίᾳ ἠκολούθουν αὐτῷ καὶ διηκόνουν αὐτῷ, καὶ ἄλλαι πολλαὶ αἱ συναναβᾶσαι αὐτῷ εἰς Ἱεροσόλυμα.

v 34   καὶ τῇ ᵃ[ἐνάτῃ ὥρᾳ] ἐβόησεν ᵇ[ὁ Ἰησοῦς] φωνῇ μεγάλῃ· ᶜ[ελωι ελωι] ᵈ[λεμα σαβαχθανι]; ὅ ἐστιν μεθερμηνευόμενον· ὁ θεός ᵉ[μου] ᶠ[ὁ θεός μου] εἰς τί ᵍ[ἐγκατέλιπές με];

ᵃωρα τη ενατη A C 33 *Maj*
    Text ℵ B D L Θ Ψ 059 083 *f*¹·¹³ (565) 579 892 1424 2427 2542ˢ *l* 844 *al* c ff² Eus

ᵇ[ ] D Θ *pc* i k syˢ boᵖᵗ

ᶜηλι ηλι D Θ 059 565 *pc* it vgᵐˢˢ Eus

ᵈλαμα σαβαχθανι Θ 059 1 565 2427 2542ˢ *l* 844 *pc* vg
λαμα ζαβαφθανι B
λιμα σαβαχθανι *f*¹³ 33 *Maj* syʰ
λιμα σαβακτανι A
λαμα ζαφθανι D (i) vgᵐˢˢ
λεμα σαβακτανι ℵ*
λεμα ζαβαχθανι 083
    Text λεμα σαβαχθανι ℵ C L Δ Ψ 892 *pc* c l vgᵐˢˢ Eus

ᵉ[ ] A K P Γ Δ Θ 059 *f*¹·¹³ *l* 844 *pm* i vgᵐˢˢ saᵐˢˢ Eus

ᶠ[ ] B 565 boᵐˢ

ᵍ2 1 C (K) Θ *f*¹·¹³ 33 *Maj* it vgᵐˢˢ
με εγκατελειπες A *al*
ωνειδισας με D c (i) k
εγκατελειπες με L 083 565 892 2427 *pc*
    Text ℵ B Ψ 059 *pc* vg Ptolⁱʳ Ju Eus

אֵלִי אֵלִי לָמָה עֲזַבְתָּנִי MT Ps 22,2a
אֱלָהִי אֱלָהִי לְמָה שְׁבַקְתָּנִי Aramaic²
Ὁ θεὸς ᾽ο θεός μου, πρόσχες μοι· ἵνα τί ἐγκατέλιπές με; LXX Ps 21,2a

Because this verse records what the gospel writer considers the last words of Christ, it has been the object of a great deal of attention which in turn is responsible for its many divergent readings. The inclusion of τη between ἐνάτῃ ὥρᾳ is a later interpolation. The other variants are more complicated.
    The problems with the text can be divided into two parts, the Greek transliteration of Hebrew/Aramaic Ps 22,2a and the Greek translation of the

----

² The Aramaic cited here and throughout this discussion is a reconstruction based on entries in BDB 1080, 1099, 1114 unless otherwise noted.

same. The first point is further refined by separating those Greek transliterations based on Hebrew from those grounded on Aramaic, and it is this issue I would like to address first.

The interrogative λαμα is the Greek transliteration of the Hebrew לָמָה in most cases, although the mobile schewa in Hebrew can also be rendered by λεμα in this Greek transcription.[3] The alternative, λιμα, is from the Aramaic. The Alexandrian tradition, the basis of the translation for this verse, instances a phrase with a mixture of both Hebrew and Aramaic. Moreover, one of the prime witnesses for the Alexandrian text, Vaticanus, evidences a mixture of two languages in a single word, ζαβαφθανι. Most of the other variants offer little clarity. In addition to the Alexandrian tradition, Θ contains a Hebrew and Aramaic mix. Part of the Byzantine family, A and *Maj*, along with Alexandrine ℵ* are purely Aramaic. Only the Western text, principally Bezae, offers the closest transliteration of the Hebrew, but even its ζαφθανι lacks a consonant corresponding to the ע in the Hebrew עֲזַבְתָּנִי. Nonetheless, the Western text provides the closest, unadulterated transliteration of either the Aramaic or the Hebrew; this is corroborated by its instance of ηλι ηλι and λαμα.

The following schema helps to clarify the discussion.[4]

Mark 15,34b   ελωι ελωι λεμα σαβαχθανι

Aramaic		אֱלָהִי אֱלָהִי לְמָה שְׁבַקְתָּנִי
ℵ*		ελωι ελωι (λεμα) σαβακτανι
ℵ C L Δ Ψ 892 *pc* c vg^{mss}		ελωι ελωι (λεμα) σαβαχθανι
A		ελωι ελωι λιμα σαβακτανι
083		ελωι ελωι (λεμα) ζαβαχθανι
*f*¹³ 33 *Maj* sy^h		ελωι ελωι λιμα σαβαχθανι

MT Ps 22,2a	אֵלִי אֵלִי לָמָה עֲזַבְתָּנִי
D vg^{mss}	ηλι ηλι λαμα ζαφθανι

MT Ps 22,2a	... ...בְתָּנִי... לָמָה	Aramaic שְׁב... ... אֱלָהִי אֱלָהִי
B	... ... λαμα ...φθανι	ελωι ελωι ... ζαβα...

MT Ps 22,2a	... לָמָה אֵלִי אֵלִי	Aramaic שְׁבַקְתָּנִי ... ...
θ 059 565 *pc*	ηλι ηλι λαμα ...	... ... σαβαχθανι

---

[3] Paul Joüon, S.J., *A Grammar of Biblical Hebrew* (trans. T. Muraoka, 14/1; Roma: Editrice Pontificio Istituto Biblico, 1991) 51-2.

[4] Major witnesses for the Hebrew or Aramaic versions of Ps 22,2a in Mark 15,34 are written to reflect the Greek transliterations. For those cases in which the passages are divided between Hebrew and Aramaic, the Semitic readings are approximations. Parentheses indicate that λεμα transliterates the interrogative לְמָה, a reading which can be either Hebrew or Aramaic.

MT Ps 22,2a	... לָמָה	Aramaic שְׁבַקְתַּנִי ... אֱלָהִי אֱלָהִי
1 2427 2542ˢ	... λαμα	ελωι ελωι...σαβαχθανι
l 844		

MT Ps 22,2a	... ... אֵלִי אֵלִי	Aramaic שְׁבַקְתַּנִי לָמָה ... ...
Eus	ηλι ηλι	... ... λεμα σαβαχθανι

LXX Ps 21,2a   Ὁ θεὸς ὁ θεός μου, πρόσχες μοι· ἵνα τί ἐγκατέλιπές με;

Mark 15,34c	ὁ θεός μου ὁ θεός μου εἰς τί ἐγκατέλιπές με
ℵ Ptolᴵʳ	ο θεος μου ο θεος μου εις τι εγκατελιπες με
A	ο θεος ο θεος μου εις τι με εγκατελειπες
B	ο θεος μου εις τι εγκατελιπες με
D c k	ο θεος μου ο θεος μου εις τι ωνειδισας με
P Γ Δ 059	ο θεος ο θεος μου εις τι εγκατελιπες με
l 844 Eus	
K	ο θεος ο θεος μου εις τι με εγκατελειπες
L 083 892	ο θεος μου ο θεος μου εις τι εγκατελειπες με
2427 pc	
Θ f¹·¹³ vgᵐˢˢ	ο θεος ο θεος μου εις τι με εγκατελιπες
Ψ pc	ο θεος μου ο θεος μου εις τι εγκατελιπες με
33 Maj	ο θεος μου ο θεος μου εις τι με εγκατελιπες
565	ο θεος μου εις τι εγκατελειπες με
i	ο θεος ο θεος μου εις τι ωνειδισας με
Justin	Ὁ θεός, ὁ θεός, ἵνα τί ἐγκατέλιπές με;[5]

There are two possibilities which can explain the evidence of two languages in this verse and the subsequent resulting confusion. First, it is possible that there existed, at the time of the composition of the gospel, Aramaic and Hebrew copies of Ps 22; the quotation entered the text according to the copy of a particular language a respective scribe had at hand. Subsequent scribes then corrected and rewrote the reading according to whichever language version they preferred. The second possibility is that, if this verse witnesses the original language of the quotation, there is no way to decide conclusively what that language, either Aramaic or Hebrew, actually was. If so, the mixed nature of the text is the result of various scribes correcting each other's versions based on written Hebrew in some cases and "targumized" Hebrew in others.

Of the strongest witnesses, Vaticanus and Bezae evidence the most difficult readings to explain. The former features elements of both Hebrew and Aramaic, while the latter follows the Hebrew exclusively.

Bruce M. Metzger maintains ελωι as the correct transliteration in v 34, stating that it is the reading of the great majority of uncials and minuscule manuscripts which are in turn copying the Aramaic אֱלָהִי.[6] This certainly explains the first half of the reading in Vaticanus. Metzger's conclusion

---

[5] Justin, *Dialogue avec Tryphon* 99,1 ([éd. Georges Archambault, Tome 2; Paris: Librairie Alphonse Picard et Fils, 1909] 116).

[6] Metzger, *Textual* 2ⁿᵈ 99-100.

regarding the second half, however, is not as sound.

First, B Θ 059 1 565 2427 2542ˢ · l 844 *pc* vg hardly constitute the great majority of uncials and minuscules, particularly when *the* major Alexandrian uncial, Vaticanus, contains elements from both Aramaic and Hebrew. Second, one of the bases of Metzger's conclusion depends upon reading ζαβαφθανι in Vaticanus as a transliteration of the Aramaic שְׁבַקְתָּנִי instead of the Hebrew עֲזַבְתָּנִי,[7] an argument difficult to sustain. This is in no small way complicated by the fact that the strong guttural ע in Hebrew has no exact Greek equivalent. Metzger suggests that the initial *a* sound in the ע dropped out because of its proximity to the final *a* in λαμα.[8] This is a valid point which also confirms that with ζαβαφθανι Vaticanus has a Hebrew element. That the reading ζαφθανι in D is a "scholarly correction representing the Hebrew of Ps 22,1 עֲזַבְתָּנִי..."[9] is an explanation which makes sense given the singularity of Bezae's witness for this reading.

The fluctuations between Hebrew and Aramaic in this verse, even among the strongest witnesses, reflect a desire to know and to establish conclusively whether Jesus spoke Hebrew or Aramaic when he cried out from the cross. Richard T. A. Murphy addresses this language question in his dissertation, *The Dereliction of Christ on the Cross*.[10] Although the linguistic study in this work is detailed, its basis is the written Targumic literature of the Tenth Century AD. Another study by Martin Rehm also treats the matter, but like Murphy, he addresses the issue without recourse to an early Aramaic text,[11] and this points to the major difficulty in analyzing this verse. Brown maintains that Mark was writing for readers who did not know a Semitic language. Since the second evangelist regularly translated Aramaic for his readers and explained Jewish customs (7,3-4), in 15,34 he was simply doing the same.[12]

If written Aramaic translations of the Psalms and historical books existed in the intertestamental period, either at Qumran or elsewhere, they have not yet been discovered. The oldest official translation of the Hebrew Bible into Aramaic is the *Targum Onkelos* of the Third Century AD, and this is only of the Pentateuch.[13] Targums of the psalms did not exist until much later, owing to their unofficial status in public synagogue services.[14] Indeed, the final redaction

---

[7] Metzger, *Textual* 2ⁿᵈ 100.

[8] Metzger, *Textual* 2ⁿᵈ 100 n 1.

[9] Metzger, *Textual* 2ⁿᵈ 100.

[10] Reflecting the times in which he was writing, Murphy opts for the reading which comes closest to the Matthean one (Richard T. A. Murphy, O.P., *The Dereliction of Christ on the Cross* [Washington, DC: Pontificium Institutum Angelicum, 1940] 12).

[11] Martin Rehm, "Eli, Eli lamma sabacthani," *BZ* 2 (1958) 275-78.

[12] Brown, *Messiah* 2; 1061-2.

[13] Bernard Grossfeld, "Aramaic: the Targumim," *Encyclopedia Judaica* (4; New York: The Macmillan Company, 1971) 842.

and official recognition of a written Targum belong to the post-Talmudic period, thus placing the work not earlier than the Fifth Century AD.[15] Appealing to the name Ἠλίας in v 36 as an indication that what the people hear is closer to the Hebrew than the Aramaic proves equally unconvincing for similar reasons.[16]

On this basis, one of the reasons explaining the occurrence of two Semitic languages in a four-word sentence is eliminated. If there are Aramaic sources or proto-Targumic editions of Psalm 22, they have not yet been brought to light; conclusions based on such a possibility are faulty without them. That Bezae is the only witness for an unadulterated Hebrew reading is more than likely due to a learned scribe who saw the connection between the gospel verse and Hebrew Ps 22,2. Based on the textual witness, the most probable explanation is that the quotation was originally written in Aramaic.[17] Subsequent scribes saw the relationship these words have with Ps 22 and altered them accordingly; not to be discounted is the attempt to harmonize the verse with Matthew 27,46.

The second and more important problem in this verse is the Greek translation of Jesus' last words. Both MT Ps 22,2 and the Aramaic express the vocative and genitive in a single construction (אֵלִי, אֱלָהִי) which LXX Ps 21,2 writes as Ὁ θεός μου. That the first occurrence of μου is omitted in many witnesses indicates a tendency to assimilate the last words of Jesus in Mark to Ps 21,2 in the LXX. The similarity was already established by the phrase ἐγκατέλιπές με. Mark is not, however, simply quoting the LXX. The μου after the first evocation of θεός reflects an attempt to translate precisely the first person singular genitive suffix in the Hebrew אֵלִי. Furthermore, Mark has no equivalent of πρόσχες μοι which occurs immediately after the vocative in LXX Ps 21,2a. Even though Mark reads ἐγκατέλιπές με, the word order of LXX Ps 21,2, it does not necessarily mean he is copying from the psalm. For one thing, the word order does not change the meaning, and secondly, having the object after the verb is closer to the Hebrew form עֲזַבְתָּנִי. Since Mark would have had no Aramaic copy of the psalm, a strong possibility is that he based the Greek transliteration on MT Ps 22,2a.[18]

---

[14] Grossfeld, "Aramaic" 848.

[15] Grossfeld, "Aramaic" 842.

[16] The prophet's name in Hebrew is אֵלִיָּהוּ which, as Murphy explains, many consider closer to the Hebrew אֵלִי than אֱלָהִי (10). I believe that this point is untenable, particularly in light of the fact that qames represents in Hebrew and Aramaic both an a-class and u-class vowel (Joüon, Grammar 14/1; 42-5). In addition, the historical books did not exist as Targums at the period of gospel composition; it is impossible to know how people would have written the prophet's name which they heard.

[17] For further discussion on the question of Aramaic in the New Testament, cf. Joseph A. Fitzmyer, S.J., "Methodology in the Study of the Aramaic Substratum of Jesus' Sayings in the New Testament," Jésus aux origines de la christologie (ed. J. Dupont, Leuven: Leuven University Press, 1975) 73-102.

[18] As Brown explains, that it is unclear whether Mark knew Hebrew or Aramaic does not deny the possibility that the evangelist was familiar with Semitic sayings prevalent in the tradition (Messiah 2; 1061-2).

Justin Martyr provides another possibility, however. The *Dialogue with Trypho* reads, Ὁ θεός, ὁ θεός, ἵνα τί ἐγκατέλιπές με;[19] there is no personal pronoun altogether, a fact which does not fully respect the MT or the LXX. Indeed, Justin's quotation seems to be a cross between the Hebrew and Greek versions of the psalm. That Justin had a pre-canonical, written copy of the gospel or a gospel harmony at his disposal allows that this mix between Hebrew and Greek already existed in the late stages of the oral tradition.[20] In all probability almost as soon as this logion was recorded, correctors and scribes began to shape it into a replicate of either the Hebrew or septuagintal version of the psalm, hence the many variations of this verse.[21] The most important point to keep in mind about Mark 15,34 is that, from the very beginning, it was subject to so many alterations that the resulting composite structure makes it virtually impossible to establish the reading.[22]

Metzger, considering that the reversed order of the two words reflects a copyist's desire to harmonize the LXX reading with the one in the Matthean text, holds to the word order, ἐγκατέλιπές με (v 34).[23] There is no reason to disagree with him on this point. It should be noted as well that the alternative

---

[19] Justin, *Dialogue avec Tryphon* 99,1 (Tome 2; 116).

[20] For the view that Justin utilized such a copy of at least the synoptic gospels, cf. Arthur J. Bellinzoni, Jr., "The Source of the Agraphon in Justin Martyr's Dialogue with Trypho 47:5," *VC* 17 (1963) 65-70; Charles Cosgrove, "Justin Martyr and the Emerging Christian Canon," *VC* 36 (1982) 209-232; Donald A. Hagner, "The Sayings of Jesus in the Apostolic Fathers and Justin Martyr," in *Gospel Perspectives* (ed. David Wenham, 5; Sheffield: *JSOT* Press, 1985) 233-68.
That Justin had a gospel harmony which was developed by Tatian in his *Diatessaron* is argued by M.-É. Boismard, O.P. (*Le Diatessaron de Tatien à Justin*, EBib 15; Paris: J. Gabalda et Cie, 1992).

[21] In this regard note as well *Gos. Pet.* 5 which reads Ἡ Δύναμις μου, ἡ Δύναμις, κατέλειψας με. In addition to the substitution of Δύναμις for θεός, this piece changes the interrogative of the psalm to a declarative.

[22] Editions of the Greek text reflect this difficulty. The 26th and 27th editions of the *NA* and the 3rd and 4th of the *UBSGNT* disagree with the *Synopsis Quattuor Evangeliorum* (ed. Kurt Aland [4/5; Stuttgart: Biblia-Druck, 1975]) on whether the interrogative should be λεμα or λαμα. To resolve the issue they split the Alexandrian text; א is the primary witness for *NA* and *UBSGNT*, while B offers chief testimony for the *Synopsis*. It should be noted that the Alexandrian witness for the *NA* and *UBSGNT*, λεμα σαβαχθανι, is identical to the Matthean reading (27,46). The *Synopsis*, on the other hand, further divides its foundation by accepting Vaticanus's λαμα but abandoning its ζαβαφθανι. It is difficult to see how the editors of the *Synopsis* could justify such an action especially when, in this case, there is no problem with the Vaticanus text itself (*Codex Vaticanus Graecus 1209 [Codex B]*, ΤΑ ΙΕΡΑ ΒΙΒΛΙΑ [In Civitate Vaticana 1965] 1302).

[23] Metzger, *Textual* 2nd 100.

reading lacks the support of major witnesses, i.e., ℵ B D.

v 36 δραμὼν δέ τις ᵃ[καὶ] ᵇ[γεμίσας] σπόγγον ὄξους περιθεὶς καλάμῳ
ᶜ[ἐπότιζεν αὐτὸν λέγων]· ᵈ[ἄφετε] ἴδωμεν εἰ ἔρχεται Ἠλίας καθελεῖν αὐτόν.

ᵃ[ ] B L Ψ (ƒ¹³ 2542 l 844) 2427 pc c vgᵐˢ
    Text ℵ A C D Θ 059 083 565 700 ƒ¹ 33 Maj

ᵇπλησας D Θ 565 700
    Text ℵ A C 059 083 ƒ¹ 33 Maj

ᶜ[ ] D

ᵈαφες ℵ D N Θ ƒ¹·¹³ 28 565 579 700 2542ˢ l 844 al it
    Text A B C L Ψ 083 33 2427 Maj vg sy

    These variations, like those in the preceding verse, bring to the fore the
emphasis on quotations and the corresponding desire to clarify, magnify, and
correct certain details, particularly when several traditions flow together, as
seems to be the case here. Brown concludes that this reading resulted when a
pre-Marcan passage involving the offering of wine to Jesus was combined with an
eschatological reference to Elijah.[24] This verse does betray a redactional hand
combining two traditions or "fixed points," but the traditions so joined, in all
probability, pre-date any mention of the offering of wine or an eschatological
reference.[25]
    There are no literary problems evident, thus the *lectio brevior* produces
the best reading. There are, however, some changes in vocabulary which cannot
be determined on the principle of *lectio brevior*, for example: γεμίσας/πλησας
and ἄφετε/αφες; the more important for the text is the latter pair.
    The major problem in the verse lies with the attempt to ground the
opening participial phrase with a finite verb. As read, connecting it to ἄφετε
ἴδωμεν εἰ ἔρχεται Ἠλίας καθελεῖν αὐτόν does not work. The imperative is
plural, while the subject of the participial phrase, and thus the object of the
imperative, is singular. If the one speaking is a single individual with the reed,
why does this person tell the bystanders, who are not doing anything, to wait?
When the imperative is read in the singular, who is the subject of the sentence?
There seem to be two solutions.
    The first is to make the participial phrase, from δραμὼν to καλάμῳ,
dependent on v 35. In this case, the vinegar on the reed is merely mentioned to
draw attention to MT Ps 69,22b (LXX Ps 68,22b) as an indication of cruelty and
intimation of prophetic fulfillment. Hence, the subject of the verb in v 36 is
those in v 35, and they are talking to each other in mockery or in veiled hope of
seeing some miracle. The problem with this solution is that the subject demands

---

[24] Brown, *Messiah* 2; 1060.

[25] Cf. below, Chapter Four.

a cohortative, not an imperative, as ἴδωμεν suggests. The conjunction δέ in v 36a militates against such a grammatical construction as well.

The second is to make the participial phrase dependent on v 36b. The subject is still the crowd in v 35, but the one who fetched the vinegar is now the object of the plural imperative. The verb does not have to be read in the plural, however. That א, an Alexandrian witness, agrees with Western and Caesarean texts for reading αφες, a choice which makes grammatical and logical sense, dictates a preference for the singular imperative. Bezae, however, frequently harmonizes the Marcan and Matthean texts, and that appears to be the case here with other witnesses following suit. The *lectio difficilior* shows ἄφετε. The plural imperative in part of the tradition can also be explained by the confusion between τινες in v 35 and τις in v 36; a scribe, reading the former for the latter, changed the singular imperative to the plural.

Précis

Mark 15,34 has a twofold problem. First, there is the question of Hebrew and Aramaic vocabulary in the cry from the cross, and second, the translation of this Hebrew/Aramaic combination into Greek. The pre-canonical gospel witnessed by Justin seems to be the most likely possibility for the origin of the composite Hebrew and Aramaic reading in Mark 15,34. In addition, the many and varied versions of this verse in the textual tradition indicate a great deal of fluidity in its transmission.

Linked to the problem in 15,34 is the confusion between the singular and plural imperative of ἀφίημι in v 36. The textual difficulties in these two verses reflect the blending of two traditions or "fixed points". The question of Hebrew or Aramaic usage in the cry from the cross occurs in the respective Matthean parallel as well, a reading which, like Mark, also results from the combining of two traditions.

Matthew 27,45-56

Matthew 27,46, like its Marcan parallel, exhibits a problem centering around Jesus' last words. In addition, Matthew contains its own set of textual difficulties such as the piercing of the side (v 49) and the rending of the temple curtain (v 51). This discussion concentrates on these three verses.

Matthew 27,45-56

45Ἀπὸ δὲ ἕκτης ὥρας σκότος ἐγένετο ἐπὶ πᾶσαν τὴν γῆν ἕως ὥρας ἐνάτης. 46περὶ δὲ τὴν ἐνάτην ὥραν ἀνεβόησεν ὁ Ἰησοῦς φωνῇ μεγάλῃ λέγων, Ηλι ηλι λεμα σαβαχθανι; τοῦτ' ἔστιν· Θεέ μου θεέ μου, ἱνατί με ἐγκατέλιπες; 47τινὲς δὲ τῶν ἐκεῖ ἑστηκότων ἀκούσαντες ἔλεγον ὅτι Ἠλίαν φωνεῖ οὗτος. 48καὶ εὐθέως δραμὼν εἷς ἐξ αὐτῶν καὶ λαβὼν σπόγγον πλήσας τε ὄξους καὶ περιθεὶς καλάμῳ ἐπότιζεν αὐτόν. 49οἱ δὲ λοιποὶ ἔλεγον, ἄφες ἴδωμεν εἰ ἔρχεται Ἠλίας σώσων αὐτόν. 50ὁ δὲ Ἰησοῦς πάλιν κράξας φωνῇ μεγάλῃ ἀφῆκεν τὸ πνεῦμα. 51Καὶ ἰδοὺ τὸ καταπέτασμα τοῦ ναοῦ ἐσχίσθη ἀπ' ἄνωθεν ἕως κάτω εἰς δύο καὶ ἡ γῆ ἐσείσθη καὶ αἱ πέτραι ἐσχίσθησαν, 52καὶ τὰ μνημεῖα ἀνεῴχθησαν καὶ πολλὰ σώματα τῶν κεκοιμημένων ἁγίων ἠγέρθησαν, 53καὶ ἐξελθόντες ἐκ τῶν μνημείων μετὰ τὴν ἔγερσιν αὐτοῦ εἰσῆλθον εἰς τὴν ἁγίαν πόλιν καὶ ἐνεφανίσθησαν πολλοῖς. ⁵⁴Ὁ δὲ ἑκατόνταρχος καὶ οἱ μετ' αὐτοῦ τηροῦντες τὸν Ἰησοῦν ἰδόντες τὸν σεισμὸν καὶ τὰ γενόμενα ἐφοβήθησαν σφόδρα, λέγοντες, ἀληθῶς θεοῦ υἱὸς ἦν οὗτος. ⁵⁵Ἦσαν δὲ ἐκεῖ γυναῖκες πολλαὶ ἀπὸ μακρόθεν θεωροῦσαι, αἵτινες ἠκολούθησαν τῷ Ἰησοῦ ἀπὸ τῆς Γαλιλαίας διακονοῦσαι αὐτῷ· ⁵⁶ἐν αἷς ἦν Μαρία ἡ Μαγδαληνὴ καὶ Μαρία ἡ τοῦ Ἰακώβου καὶ Ἰωσὴφ μήτηρ καὶ ἡ μήτηρ τῶν υἱῶν Ζεβεδαίου.

    v 46   περὶ δὲ τὴν ἐνάτην ὥραν ᵃ[ἀνεβόησεν] ὁ Ἰησοῦς φωνῇ μεγάλῃ λέγων· ᵇ[ηλι ηλι] ᶜ[λεμα σαβαχθανι]; τοῦτ' ἔστιν· θεέ μου θεέ μου, ἱνατί με ἐγκατέλιπες;

ᵃεβοησεν B L W 33 700 al

ᵇελωι ελωι ℵ B 33 vgᵐˢˢ co
   Text A D (L) W Θ f¹·¹³ Maj lat

ᶜλαμα ζαφθανι D* b ff² h
 λαμα σαφθανι Dᶜ
 λαμα σαβαχθανι Θ f¹ pc vgᶜˡ mae
 λιμα σαβαχθανι A (W) f¹³ Maj (f q)
 λεμα σαβακτανει B (892) pc lat boᵖᵗ
   Text ℵ L 33 700 pc ff¹

אֵלִי אֵלִי לָמָה עֲזַבְתָּנִי MT Ps 22,2a
אֱלָהִי אֱלָהִי לְמָה שְׁבַקְתַּנִי Aramaic²⁶
Ὁ θεὸς ὁ θεός μου, πρόσχες μοι· ἵνα τί ἐγκατέλιπές με; LXX Ps 21,2a

    ἀναβοάω, cry out,²⁷ is less descriptive than βοάω, cry of anguish or for help,²⁸ which suggests that βοάω is most likely copied from Mark 15,34. In addition, one of the primary witnesses of the Alexandrian text, Vaticanus, is in accord with several of the Byzantine and Caesarean manuscripts for reading εβοησεν.
    The last words of Christ instance several variants of the transliterated Hebrew and Aramaic which originate in the attempt to match the quotation with MT Ps 22,2a.
    Although the majority of uncials and other witnesses show ηλι as representing Hebrew אֵלִי, only D Θ f¹ b ff² h pc vgᶜˡ mae reproduce the Hebrew לָמָה as λαμα. The variations of this interrogative show a reliance on לְמָה, which can be either Hebrew or Aramaic.²⁹

---

²⁶ The Aramaic cited here and throughout this discussion is a reconstruction based on entries in BDB 1080, 1099, 1114 unless otherwise noted.

²⁷ BAGD 51.

²⁸ BAGD 144.

²⁹ Cf. above.

When the verb עֲזַבְתָּנִי is transliterated, several Greek spellings result, representing the influence of two different Semitic roots: the Hebrew עֽזב,[30] and the Aramaic שׁבק.[31] Only Bezae with λαμα ζαφθανι comes close to simulating the Hebrew לָמָה עֲזַבְתָּנִי; this is coupled with its witness of ηλι. On the other hand, the Alexandrian, Byzantine, and Caesarean texts are influenced by the Aramaic.

Here too, a schema of the textual variants aids the discussion.[32]

Matthew 27,46 ηλι ηλι λεμα σαβαχθανι

Aramaic		אֱלָהִי אֱלָהִי לְמָה שְׁבַקְתַּנִי
א 33		ελωι ελωι (λεμα) σαβαχθανι
B		ελωι εωλι (λεμα) σαβακτανει

MT Ps 22,2a	אֵלִי אֵלִי לָמָה עֲזַבְתָּנִי	
D* b ff² h	ηλι ηλι λαμα ζαφθανι	
Dᶜ	ηλι ηλι λαμα σαφθανι	

Mt Ps 22,2a	אֵלִי אֵלִי	Aramaic	לְמָה שְׁבַקְתַּנִי ... ...
A W f¹³ Maj	ηλι ηλι		λιμα σαβαχθανι ... ...
L	ηλι ηλι		(λεμα) σαβαχθανι ... ...

MT Ps 22,2a	אֵלִי אֵלִי לָמָה ...	Aramaic	... ... שְׁבַקְתַּנִי
θ f¹	ηλι ηλι λαμα ...		σαβαχθανι ... ...

LXX Ps 21,2a ʽΟ θεὸς ʼο θεός μου, πρόσχες μοι· ἵνα τί ἐγκατέλιπές με;

Matthew 27,46c θεέ μου θεέ μου, ἰνατί με ἐγκατέλιπες;

Witness with identical reading in both Mark 15,34b and Matthew 27,46b

D ηλι ηλι λαμα ζαφθανι

The text as it appears in the NA²⁷ is based upon a great amount of shifting between Hebrew and Aramaic among the witnesses. Moreover, Sinaiticus copies from the Marcan reading, and only D shows a correspondence to a Marcan variant. These facts make it difficult to establish with absolute certitude which

---

[30] BDB 736.

[31] BDB 1114.

[32] Major witnesses for the Hebrew or Aramaic versions of Ps 22,2a in Matthew 27,46 are written to reflect the Greek transliterations. For those cases in which the passages are divided between Hebrew and Aramaic, the Semitic readings are approximations. Parentheses indicate that λεμα transliterates the interrogative לְמָה, a reading which can be either Hebrew or Aramaic.

version of Ps 22,2 Matthew tried to transliterate into Greek, the Hebrew or the Aramaic. All the more confusing is why the *NA*[27] would read with the Western text for ηλι but shift to the Alexandrian tradition for λεμα σαβαχθανι.

The editors of the *UBSGNT*[4] mention that the text of several witnesses, i.e., א B 33 co were assimilated to the reading ελωι of Mark 15,34; this represents the Aramaic אֱלָהִי.[33] While they note confusion between Aramaic and Hebrew as seen in the variations of ηλι and λαμα, they do not explain the reasons behind a half Hebrew and half Aramaic reading for this verse.[34]

One reason for the difficult readings goes back to the scribes themselves. Seen here is the same tendency found in Mark; some scribes insisted upon the written Hebrew while others preferred to "targumize" the quotation. They then made numerous revisions and corrections accordingly. For example, as it does in Mark, Bezae's precise hand also replaces the Aramaic with a Hebrew transliteration here in Matthew. In addition, subsequent scribes and redactors tried to justify the Matthean and Marcan accounts with each other as well as with the MT, LXX, and any "targumized" versions of the psalm. This produced a reading in which the first half of the quotation instances the transliterated Hebrew ηλι while the second half shows the transliterated Aramaic λεμα σαβαχθανι.[35]

Despite the problems with establishing the Semitic source for this phrase, its Greek translation is stable in all the witnesses. The Matthean account uses the vocative of Θεός and omits πρόσχες μοι. The LXX Ps 21,2 has no variants; MT Ps 22,2 shows no equivalent to the LXX vocative Ὁ but includes a genitive suffix for each evocation of God (אֵלִי, אֱלֹהִי), something which θεέ μου replicates. It should be noted as well that, for the phrase με ἐγκατέλιπες, Matthew does not follow the word order found in LXX Ps 21,2. These facts confirm that Matthew is not drawing from the LXX but rather from a Semitic source, and since there is no extant Aramaic version of this psalm from the intertestamental period, it is more prudent to say that Matthew is translating Hebrew Ps 22,2.

  v 49   οἱ δὲ λοιποὶ ᵃ[ἔλεγον·] ἄφες ἴδωμεν εἰ ἔρχεται Ἠλίας σώσων αὐτόν. ᵇ[ ]

ᵃειπαν B (D) f¹³ pc
    Text א A C L W Θ ε̄¹ 33 *Maj*
ᵇαλλος δε λαβων λογχην ενυξεν αυτου την πλευραν, και εξηλθεν υδωρ και αιμα א B C L Γ pc vgᵐˢˢ mae
    Text A D W Θ f¹·¹³ 33 *Maj* lat sy sa bo

The insertion of αλλος δε λαβων λογχην ενυξεν αυτου την πλευραν, και εξηλθεν υδωρ και αιμα in this text has Alexandrian and Egyptian witness; the

---

[33] Metzger, *Textual* 2ⁿᵈ 58.

[34] Metzger, *Textual* 2ⁿᵈ 58-9.

[35] As in Mark, that the bystanders in v 47 hear the name as Ἠλίας cannot be used to substantiate a Hebrew reading. Cf. above.

textual evidence for its exclusion is provided by Western, Byzantine, and Caesarean traditions. That both ℵ and B particularly are among the witnesses for its inclusion shows a strong tradition for its position in the verse, the editing of NA^{27} notwithstanding. If indeed it belongs here, then Jesus dies not from crucifixion but from a stabbing in the side. Despite the concord among some major uncials for this addition, there is very little support for it elsewhere. Not only do the Latin codices omit it, but the sahidic and bohairic witnesses of the Alexandrian tradition do not show it either. The verse αλλος...αιμα makes no sense in this context particularly before v 50. The story of the piercing of the side exists in John (19,34), and some scribe or redactor copied it here.

Metzger's explanation for αλλος δε λαβων λογχην ενυξεν αυτου την πλευραν, και εξηλθεν υδωρ και αιμα in v 49 states that a particular reader probably wrote this Johannine passage in the margin of Matthew's gospel, and this piece eventually was copied into the text. The fact that the reader did not have a copy of John 19,34 alongside the Matthean text explains the minor differences.[36]

v 51 Καὶ ἰδοὺ τὸ καταπέτασμα τοῦ ναοῦ ἐσχίσθη ᵃ[ἀπ᾽ ἄνωθεν ἕως κάτω εἰς δύο] ᵇ[καὶ] ἡ γῆ ἐσείσθη καὶ αἱ πέτραι ἐσχίσθησαν,

ᵃ5 6 1-4 A C³ W f¹·¹³ Maj syᵖ·ʰ mae
5 6 2-4 ℵ Θ
2-6 L saᵐˢˢ
απ ανω εως κατω 1424
εις δυο μερη απο ανωθεν εως κατω D ex latt?
Text B C* 33 saᵐˢˢ bo

ᵇThe beginning of an early division

The phrase ἀπ᾽ ἄνωθεν ἕως κάτω εἰς δύο appears to be an interpolation. Its word order is unstable in this verse, particularly in regard to the position of εἰς δύο, two words which make the phrase all the more clumsy. Nonetheless, some version of it is witnessed in Alexandrian, Byzantine, Western, and Caesarean traditions. Even Latin manuscripts show *et ecce velum templi scissum est in duas partes a summo usque deorsum* with negligible variants in two texts,[37] a reading which may have influenced Bezae.

---

[36] Metzger, *Textual* 2ⁿᵈ 59. The vocabulary of the variant provides a key for understanding how a phrase which originated as a gloss can be supported by so many witnesses. First, v 48 features an individual placing a vinegar-soaked sponge on a κάλαμος which is then presumably lifted to Christ's mouth. The variant in v 49 describes a λογχη; both κάλαμος and λόγχη are long poles, a fact which could have triggered the imagination of a scribe or redactor. Second, v 48 features two active participles, δραμών and λαβών. The Matthean variant evidences the participle λαβων, a word which would yet again prompt the mind of a scribe or redactor, thus leading the copier to make a parallel construction. These two elements, the κάλαμος/λόγχη image and the δραμών/λαβών participles, provided a text able to receive an interpolation from the gospel of John.

Moreover, although he does not state to which gospel he is alluding, Irenaeus gives a description of the death of Christ with much of the Matthean imagery. While Irenaeus includes the rending of the temple curtain along with the shaking of the land, splitting of rocks, and the raising of the dead, there is nothing about the veil being torn in two from top to bottom.[38] In addition, the disputed word order of the phrase serves to highlight its awkward position in the verse; ἀπ᾽ ἄνωθεν ἕως κάτω εἰς δύο is not original to the text. The witness of ℵ θ matches the Marcan reading thereby suggesting that a scribe copied them in to harmonize the account with Mark's.

That this phrase is an interpolation is a conclusion also evident from reading vv 51-52 as a single unit. Verse 50 opens with the definite article ὁ plus the post-positive conjunction δέ; the same is true for v 54. On the other hand, when the disputed text is excised, verse 51, itself beginning with καί, initiates a pattern of finite passive verbs followed by καί. This style continues throughout v 52. In v 53 the active verb εἰσῆλθον breaks the pattern, and in v 54 the particle δέ shifts the scene to the reaction of the centurion. This pattern paints an apocalyptic picture running from the tearing of the curtain, to the splitting of rocks, to the opening of tombs, to the raising of the dead. The phrase ἀπ᾽ ἄνωθεν ἕως κάτω εἰς δύο is an intrusion which interrupts the flow, and this fact explains the reason for the appearance of a major break at καὶ ἡ γῆ ἐσείσθη in part of the tradition.

Why the phrase was written into the text can be answered by examining the verb σχίζω. Since it signifies *to split, divide, separate, tear apart, tear off*,[39] scribes and redactors, very early in the tradition, wanted to leave no doubt in anyone's mind that the temple curtain was irreparably damaged; a reading from Mark remedied the problem. Hence, the phrase appears in Alexandrian, Byzantine, Western, and Caesarean texts.

Précis

The textual critique of the death account in Mark has concentrated on 15,34.36 while that in Matthew has centered on 27,46.49.51. The textual tradition witnessing both the cry from the cross and events surrounding it (Matt 27,46.49; Mark 15,34.36) stands as the greatest problem common to both gospels; the melding of two traditions seen in Mark has also affected the Matthean reading. Despite the strong textual witness for the inclusion of the phrase αλλος δε λαβων λογχην ενυξεν αυτου την πλευραν, και εξηλθεν υδωρ και αιμα at Matt 27,49, it is not part of the Matthean death account; it is a gloss which was eventually interpolated into the text.

---

[37] Matthäusevangelium, *Itala Das Neue Testament in altlateinischer Überlieferung*, Hrsg. A. Jülicher (1; Berlin: Walter de Gruyter, 1972) 208.

[38] Irénée de Lyon, *Contre les Hérésies* 3,60-64.4,34 ([SC 100; Paris: Cerf 1965] 855).

[39] BAGD 797.

These two gospels also have their individual difficulties. One peculiar to Mark is the use of the plural imperative in 15,36; as the *lectio difficilior*, it lacks a certain coherence when read with the surrounding narrative. More than likely, its presence is the result of contamination from the parallel account in Matthew. Likewise, the phrase ἀπ᾽ ἄνωθεν ἕως κάτω εἰς δύο in Matt 27,51 was probably copied from Mark in order to dispel any ambiguity caused by the verb σχίζω. The very fact that this phrase characterizes an effort to clarify and polish the text signals that it is a later interpolation.

The textual problems in the Marcan and Matthean death accounts highlight the similarity between these two synoptics; this point becomes more apparent when compared to the Lucan and even Johannine parallels.

Luke 23,44-49

In the textual analysis of this text, three tendencies come to the fore. First, vv 45 and 46 witness the greatest textual variation owing in large part to the fact that they describe the final moments of Christ's life. The darkening of the sun in the variant readings shows a dependency on the prophecy in LXX Amos 8,9 and Isa 13,10 while Christ's last words in v 46 are a paraphrase of LXX Ps 30,6. Second, there is a paraphrase from the *Gos. Pet.* in part of the tradition (v 48).

Luke 23,44-49
⁴⁴Καὶ ἦν ἤδη ὡσεὶ ὥρα ἕκτη καὶ σκότος ἐγένετο ἐφ᾽ ὅλην τὴν γῆν ἕως ὥρας ἐνάτης ⁴⁵τοῦ ἡλίου ἐκλιπόντος, ἐσχίσθη δὲ τὸ καταπέτασμα τοῦ ναοῦ μέσον. ⁴⁶καὶ φωνήσας φωνῇ μεγάλῃ ὁ Ἰησοῦς εἶπεν, πάτερ, εἰς χεῖράς σου παρατίθεμαι τὸ πνεῦμά μου. τοῦτο δὲ εἰπὼν ἐξέπνευσεν. ⁴⁷Ἰδὼν δὲ ὁ ἑκατοντάρχης τὸ γενόμενον ἐδόξαζεν τὸν θεὸν λέγων, Ὄντως ὁ ἄνθρωπος οὗτος δίκαιος ἦν. ⁴⁸καὶ πάντες οἱ συμπαραγενόμενοι ὄχλοι ἐπὶ τὴν θεωρίαν ταύτην, θεωρήσαντες τὰ γενόμενα, τύπτοντες τὰ στήθη ὑπέστρεφον. ⁴⁹Εἱστήκεισαν δὲ πάντες οἱ γνωστοὶ αὐτῷ ἀπὸ μακρόθεν καὶ γυναῖκες αἱ συνακολουθοῦσαι αὐτῷ ἀπὸ τῆς Γαλιλαίας, ὁρῶσαι ταῦτα.

v 45   ᵃ[τοῦ ἡλίου ἐκλιπόντος], ᵇ[ἐσχίσθη δὲ τὸ καταπέτασμα τοῦ ναοῦ μέσον.][40]

ᵃκαι εσκοτισθη ο ηλιος A C³ (D) W Δ Θ Ψ f¹.¹³ *Maj* lat sy (itᵃ,ᵇ,ᶜ,ᵉ arm geo Diatessaron omit και) eth Mcion^Evid Or^lat'mss
[   ] 33 vg^ms
εσκοτισθη δε ο ηλιος D itᵈ
του ηλιου εκλειποντος P⁷⁵ᶜ B 597 *al* Or
του ηλιου εκλιποντος και εσκοτισθη ο ηλιος C²ᵛⁱᵈ
   Text P⁷⁵* ℵ C*ᵛⁱᵈ L 070 579 2542 *pc* sy^hmg Or^lat'mss
ᵇ[   ] D
και το καταπετασμα του ναου εσχισθη Ψ

---

[40] The *NA²⁷* apparatus is supplemented in part by that of the *UBSGNT⁴* in this verse.

The Byzantine, Western, and Caesarean traditions evidence σκοτίζομαι while the Alexandrian shows ἐκλείπω. The chief witness of the Western text, Bezae, omits 45b.

The problem in the first half of this verse centers around the two verbs, ἐκλείπω and σκοτίζομαι. Good Greek is not averse to redundancy, the verb σκοτίζομαι, *to be or become dark*,[41] as a cognate of σκότος, *darkening of the sun*,[42] would be expected in this verse. In addition, two OT prophecies provide a basis for reading the verb σκοτίζομαι. LXX Isa 13,10 instances οἱ γὰρ ἀστέρες τοῦ οὐρανοῦ καὶ ὁ Ὠρίων καὶ πᾶς ὁ κόσμος τοῦ οὐρανοῦ τὸ φῶς οὐ δώσουσιν, καὶ σκοτισθήσεται τοῦ ἡλίου ἀνατέλλοντος, καὶ ἡ σελήνη οὐ δώσει τὸ φῶς αὐτῆς. Likewise, LXX Amos 8,9b has καὶ δύσεται ὁ ἥλιος μεσημβρίας, καὶ συσκοτάσει ἐπὶ τῆς γῆς ἐν ἡμέρᾳ τὸ φῶς· These two texts are situated in a context of judgment and destruction. The question turns to τοῦ ἡλίου ἐκλιπόντος.

A genitive absolute associated with the verb ἐγένετο (v 44), as appears here, is not unknown in the Lucan gospel.[43] This singularity of the eclipsing of the sun *vis-à-vis* the other two synoptics makes τοῦ ἡλίου ἐκλιπόντος the *lectio difficilior*. The compilers of the *UBSGNT⁴*, commenting on their choice for the reading τοῦ ἡλίου ἐκλιπόντος in v 45a, grade its inclusion as *B*, i.e. the text is almost certain.[44] In his commentary on the *UBSGNT⁴* Metzger holds that καὶ ἐσκοτίσθη ὁ ἥλιος is an easier reading than τοῦ ἡλίου ἐκλιπόντος and is therefore probably not original.[45]

If ἐκλείπω is the original reading, a scribe or redactor must have found reason to contest it to the point of substituting σκοτίζομαι. The primary definition of ἐκλείπω is *fail* or *die out*.[46] Verse 44 explains that there was darkness over the whole land for a three-hour span. It seems that ἐκλείπω overstates the case; a sun which dies at the sixth hour is unlikely to return at the ninth hour. Such a cataclysm, an interpretation which arises from viewing the genitive absolute as a causal phrase,[47] would overshadow the central action of the narrative, the death of Christ. A copyist, seeing this problem, and wishing to emphasize the apocalyptic prophecies in LXX Isa 13,10 and LXX Amos 8,9b, wrote the verb σκοτίζομαι.[48] If, however, the genitive absolute, τοῦ ἡλίου

---

[41] BAGD 757.

[42] BAGD 757.

[43] Cf. 9,34; 11,14; 15,14; 20,1.

[44] *UBSGNT⁴* 3*.

[45] Metzger, *Textual* 2nd 155.

[46] BAGD 242.

[47] In koine Greek, the causal participle, as in classical Greek, is equivalent to an adverbial clause (BDF 215 para. 418). This in turn can be a function of a genitive absolute in that "it expresses some secondary determination of the main sentence in a syntactically independent form" (Maximilian Zerwick, S.J., *Biblical Greek* [Rome: Pontificio Istituto Biblico 1963, reprinted 1987] 18 para. 48).

[48] The context for each of these two OT citations is the day of the Lord. In

ἐκλιπόντος, is read as a circumstantial instead of a causal phrase,[49] the idea of the sun failing or dying out simply becomes additional information which mitigates any overtones of absolute cosmic destruction the verb ἐκλείπω might bear: "It was around the sixth hour, and there was darkness over the whole land until the ninth hour, while the sun's light failed". The Alexandrian reading, the *lectio difficilior*, is also the original one, τοῦ ἡλίου ἐκλιπόντος.[50]

Verse 45b presents particular difficulties. Of all the witnesses only D does not show ἐσχίσθη δὲ τὸ καταπέτασμα τοῦ ναοῦ μέσον. In v 46, however, D reads καὶ τὸ καταπετασμα του ναου εσχισθη.[51] Either Bezae is harmonizing this text with Matthew and Mark, where the rending of the temple curtain comes after Christ's death, or Bezae represents the original reading which other witnesses have altered and placed in v 45b.

In terms of the narrative, placing this phrase in v 46 adds a sense of finality to the scene thus heightening the dramatic effect of the death, while its position in this verse after the failing of the sun emphasizes the natural upheavals and makes Jesus' last breath anticlimactic. For a fine literary style, there is a strong case for reading Bezae's reconstituted version of ἐσχίσθη δὲ τὸ καταπέτασμα τοῦ ναοῦ μέσον in v 46. On textual evidence, however, the fact that ἐσχίσθη δὲ τὸ καταπέτασμα τοῦ ναοῦ μέσον opened a division early in the tradition would suggest that it belongs in v 45; early witnesses save D are unanimous in this position. Based on the textual evidence, and by reason of *lectio difficilior*, ἐσχίσθη δὲ τὸ καταπέτασμα τοῦ ναοῦ μέσον belongs in v 45b. Bezae harmonizes the text with Matthew and Mark.

v 46   καὶ φωνήσας φωνῇ μεγάλῃ ὁ Ἰησοῦς εἶπεν· πάτερ, εἰς χεῖράς σου [a][παρατίθεμαι] τὸ πνεῦμά μου. τοῦτο δὲ εἰπὼν ἐξέπνευσεν. [b][ ]

[a]παρατιθημι D f[1] 892 2542 *al*
παραθησομαι L f[13] *Maj* vg[ms]
Text P[75] ℵ A B C K P Q W Θ Ψ 070 33 579 1241 *l* 844 *al* Cl[ex] [Thd] Eus

---

Isaiah 13, the earth will be made a desolation as it is purged of evil; in Amos 8, there will be tremendous mourning as for a loved one. Of course, allusion to these prophecies does not depend solely on the verb σκοτίζομαι; ἥλιος, γῆ, and σκότος can evoke the same thoughts.

[49] In koine Greek, either the circumstantial participle can refer to a noun in the same sentence and be in agreement with it, or the participle can be in absolute form in which its logical relation to the rest of the sentence is deduced from the context (BDF 215 para. 417).

[50] Rufino María Grández holds to the σκοτίζομαι reading. He bases this on 1) Lucan use of genitive participles, 2) the internal criticism of the biblical tradition which he sees as consonant with σκοτίζειν, and 3) the allusion σκοτίζομαι makes with Amos 8,9 (*Las Tinieblas en la Muerte de Jesus, Estudio sobre Lc 23,44-45a* [Jerusalem: Studium Biblicum Franciscanum, 1989] 73).

[51] Cf. below.

ᵇκαι το καταπετασμα του ναου εσχισθη D

A reference to LXX Ps 30,6 (MT Ps 31,6), εἰς χεῖράς σου παρατίθεμαι τὸ πνεῦμά μου exhibits variations in the reading of the verb παρατίθημι. While the text, with support from Alexandrian, Byzantine, and Caesarean traditions, employs the present indicative middle form, the major witness of the Western recension, Bezae, uses the present indicative active, παρατίθημι. The former shows a reliance on classical grammar. LXX Ps 30,6 reads παραθήσομαι, a future indicative middle which is found in several of the Lucan witnesses. The switch from the future tense in LXX Ps 30,6 to the present in this verse suggests a connection the writer is trying to make; what was predicted in the Psalms is fulfilled in the gospel. The strong witness for παρατίθεμαι, coupled with its grammatical correctness and the fact that LXX Ps 30,6 also evidences the middle voice, uphold it as the preferred reading.

Here, as in Mark 15,34 and Matt 27,46, the discrepancies center around the last words of Christ. At this point, the textual tradition in all three synoptics reflects the elaboration of a "fixed point".

v 48   καὶ πάντες οἱ συμπαραγενόμενοι ὄχλοι ἐπὶ τὴν θεωρίαν ταύτην, θεωρήσαντες τὰ γενόμενα, τύπτοντες τὰ στήθη ᵃ[ ] ὑπέστρεφον ᵇ[ ].

ᵃκαι τα μετωπα D (c)

ᵇdicentes: vae nobis quae facta sunt hodie propter peccata nostra; appropinquavit enim desolatio Hierusalem gˡ (syˢ·ᶜ·)

The Codex D addition of και τα μετωπα after στήθη is an embellishment of the text. The same may be true for the translation from the *Gos. Pet.* 7 found in the Latin and Syriac manuscripts, "dicentes: vae nobis quae facta sunt hodie propter peccata nostra; appropinquavit desolatio Hierusalem". None of these evidences a major textual problem. It is most likely that the material from the *Gos. Pet.*, gˡ, and syˢ·ᶜ reflects emendation of the text in an age subsequent to the writing of the gospel; it does not witness part of the Lucan tradition that has been lost.

Gospel of Peter

The *Gos. Pet.* appears to have been composed at a date later than any of the four canonical Gospels. First, the cry from the cross in *Gos. Pet.* shows great similarity with the Marcan and Matthean versions despite the slight change in vocabulary.[52] A liaison between Luke and *Gos. Pet.* should exhibit a stronger affinity in citing Christ's last words. Second, whereas in the Lucan account the crowd follows Jesus from the trial to the crucifixion (23,24-27.48) thus giving the story line internal consistency, in *Gos. Pet.* the crowd is set *in medias res*, is

---

[52] *Gos. Pet.* 5 reads Ἡ δύναμις μου, ἡ δύναμις, κατέλειψάς με·

defined as Jews, and is included with the elders and priests (7). Third, the *Gos. Pet.* quotation itself, Οὐαὶ ταῖς ἁμαρτίαις ἡμῶν· ἤγγισεν ἡ κρίσις καὶ τὸ τέλος Ἰερουσαλήμ (7), interprets the destruction of Jerusalem in AD 70 as a result of that city's role in Jesus' death. This fact betrays a late date of composition for *Gos. Pet.* Neither Luke, nor any of the other evangelists for that matter, make such a connection between the passion of Christ and the outcome of the first Jewish revolt. Fourth, the *Gos. Pet.* overuses the term *Lord* when speaking about Jesus, to the point of speaking of the first day of the week as the *Lord's Day.* This indicates a late composition.

Above all, concerning the citation itself, Rendel Harris demonstrates that it originates in a Syriac text which was redacted into the *Diatessaron*, and the *Diatessaron* heavily influenced the *Gos. Pet.*.[53]   Harris' findings are substantiated by recent research which proves that there is no evidence of a "reliable second-century *Vorlage*" of the Akhmim fragment and that traditions peculiar to the *Gos. Pet.* continued to develop after the second century.[54] On this basis, it appears that the *Gos. Pet.* first copied material from the *Diatessaron*. In addition, the *UBSGNT*[4] editors maintain that the interpolations in v 48 stem from a desire to heighten the account, and they cite Ephraem's commentary on the *Diatessaron* as an example.[55]

Hence, with regard to Luke 23,48, the Latin version of the quotation from the *Gos. Pet.*, the language itself being an indication of its late composition, was recopied into the g[1] and sy[s.c] versions of the Lucan text by a scribe who knew of the *Gos. Pet.* The crowd mentioned in v 48 would easily engage the imagination of a scribe to include this *Gos. Pet.* reading in the Lucan account.

Précis

Two points arise from this textual analysis of Luke 23,44-49. First, Jesus' last words in v 46, as well as the events leading up to that moment (v 45) show the greatest textual variation among the verses in the pericope. These verses also rely on three septuagintal references, Amos 8,9, Isa 13,10, and Ps 30,6. As with the last words recorded in Mark 15,34 and Matt 27,46, the textual variations in Luke 23,46 characterize the development of a "fixed point". Second, the elaborations from the *Gospel of Peter* found at v 48 in some of the Syriac and Latin codices do not pre-date the Lucan gospel.

---

[53] Rendel Harris, "The Origin of a Famous Lucan Gloss," *ExpTim* 35 (1923-24) 7-10.

[54] Jay C. Treat, "The Two Manuscript Witnesses to the *Gospel of Peter*," *SBL Seminar Papers* (1990) 399.

[55] Metzger, *Textual* 2nd 155-6.

John 19,25-30

The death of Christ in John's gospel has very few textual problems and certainly no major one. The discrepancies are confined to Byzantine, Caesarean, and Egyptian texts *vis-à-vis* the Alexandrian tradition. When these witnesses disagree with ℵ B C *et al*, it is usually when the non-Alexandrian texts elaborate and interpolate certain readings. Bezae, the principal witness of the Western tradition, lacks a certain degree of dependability since its witness for this gospel is to be found only in later supplements. Complications in the textual tradition for this Johannine pericope are confined mainly to vv 25 and 29, but vv 28 and 30 have some points necessitating mention.

John 19,25-30
25Εἱστήκεισαν δὲ παρὰ τῷ σταυρῷ τοῦ Ἰησοῦ ἡ μήτηρ αὐτοῦ καὶ ἡ ἀδελφὴ τῆς μητρὸς αὐτοῦ, Μαρία ἡ τοῦ Κλωπᾶ καὶ Μαρία ἡ Μαγδαληνή. 26Ἰησοῦς οὖν ἰδὼν τὴν μητέρα καὶ τὸν μαθητὴν παρεστῶτα ὃν ἠγάπα, λέγει τῇ μητρί, γύναι, ἴδε ὁ υἱός σου. 27εἶτα λέγει τῷ μαθητῇ, ἴδε ἡ μήτηρ σου. καὶ ἀπ᾽ ἐκείνης τῆς ὥρας ἔλαβεν ὁ μαθητὴς αὐτὴν εἰς τὰ ἴδια. 28Μετὰ τοῦτο εἰδὼς ὁ Ἰησοῦς ὅτι ἤδη πάντα τετέλεσται, ἵνα τελειωθῇ ἡ γραφή, λέγει, Διψῶ. 29σκεῦος ἔκειτο ὄξους μεστόν· σπόγγον οὖν μεστὸν τοῦ ὄξους ὑσσώπῳ περιθέντες προσήνεγκαν αὐτοῦ τῷ στόματι. 30ὅτε οὖν ἔλαβεν τὸ ὄξος ὁ Ἰησοῦς εἶπεν, τετέλεσται, καὶ κλίνας τὴν κεφαλὴν παρέδωκεν τὸ πνεῦμα.

v 25   Εἱστήκεισαν δὲ παρὰ τῷ σταυρῷ a[τοῦ Ἰησοῦ] ἡ μήτηρ αὐτοῦ καὶ ἡ ἀδελφὴ τῆς μητρὸς αὐτοῦ, b[c(Μαρία) ἡ τοῦ Κλωπᾶ καὶ] d[Μαρία] ἡ Μαγδαληνή.

a[ ] W

b[ ] P60vid

cΜαριαμ ℵ (L) Ψ 1 33 565 *l* 844 *pc*

dΜαριαμ ℵ (L) Ψ 1 33 565 *l* 844 *pc*

A textual variation centers around the phrase Μαρία ἡ τοῦ Κλωπᾶ; P60vid does not show the term. This textual discrepancy raises three questions. If such an early witness as P60 does not evidence the phrase, can it be considered part of the tradition? If so, should this phrase be read as an appositive for ἡ ἀδελφὴ τῆς μητρὸς αὐτοῦ? Finally, why is John the only evangelist to include this woman? The answer to the first question is the least difficult. Since the omission by P60 is uncertain anyway, and since the other major witnesses show the phrase, to consider it part of the original text is a sound conclusion.

The second question is more complex. Parents generally would not give two daughters the same name; on this basis, Μαρία ἡ τοῦ Κλωπᾶ cannot be an appositive of ἡ ἀδελφὴ τῆς μητρὸς αὐτοῦ. John, however, is the only evangelist not to specify Μαρία as the name of Jesus' mother; indeed, she goes unnamed throughout the fourth gospel.[56] On this basis, the possibility that Μαρία ἡ τοῦ

Κλωπᾶ is an appositive phrase identifying the sister of Jesus' mother, although unlikely, cannot be excluded. This verse witnesses the only gospel occurrence mentioning the sister of Jesus' mother.[57] If in fact the mother of Jesus was known by another name, it seems more than likely that it serves to identify further both the sister and the wife of Klopas; they are one and the same. If, on the other hand, Μαρία ἡ τοῦ Κλωπᾶ is not an appositive of ἡ ἀδελφὴ τῆς μητρὸς αὐτοῦ, the importance of Mary, wife of Klopas witnessing the death is in no way diminished.

The last question, why does John include her, can best be answered by looking to the third gospel. Luke 24,18 relates that Κλεοπᾶς is the name of one of the disciples on the road to Emmaus, the only occurrence of such a person in the NT; likewise for this Johannine verse, Κλωπᾶς does not occur in any other NT book.[58] It is possible to surmise that in the Lucan reading, the other disciple with Κλεοπᾶς could be his wife, Μαρία. If Κλωπᾶς is the same person as Κλεοπᾶς, and if the other disciple in Luke's Emmaus pericope is his wife, then the importance of specifying her presence at the cross in John 19,25 becomes evident: There may have been a tradition in which Μαρία ἡ τοῦ Κλωπᾶ was considered a witness of both the crucifixion and the resurrection, a "fixed point". This last factor evidences a possible link between Luke and John in their respective passion and resurrection narratives.

The textual problems in this verse, as slight as they may be, not only reflect an attempt to clear up any ambiguities concerning which women named Mary were at the cross, but they evidence the process of the Johannine redaction.

v 28   Μετὰ τοῦτο ᵃ[εἰδὼς ὁ Ἰησοῦς] ὅτι ᵇ[ἤδη πάντα] τετέλεσται, ᶜ[ἵνα ᵈ(τελειωθῇ) ἡ γραφή], λέγει, Διψῶ.

ᵃ3 1 B it
ιδων ο Ιησους Κ Γ Ψ f¹³ (892ˢ) 1424 pm a bo
Text ℵ A Dˢ L N W Θ f¹ 33 565 579 700 1241 l 844 pm vg

ᵇ2 1 ℵ Θ f¹³ Maj f q

2 W f¹ 565 (579) 700 1424 pc it vgᶜˡ syᵖ sa ac² pbo
Text P⁶⁶ A B Dˢ L Ψ 33 l 844 al lat bo

ᶜp66* ac² boᵐˢ

ᵈπληρωθη ℵ Dˢ Θ f¹.¹³ (565) al it

The great majority of the omissions and additions are confined to

---

57 VKGNT 1/2; 760.

57 VKGNT 1/1; 13.

58 VKGNT 1/1; 693-4.

Byzantine and Caesarean witnesses. Of particular note is the absence of ἵνα
τελειωθῇ ἡ γραφή in P⁶⁶*, a variant which suggests that the phrase was a later
interpolation. That ℵ Dˢ and others show πληρωθη instead of τελειωθῇ in this
section corroborates the conclusion that this part of the verse is a later addition.

<u>v 29</u>   σκεῦος ᵃ[ ] ἔκειτο ὄξους μεστόν· ᵇ[σπόγγον οὖν μεστὸν τοῦ ὄξους
ᶜ(ὑσσώπῳ) περιθέντες] προσήνεγκαν αὐτοῦ τῷ στόματι.

ᵃουν Dˢ Θ f¹·¹³ *Maj* lat syʰ
δε ℵ saᵐˢˢ pbo bo
    Text A B L W Ψ 579 *pc* it

ᵇσπογγον ουν μεστον οξους υσσωπω περιθεντες ℵ*
οι δε πλησαντες σπογγον οξους και υσσωπω περιθεντες A Dˢ f¹³ *Maj* f
q sy bo

οι δε πλησαντες σπογγον οξους μετα χολης και υσσωπω περιθεντες f¹³
q syʰ**

οι δε πλησαντες σπογγον του οξους μετα χολης και υσσωπου, και
περιθεντες καλαμω Θ 892ˢ *pc*

ᶜυσσω (*cf* it) [Camerarius *cj*]
    Text P⁶⁶ᵛⁱᵈ ℵ B L W Ψ f¹ 1 33 565 (579) *pc* (lat) saᵐˢˢ ac² pbo

According to Metzger, υσσω is a haplographic mistake,[59] but it calls
attention to the presence of ὕσσωπος in this verse, particularly since John is the
only evangelist to include it.
    The Byzantine and Caesarean texts evidence many interpolations centered
around the sponge. This verse contains allusions to MT Ps 69,22 and LXX Ps
68,22; the latter explains the addition of χολης. The Alexandrian witnesses for
the text, while not including the gall, show hyssop as the instrument for raising
the sponge to the mouth. MT Exod 12,22 states that the head of the house is to
use אֵזוֹב for placing the blood of the paschal lamb on the lintel, a plant which
LXX Exod 12,22 shows as ὑσσώπου. In several other books of the Pentateuch,
אֵזוֹב is used for purification.[60]
    Of all the MT references to אֵזוֹב (LXX ὕσσωπος), the citations from Exod
12,22 and Num 19,6 are the ones most likely to have influenced the occurrence

---

[59] Metzger, *Textual* 2ⁿᵈ 217-8.

[60] אֵזוֹב, *hyssop...an herb of purging qualities* (BDB 23), is used for the
purification of lepers in Lev 14,4.6.49.51.52, although it is spelled without the
mater lectionis ו. In MT Ps 51,9 it appears in a context of purification. It is
included in the ceremony of the red heifer (Num 19,6), and in MT 1 Kgs 5,13 it
forms part of a synecdoche describing the wisdom of Solomon: "He would speak
of trees, from the cedar that is in the Lebanon to the hyssop that grows in the
wall" (*NRSV* 1 Kgs 4,33).

of ὕσσωπος in this verse. Such a conclusion is based on John's description and setting of the crucifixion[61] as well as the fact that ὕσσωπος, while symbolically associated with the rites of purification, as a leafy bush is highly impractical for the task described by John. In addition, hyssop, a plant of southern Europe, is not native to the Holy Land.[62] No doubt others saw these inconsistencies as well, hence the reading with Θ 892^s et al. The variations of this verse mainly reflect attempts to offset any confusion surrounding the sponge, vinegar, and hyssop.

v 30   ὅτε οὖν ἔλαβεν τὸ ὄξος ^{a}[ὁ Ἰησοῦς] εἶπεν, τετέλεσται, καὶ κλίνας τὴν κεφαλὴν παρέδωκεν τὸ πνεῦμα.

^{a}Ιησους B W
[ ] ℵ* a pbo
Text *rell*

The absence of Ἰησοῦς by Sinaiticus, a major witness, indicates that early in the tradition the name Ἰησοῦς in v 28 sufficed as the subject for this verse. This circumstance in turn suggests that at one point there was less material between vv 28 and 30.

Précis

John 19,25-30 evidences few difficulties in the textual tradition; the *dubium* surrounding Mary, wife of Klopas raised by P^{60} in v 25 is dispelled by the overwhelming testimony of other manuscripts, most notably ℵ. Variants in v 28 are confined in the main to Byzantine and Caesarean witnesses. Because the fourth gospel includes hyssop in the sponge episode, an addition not found in the parallel synoptic accounts, verse 29 exhibits various interpolations and elaborations, particularly within the Byzantine tradition. An important observation is the discrepancy involving the presence of the name Ἰησοῦς in v 30. In its absence, the subject in v 28, also Ἰησοῦς, must govern v 30. This leads to the conclusion that parts of vv 28-30 contain supplementary material, something which the elaborations in v 29 substantiate.

Summary

The textual questions in the death account among all four gospels help to identify those points in the tradition where the joining of several pieces of

---

[61] There is a decidedly paschal thrust to the Johannine passion account. Cf. John 12,1; 13,1; 19,14.31.33.

[62] J. C. Trevor, "Hyssop," *The Interpreter's Dictionary of the Bible* (2; New York: Abington Press, 1962) 669-70.

information called for greater explanation or clarification. Most elaborations center around two "fixed points," the last words of Christ and the description of the witnesses; this is seen in all four gospel accounts.

Mark 15,34 and Matt 27,46 provide evidence for the many discrepancies over the transliteration of the Hebrew/Aramaic cry from the cross and its Greek translation. The textual problems in Mark 15,36 are related to the cry of dereliction in v 34; both result from the blending of two traditions. These two traditions surface in Matthew, and, as in Mark, they cause some textual difficulties. In Matt 27,49, however, the addition of a gloss is the central issue.

Luke 23,45-46 records Christ's last words. As such, it has affinity with Mark 15,34 and Matt 27,46 in so far that it shows the development of a "fixed point". Furthermore, Luke 23,45 is related to Christ's last words by virtue of supplying the background to the death. The same "fixed point" in John 19,30 features the omission of the name *Jesus* in part of the textual tradition. The trace of two interpolations in Luke 23,48 suggests that the verse stands as a redactional seam, a point which will become clearer in the following literary and source analysis of the "fixed points" in Luke 23,44-49.

Chapter Four

Source Criticism of Luke 23,44-49

State of the problem

In discussions of source criticism, observes Joseph B. Tyson, it is possible to "paint a credible picture of Luke on the basis of any source hypothesis."[1] Noting that such an approach lacks accuracy, for there are no criteria for making judgments about the merit of a particular work, Tyson prefers to leave the source question unresolved, at least for the time being.[2] Tyson, however, does not believe that literary criticism is the substitute for source analysis; he feels that, although literary criticism asks the right questions, it does not provide the means to answer them;[3] hence, Tyson proposes the aforementioned approach of a "holistic" reading.[4]

Martin Kähler posits that the gospels are "...passion narratives with extended introductions."[5] If the core of the passion narratives is the death itself, to which the stories of the arrest, trial, and resurrection were soon added, then the theology of each evangelist becomes evident in his respective treatment of the death of Jesus, first, in terms of the passion and resurrection, and second, in the whole gospel narrative. Thus, working with the final redaction is the only way to uncover the particular theology of the evangelist.

The holistic approach put forth by Tyson has much to commend it. To rely solely on source analysis can lead to a lack of respect for the literary integrity of the final piece. On the other hand, it is difficult to understand the final product without being attentive to what went into its composition. On this basis, for the death account in Luke, two methods are used in this study. The source and redactional questions are examined first; this exercise is limited to Luke 23,44-49 and its parallels. The results of this section are then applied in Chapter Five to a synchronic reading of the death of Jesus in the Lucan corpus.

Complexities of the pericope

Introduction

The Lucan account of Jesus' death is the shortest of the synoptics. Despite its brevity, there are many elements contained in Luke 23,44-49 which

---

[1] Tyson, *Death* 8.

[2] Tyson, *Death* 9.

[3] Tyson, *Death* 6.

[4] Tyson, *Death* 9. Cf. also above, Chapter One.

[5] Martin Kähler, *The So-Called Historical Jesus and the Historic Biblical Christ*, trans. Carl E. Braaten (Philadelphia: Fortress Press, 1964) 80 n 11.

also appear in the parallel accounts of Mark and Matthew; there are also
significant departures from the first two evangelists.

The redactional study of this pericope consists of several sections:
examination of synoptic similarities, an analysis of Lucan differences, the state of
the redactional question, and a reading of Luke's internal structure. Luke is
compared first to Mark. The results of this study will show that Luke and John
represent a primitive account of the death narrative which was independent of the
synoptics. Borrowing from this common source, and at an early stage, a Lucan
and Johannine redactor made respective changes on a "fixed point"[6] to the extent
that, notwithstanding the similarities, two independent death narratives evolved,
one Lucan and the other Johannine.

Finally the hypothesis will be proposed and tested that these redacted
Lucan and Johannine accounts, in their primitive form, have been combined to
provide the basis of the accounts in Mark and Matthew. The work of other
redactors at various stages of the development of the texts is also studied. It will
be seen that, at a certain point, a Lucan redactor used an intermediate Marcan and
Matthean version in the final recension of the third gospel.

Similarities among the synoptics

Among the synoptics, the similarities in the death narratives exist in
context, narrative sequence, and vocabulary.

The death of Jesus has an identical context in each of the synoptics.
Although there are differences among them in relating how those crucified with
Jesus curse him, Matthew, Mark, and Luke begin their respective death
narratives immediately after each has related the criminals' reviling of Jesus.[7]
After Jesus has died, the three evangelists continue by noting the women from
Galilee who witness the crucifixion. The burial then follows.

The narrative sequence of each synoptic death account shows similar
traits: a) there is darkness from the sixth hour to the ninth hour, b) this darkness
covers the whole land, c) Jesus cries out with a loud voice and expires, d) the
centurion makes a declaration about Jesus, and e) the women who followed Jesus
from Galilee stand afar off and witness these happenings.

Similarities in vocabulary exist among the synoptic versions although
often there are differences in tense and voice among the verbs. Verbs common to
each include:

a) $\gamma\acute{\iota}\nu o\mu\alpha\iota$ in aorist middle
  ($\grave{\epsilon}\gamma\acute{\epsilon}\nu\epsilon\tau o$ in Matthew, Mark, and Luke);
b) $\sigma\chi\acute{\iota}\zeta\omega$ in aorist passive
  ($\grave{\epsilon}\sigma\chi\acute{\iota}\sigma\theta\eta$ in Matthew, Mark, and Luke);
c) $\acute{o}\rho\acute{a}\omega$ as aorist or present participle

---

[6] Cf. above.

[7] Matt 27,44 specifies that the robbers, $\lambda\eta\sigma\tau\alpha\acute{\iota}$, mock Jesus. Mark 15,32 says
that those who were crucifed with him reviled him. Luke 23,39-43 distinguishes
between one of the wrongdoers, $\kappa\alpha\kappa o\hat{\upsilon}\rho\gamma o\iota$, who insults Jesus and another who
defends him.

(ἰδών in Mark and Luke; ὁρῶσαι in Luke; ἰδόντες in Matthew);
d) εἰμί in imperfect
   (ἦν in all three);
e) θεωρέω as aorist or present participle
   (θεωρήσαντες in Luke; θεωροῦσαι in Matthew and Mark);
f) ἀκολουθέω in aorist or imperfect, or as a participle with prefix συν
   (ἠκολούθησαν in Matthew; ἠκολούθουν in Mark; συνακολουθοῦσαι in
   Luke).

The nouns common to each of the synoptics often show slight variations in case: ὥρα, σκότος, γῆ, φωνή, Ἰησοῦς, καταπέτασμα, ναός, θεός, γυνή, Γαλιλαία.

Among the adjectives common to the synoptics, ἐκτός, ἔνατος, μεγάλη, only ἐκτός varies in case.

There is one common pronoun, οὗτος.

The adverb μακρόθεν is introduced by the preposition ἀπό in Matthew, Mark, and Luke.

Differences among the synoptics

When contrasted with the other synoptics, there are some striking dissimilarities in both vocabulary and subject matter in Luke. All synoptics relate a three-hour period of darkness, all note Jesus' crying out with a loud voice immediately before the moment of death, all describe the rending of the temple curtain, all quote a statement of the centurion, and all cite the presence of the women from Galilee. On the other hand, a comparative reading of each account brings to the surface major points of divergence in Luke vis-à-vis the other two synoptics.

First, both Matthew and Mark record two cries of Jesus, one of abandonment and another at the moment of death. The latter contains neither a quotation nor indirect speech; it simply states that Jesus utters or cries out with a loud voice. Luke, on the other hand, mentions only one loud cry followed by Jesus' final words πάτερ, εἰς χεῖράς σου παρατίθεμαι τὸ πνεῦμα μου; there is no cry of abandonment. In addition, Luke does not expressly say that Jesus uttered the loud cry and died at the ninth hour. Second, Matthew and Mark narrate the incident of the vinegar-soaked sponge which does not exist in Luke. Third, although all three synoptics relate the splitting of the temple curtain, Luke places it before the death itself and, unlike Matthew or Mark, does not specify that it was torn from top to bottom. Fourth, only Luke mentions the eclipse of the sun, although all three synoptics describe a three-hour period of darkness. Fifth, whereas Matthew and Mark record the centurion's affirming that Jesus was the son of God, Luke quotes him as saying ὁ ἄνθρωπος οὗτος δίκαιος ἦν; in addition, Mark reads κεντυρίων instead of ἑκατοντάρχης. Sixth, Luke features the bystanders beating their breasts as they return home. Seventh, Luke alone does not specify by name the women who stand afar off observing the crucifixion. Eighth, he is also the only evangelist to include Jesus' acquaintances in the scene, albeit unnamed.

State of the redactional question

Exegetes studying the Lucan death narrative are divided between those who explain the death account in terms of Luke's redaction of Mark, and those who find evidence of a primitive tradition behind Luke.

There are many who defend Mark as the source of the death account. Hans Conzelmann, while maintaining the passion narrative as the core piece of the synoptic tradition, maintains that there is no source outside Mark; Conzelmann is silent on the possibility of other traditions.[8] After observing similarities and differences between the death account in the third gospel and that in Mark, I. H. Marshall states, "All of this can plausibly be explained as due to Lucan editing, and the case for a separate passion narrative used by him is at its weakest here."[9] Frank J. Matera, strongly adhering to "the basic reliability of the two-source hypothesis,"[10] attempts to explain Luke's redaction of the death account solely in terms of the third evangelist's theology. Wolfgang Reinbold resolutely maintains that no model which is more complex deserves the advantage before one that is as clear and economical as the two-source theory. On this basis, Reinbold sees the Johannine tradition as original and independent of any synoptic gospel.[11] On the other hand, Frans Neirynck views the synoptics as sources for the Johannine gospel.[12]

Joseph A. Fitzmyer, concurring with Marshall's opinion, holds that this whole death episode is inspired by Mark 15,33-40a, and believes that in his redaction, Luke has abridged the Marcan parallel.[13] This, Fitzmyer explains, the third evangelist has done by a) using the failure of the sun to explain the darkness, b) placing the tearing of the temple curtain before the death, c) omitting the cry of abandonment and its association with Elijah, d) employing a different psalm in v 46 to explain the cry in Mark 15,37, e) altering the centurion's comment, f) reworking his own ending by modifying Marcan material,[14] g) revising Marcan content for vv 48-49 by listing the women's names in 8,2-3.[15]

---

[8] Hans Conzelmann, "Historie und Theologie in den synoptischen Passionsberichten," *Zur Bedeutung des Todes Jesu* (Gütersloh: Gütersloher Verlagshaus Gerd Mohn, 1968) 49.

[9] I. H. Marshall, *The Gospel of Luke* (Exeter: The Paternoster Press, 1978) 874.

[10] Matera, "Death" 471.

[11] Wolfgang Reinbold, *Der Älteste Bericht über den Tod Jesu* (New York: Walter de Gruyter, 1994) 48.

[12] Frans Neirynck, "John and the Synoptics," *Evangelica: Gospel studies -- Études d'Évangile, collected essays* (ed. F. van Segbroeck; Lueven: University Press, 1982) 398.

[13] Fitzmyer, *Luke* 2; 1512.

[14] Fitzmyer, *Luke* 2; 1512.

[15] Fitzmyer, *Luke* 2; 1520-1. Fitzmyer's explanation is similar to Bultmann's

Rudolf Bultmann had already stated that, because Luke was offended by the cry of dereliction based on LXX Ps 21,2a, he replaced it with a reading from LXX Ps 30,6 in v 46.[16] Fitzmyer relies on Bultmann to rationalize the Lucan redaction[17] but cautiously proposes that the Lucan use of LXX Ps 30,6 may have come from early Christian liturgy.[18]

These explanations do not, however, seem to be sufficient. Was Luke really offended by the cry of dereliction, or can there be another explanation of why it is lacking in the third gospel? Furthermore, neither Fitzmyer nor Bultmann comments on the sponge episode which is found in Mark (v 36) but, like the cry of dereliction, is absent from Luke. In addition, while Fitzmyer in his analysis of vv 48-49 believes that the Lucan gospel derives part of the description from Mark,[19] Bultmann does not even address these verses. Matera's approach, though an interesting word study, fails to tackle the source and literary problems inherent in the texts. Without denying that a writer's theology would certainly influence a redaction, to use theology to explain the abandoning of so much material overly burdens the final recension. This is especially so when Matera does not give his reason for such a point of departure, a weakness which is manifest both in his failure to address adequately the problems in v 48 and in his omitting v 49 from the discussion altogether.

Some, such as Adela Yarbro Collins,[20] view a a pre-Marcan PN which includes the death account. Julius Schniewind holds that there was an oral tradition common to both Luke and John.[21] Likewise, Anton Dauer believes that John had a definite and independent, oral passion narrative at his disposal which was influenced by the written synoptic accounts to the extent that a separate, parallel narrative developed.[22] Bailey, while reaching findings similar to Dauer's, broadens them. Bailey does not see a particular source available to either Luke or John. Instead, many isolated oral and written accounts were in circulation; the latter were associated with the Church's liturgy and catechesis. In addition to relying on Mark, both Luke and John drew upon these traditions.[23]

---

which states that Luke had already noted the Galilean women's identity (Rudolf Bultmann, *The History of the Synoptic Tradition* [Oxford: Basil Blackwell, 1968] 274).

[16] Bultmann, *History* 274.

[17] Fitzmyer, *Luke* 2; 1513.

[18] Fitzmyer, *Luke* 2; 1519.

[19] Fitzmyer, *Luke* 2; 1520-1.

[20] Adela Yarbro Collins, "From Noble Death to Crucified Messiah," *NTS* 40 (1994) 497-9.

[21] Schniewind, *Parallelperikopen* 96.

[22] Anton Dauer, *Die Passionsgeschichte im Johannesevangelium* (München: Kösel-Verlag, 1972) 336.

[23] Bailey, *Traditions* 115.

Boismard explains that the literary contacts between the third and fourth evangelists are especially numerous in the passion and resurrection narratives; he demonstrates that many of these contacts are characterized by common themes and vocabulary.[24]   Although some of the episodes in the Lucan gospel are truncated, transferred, or even absent in John,[25] Boismard holds that the similarities between them nonetheless can be explained by mutual dependence on a common source, proto-Luke.[26]

To approach this discussion on sources, a middle position outlined by Green is taken.   In a recent study, Green presupposes the two-document hypothesis[27] but searches for a single pre-canonical passion narrative among the first, third, and fourth evangelists[28] in order to construct Mark's source.[29] Green finds a probable, non-Marcan, pre-Lucan passion source which Luke employed along with the Marcan narrative.   The author also sees a non-synoptic, pre-Johannine passion account used by the fourth evangelist.[30] Green believes that no more than two or three passion episodes circulated independently of the passion narrative as a whole;[31] he also views Mark as a "conservative redactor".[32]

A comparison of Luke 23,44-49 with Matthew 27,45-56, Mark 15,33-41 and John 19,25-30 challenges many of the assumptions of Conzelmann, Marshall, Matera, Fitzmyer, and Bultmann, to say nothing of those of Reinbold and Neirynck. Simultaneously it supports some of Green's findings, a point evident with regard to uncovering a pre-canonical passion narrative from Matthean, Lucan, and Johannine accounts. This investigation leads to conclusions beyond Green's, however, particularly his insistence that the third gospel also depends on Mark as a source.[33]   Furthermore, with some differences, this study reaches conclusions approaching Bailey's supposition of circulated oral and written liturgical accounts[34] as well as the "fixed point" concept of Dunn[35] and the multiple source theory of Boismard.[36]

---

[24] Boismard, *Synopse* 2; 40.

[25] E.g., the mocking by the soldiers and by Herod (Luke 23,6-12 but cf. John 19,2-3) and the interrogation by the Sanhedrin (Luke 22,66-68; John 10,24-25).

[26] Boismard, *Synopse* 2; 40.

[27] Green, *Death* 17.

[28] Green, *Death* 19.

[29] Green, *Death* 136.

[30] Green, *Death* 137.

[31] Green, *Death* 174.

[32] Green, *Death* 147.

[33] Green, *Death* 135.

[34] Bailey, *Traditions* 115.

Hypothesis

Among the synoptics, Lucan differences can be divided between those in which material found in Mark and Matthew is absent in Luke, and those in which elements existing in Luke are lacking in the other two synoptic accounts. An examination of Luke's internal consistency better highlights the demarcation.[37]

Luke 23,44-49

Luke 23,44-49

⁴⁴Καὶ ἦν ἤδη ὡσεὶ ὥρα ἕκτη καὶ σκότος ἐγένετο ἐφ᾿ ὅλην τὴν γῆν ἕως ὥρας ἐνάτης ⁴⁵ᵉτοῦ ἡλίου ἐκλιπόντος, ᵇἐσχίσθη δὲ τὸ καταπέτασμα τοῦ ναοῦ μέσον. ⁴⁶ᵃκαὶ φωνήσας φωνῇ μεγάλῃ ὁ Ἰησοῦς ᵇεἶπεν, πάτερ, εἰς χεῖράς σου παρατίθεμαι τὸ πνεῦμά μου. τοῦτο δὲ εἰπὼν ᶜἐξέπνευσεν. ⁴⁷ᵃἸδὼν δὲ ὁ ἑκατοντάρχης τὸ γενόμενον ἐδόξαζεν τὸν θεὸν ᵇλέγων, Ὄντως ὁ ἄνθρωπος οὗτος δίκαιος ἦν. ⁴⁸ᵃκαὶ πάντες οἱ συμπαραγενόμενοι ὄχλοι ᵇἐπὶ τὴν θεωρίαν ταύτην, θεωρήσαντες τὰ γενόμενα, ᶜτύπτοντες τὰ στήθη ᵈὑπέστρεφον. ⁴⁹ᵃΕἰστήκεισαν δὲ πάντες οἱ γνωστοὶ αὐτῷ ἀπὸ μακρόθεν ᵇκαὶ γυναῖκες αἱ συνακολουθοῦσαι αὐτῷ ἀπὸ τῆς Γαλιλαίας, ᶜὁρῶσαι ταῦτα.

This passage comprises two parts. The first describes the death itself (vv 44-46); and the second, the reactions of various witnesses (vv 47-49).

Verses 44-46

The ripping of the temple curtain is a problem in the narrative. Why would it tear before the death instead of after, and what causes it to tear in the first place? Its rending before the death in Luke contrasts with the tearing of the curtain *post-mortem* in Mark and Matthew. Compared with its starkly dramatic position in Mark and the much more expansive placement in Matthew, the Lucan version of the temple curtain seems clumsy and out of place, as Bezae's editing of vv 45-46 testifies. It cannot be denied that there is a logical flow to the account; three hours of darkness describe the natural setting, while the tearing of the curtain is a reference to the supernatural world. That in the narrative no one has yet died, however, may make v 46 seem anticlimactic.

---

[35] Dunn, "John" 378-9.

[36] Boismard, *Synopse* 2; 15-59.

[37] Hereafter the reader may find it beneficial to consult the Appendix.

Verses 47-49

In this second half, verse 48 is heavy with redundancy. The noun phrase τὴν θεωρίαν ταύτην and the participial phrase θεωρήσαντες τὰ γενόμενα repeat the same information in two grammatical forms. Similarly, v 49 separates Jesus' acquaintances from the women who followed him from Galilee. There is a question why Luke separates the two groups. Since Jesus lived and worked in Galilee, his friends more than likely would have followed him from there.

In the Lucan account, then, two problems are manifest. The first lies with the awkward placement of the temple curtain. The second is evident in the portrayal of the human reaction to the event; the description of the sight, the event, and the witnesses displays verbal duplication and narrative disjunction.

Luke 23,44-49 and Mark 15,33-41

While allowing for some variation between them, the death accounts in the second and third gospels show the following parallels: Mark 15,33 and Luke 23,44; Mark 15,37 and Luke 23,46ac; Mark 15,38 and Luke 23,45b; Mark 15,39a and Luke 23,47a; Mark 15,40 and Luke 23,49b. Non-Marcan material is evident in Luke 23,45a.48 (but note the Marcan θεωρίαν/θεωρήσαντες).49a. The phrase ὁρῶσαι ταῦτα (49c) is a reprise fashioned by a Lucan redactor. The proportion of Marcan material is higher in the first half of the pericope than in the second. Though many attribute these differences to Lucan editing of Marcan material, such a conclusion presents difficulties which defy such a facile explanation.[38] The Lucan death narrative, however, is not smooth nor is it an improvement on Marcan style. Despite the internal consistency of vv 44-46, the rending of the temple curtain reads better after the death, while the second half (vv 47-49) features the verbal tangle of v 48. Moreover, Mark 15,34-36 has no parallel within the Lucan narrative.

That Luke 23,44-49 is the shorter and the more difficult text suggests another explanation other than Marcan priority for the death account in the third gospel. Luke, the author of the shortest of the synoptic death accounts, drew upon another source which was originally independent of Mark. This Lucan source is called *a*. To *a* is ascribed some material which traditionally has been assigned to Mark, namely Luke 23,44.45b.46ac.47a.48ad.49a. Some Marcan influences can be seen, notably in vv 47b.48b.49b. Mark, it seems, had access to *a* into which he interpolates another tradition (15,34-36). A Lucan redaction, *L*, shows retouching of both *a* and Marcan material as well as additions of its own, especially in 23,45a.46b.47b.48c.49c.

A more detailed examination of the Lucan pericope substantiates this hypothesis. Each Lucan section is treated separately.

---

[38] Reid, *Transfiguration* 36.

Luke 23,44-46[39]

Luke 23,44-46
[44][Καὶ ἦν ἤδη ὡσεὶ ὥρα ἕκτη καὶ σκότος ἐγένετο ἐφ᾿ ὅλην τὴν γῆν ἕως ὥρας ἐνάτης] [45a](τοῦ ἡλίου ἐκλιπόντος), [b][ἐσχίσθη δὲ τὸ καταπέτασμα τοῦ ναοῦ μέσον. [46a]καὶ φωνήσας φωνῇ μεγάλῃ ὁ Ἰησοῦς [b](εἶπεν, πάτερ, εἰς χεῖράς σου παρατίθεμαι τὸ πνεῦμά μου. τοῦτο δὲ εἰπὼν) [c][ἐξέπνευσεν].

Verses 44 and 45b reflect the primitive *a* account which Mark borrowed; ἐσχίσθη δὲ τὸ καταπέτασμα τοῦ ναοῦ μέσον is the basis for this statement.[40] The account of the rending of the temple curtain in Luke is briefer than in Mark. Its placement in the third gospel, after the period of darkness but before the death of Jesus, even though both Mark and Matthew situate it after the death itself, has a logic which suggests that Luke reflects the more primitive account. Unlike the other two synoptics, the phenomena in the natural and religious spheres in Luke are not reactions to any event but occurrences leading to a climax, the death of Jesus. The seemingly awkward placement of the temple curtain in Luke notwithstanding, this position serves to highlight and underscore the death of Jesus; nothing else competes for the attention of the hearer or reader. In addition, the Lucan version of the temple curtain connects the tearing to the cosmic reactions (v 44). In this Lucan context, the rending of the temple curtain before the death makes sense; it is subtle, succinct, and dramatic.

Boismard argues, however, that vv 44-45b are a Marcan insertion into the text of proto-Luke.[41] Nonetheless, I believe that literary considerations, i.e. the logical flow of the narrative, strongly suggest that vv 44-45b first arise in the *a* account which itself predates proto-Luke. Boismard's point notwithstanding, he does allow that ὡσεὶ (v 44) could have been taken from another source and added to the proto-Lucan text.[42] Similarly, Green regards the temple curtain as Marcan material while simultaneously noting that it is thematically Lucan.[43] This is to gloss over a patent difficulty, however. To be sure, a piece could be Marcan in origin and Lucan in presentation, but the placement of this curtain episode in Mark weakens that possibility. Mark's account, by expanding and repositioning the incident, bears evidence of a later redaction. This redaction was probably influenced by another source which Mark had at his disposal, a point to be demonstrated further on.

The presence of τοῦ ἡλίου ἐκλιπόντος in v 45a leaves no doubt that it can only be a later addition. First, if it were a part of *a*, it would be necessary to explain why Mark's gospel would omit it, and that is more difficult to do than to

---

[39] Square brackets [ ] represent *a*; parentheses ( ), *L*'s redaction.

[40] On this point, Boismard also demonstrates that Mark 15,33 depends on Luke 23,44 (*Marc* 226).

[41] Boismard, *Quête* 142.

[42] Boismard, *Quête* 142.

[43] Green, *Death* 96-7.

justify why a Lucan redactor would include it. It was added because someone wanted to describe the darkness.[44] Second, because it is a circumstantial and not a causal genitive absolute, it has the character of a later redaction, in this case, by the hand of L, a point confirmed by the fact that ἐκλείπω is a term peculiar to Luke.[45] The solar eclipse refines the account of the three-hour darkness, and such precisions have the hallmark of secondary editing. Green also sees the solar eclipse as a Lucan addition,[46] but he does not determine when it might have been added.

This first half of the Lucan pericope, then, has an internal harmony; its simplicity shows it to be the earliest stage of the tradition, and its unadorned style makes it ripe for an elaboration, something which Mark provides at this point.

Luke 23,44-46 and Mark 15,33-38

A comparative analysis of the death accounts (Mark 15,33-38; Luke 23,44-46) reveals another source utilized by Mark. Seeing these Lucan verses against the Marcan parallel not only accents the Marcan account of Jesus' cry from the cross, but it also highlights Mark's situating the temple curtain after the death. Indeed, these words from the cross forced a Marcan redactor to move the temple curtain further along in the narrative; the cry itself along with the sponge episode (vv 34-36) so disconnect the καταπέτασμα from its context that placing it after the death was stylistically the best choice.

Mark 15,33-38

Mark 15,33-38[47]

33[Καὶ γενομένης ὥρας ἕκτης σκότος ἐγένετο ἐφ᾽ ὅλην τὴν γῆν ἕως ὥρας ἐνάτης]. 34a(καὶ τῇ ἐνάτῃ ὥρᾳ ἐβόησεν ὁ Ἰησοῦς φωνῇ μεγάλῃ, ελωι ελωι λεμα σαβαχθανι; bὅ ἐστιν μεθερμηνευόμενον ὁ θεός μου ὁ θεός μου, εἰς τί ἐγκατέλιπές με; 35καί τινες τῶν παρεστηκότων ἀκούσαντες ἔλεγον, ἴδε Ἠλίαν φωνεῖ. 36δραμὼν δέ τις καὶ γεμίσας σπόγγον ὄξους περιθεὶς καλάμῳ ἐπότιζεν αὐτὸν λέγων, ἄφετε ἴδωμεν εἰ ἔρχεται Ἠλίας καθελεῖν αὐτόν). 37{ὁ δὲ Ἰησοῦς

---

[44] A solar eclipse cannot be an historical detail, for as Lagrange notes, an eclipse cannot take place during a full moon, nor can one last three hours (*Luc* 592).

[45] The verb ἐκλείπω occurs only four times in the NT: Luke 16,9; 22,32; 23,45 and in Heb 1,12 (*VKGNT* 1/1; 371). In addition, Joachim Jeremias assigns the verb to the category of Lucan tradition (*Die Sprache des Lukasevangeliums* [Göttingen: Vandenhoeck and Ruprecht, 1980]) 307.

[46] Green, *Death* 96.

[47]Brackets [ ] represent a; parentheses ( ), Marcan interpolation; uppercase brackets { }, Marcan reworking of a.

ἀφεὶς} [φωνὴν μεγάλην ἐξέπνευσεν].   ³⁸{Καὶ τὸ καταπέτασμα τοῦ ναοῦ
ἐσχίσθη εἰς δύο ἀπ᾽ ἄνωθεν ἕως κάτω}.

In both the second and third gospels Jesus makes a "great cry" (φωνὴ
μεγάλη),⁴⁸ and "expires" (ἐκπνέω); Matthew too has the "great cry," and there
Jesus "yields up his spirit" (πνεῦμα); compare John, where he "gives up his
πνεῦμα". The noun πνεῦμα occurs in the utterance which Luke attributes to the
dying Jesus: πάτερ, εἰς χεῖράς σου παρατίθεμαι τὸ πνεῦμα μου. All three
synoptic accounts agree in bringing together the φωνὴ μεγάλη and either the
noun πνεῦμα or its cognate verb ἐκπνέω.⁴⁹ The combination of these elements
comes from the common source, a. The quotation of LXX Ps 30,6 would be an
elaboration by L.⁵⁰ The call ελωι ελωι λεμα σαβαχθανι in Mark 15,34, is a
transliterated Aramaic paraphrase of MT Ps 22,2a.

That Mark has two cries from the cross and Luke only one is explained by
Green solely in terms of Lucan redaction.⁵¹ In addition to omitting Mark's
"offensive" cry of dereliction, Green believes that Luke interpolates MT Ps 31
into what represents Mark's second cry, a position where the second evangelist
fails to provide any particular saying.⁵² After demonstrating that particular terms
in the LXX version of Ps 30/31 differ from parallel ones in the MT, Green
concludes that v 46 in Luke is a translation of the MT and thus this quotation
represents Lucan *Sonderquelle*.⁵³

Green's explanation, however, has three attendant problems. First, that

---

⁴⁸ φωνὴν μεγάλην, Mark 15,37; φωνῇ μεγάλη, Luke 23,46.

⁴⁹ Counting all the textual variants, φωνή occurs in Matt eight times, three
times with μεγάλη; in Mark seven times, four with μεγάλη; in Luke 15 times,
seven with μεγάλη; in John 15 times, once with μεγάλη; in Acts 27 times, six
with μεγάλη (*VKGNT* 1/2; 1318).
With all the textual variants included, πνεῦμα appears in Matt 19 times, one
time in the death narrative, 27,50 (*VKGNT* 1/2; 1139); in Luke 38 times, one
time in a death context 23,46 (*VKGNT* 1/2; 1139-40); in John 24 times, one time
in a death context 19,30; in Acts 71 times, one time in a death context 7,59
(*VKGNT* 1/2; 1140-1). In Mark the cognate ἐκπνέω occurs twice, each time in
the death narrative, Mark 15,37.39; this verb also occurs in Luke 23,46 (*VKGNT*
1/1; 372). The φωνὴ μεγάλη/πνεῦμα combination occurs only in the synoptics
and only at the death of Jesus: Matt 27,50, Mark 15,37, and Luke 23,46; it never
occurs in John and Acts.
Jeremias, while acknowledging that the phrase φωνήσας φωνῇ μεγάλη is an
expression characteristic of the NT, does not address its coupling with πνεῦμα
(Jeremias, *Sprache* 307).

⁵⁰ Boismard attributes the quotation from LXX Ps 30,6 to proto-Luke (*Quête*
144).

⁵¹ Green, *Death* 98.

⁵² Green, *Death* 98.

⁵³ Green, *Death* 98.

Luke would find the cry of abandonment "offensive" cannot be sustained in light
of the third evangelist's description of the agony at 22,44. Second, that the LXX
is a translation of the MT is an assumption rather than a statement of fact. On
this basis, to hold that the quotation from Ps 31 is from the MT and thus
represents Lucan *Sonderquelle* is faulty. Third, Green nonetheless observes that
the citation from Ps 30/31 contains elements from both Greek and Hebrew
versions of the psalm.[54] I maintain that Luke follows the LXX and that the
quotation from Ps 30/31 in v 46 is not original but redactional.

The argument centers around the cry from the cross. Because Luke is the
only synoptic not to include the cry of dereliction, Boismard proposes that Mark
15,34-36 depends on Matthew 27,46-49.[55] That the Matthean version has more
Hebrew elements within it, a sign of a later redactor's reworking the material,[56]
and that Luke has a shorter account than either Matthew or Mark, however,
suggest another solution.

Brown holds that the double reference to a "loud cry" in Mark 15,34.37
actually refers to a single cry; the aorist participle ἀφείς is resumptive as is
ποιήσαντες in 15,1.[57] Thus, Brown translates Mark 15,37 as "But Jesus, having
let out *that* (*sic*) loud cry, expired".[58] Although Brown would maintain that
Luke redacts his death narrative solely from Mark, he observes an important
point. Rather than two different cries from the cross, there are really two
different versions of one cry which Mark conflates. Likewise, Collins maintains
that Mark added the Semitic cry (15,34) as well as the misunderstanding about
Elijah (15,35-37).[59] This Marcan addition is an elaboration of source material
for which the notice about the ninth hour is the redactional seam (Mark 15,34a).

Ninth hour

In addition to containing a double cry from the cross, the Marcan and
Matthean accounts also specify that Jesus dies at the ninth hour; this is not
expressly stated by Luke. There are two possibilities: either a Lucan redactor
removed this element from source *a*, or Mark, followed by Matthew, added the
notice to the *a* narrative.

In the Lucan account, Christ's death is listed as one of a series of events
along with the darkness, eclipse, and tearing of the temple curtain. The Lucan
version simply states καὶ φωνήσας φωνῇ μεγάλῃ ὁ Ἰησοῦς. Jesus could have as
easily died at the sixth hour as at the ninth. Luke is not specific on this matter,[60]

---

[54] Green, *Death* 304.

[55] Boismard, *Marc* 226-7.

[56] Cf. above.

[57] Brown, *Messiah* 2; 1079.

[58] Brown, *Messiah* 2; 1079.

[59] Collins, "Noble" 500.

[60] Matt 27,46 reads "about" the ninth hour; Mark 15,34, "at" the ninth hour.

and this may reflect the evangelist's desire to ensure the understanding that the crucifixion and burial occur before the start of the Jewish Sabbath at sunset.[61] On the other hand, a Marcan redactor could have added the specification about the ninth hour in order to highlight the death of Jesus at the hour of the afternoon temple sacrifice, a detail of which Luke is also aware.[62]

The simplest explanation, and the one I maintain, is that Luke 23,44.45b is the *lectio brevior*. There is a graduated degree of intensity in the Lucan description of Jesus' death. Everything in the PN points to the fact that these three hours belong to the dominion of darkness, a dominion so great that even the sun's light cannot penetrate through it. God's own glory then flees the temple, thereby tearing the curtain.[63] Sometime at that moment Jesus dies, but not before his final prayer of trust, and no matter when he utters it, the context demands that it happen before the end of the three-hour period. It seems most logical that, with the increasing dramatic tension inherent in the Lucan death account, the prayer comes at the ninth hour, the moment of Jesus' death.

Thus, the Marcan verse καὶ τῇ ἐνάτῃ ὥρᾳ (15,34a) functions as a reprise of 15,33, and this reprise is made necessary by the Marcan redaction of the death cry. It would be much simpler and less awkward to combine the two versions of the single death cry outside the three hours of darkness than within it, and this is what the Marcan redactor does by setting the cries before the tearing of the temple veil.

Death cry

Introducing the verse from the psalm is ἐβόησεν ὁ Ἰησοῦς φωνῇ μεγάλῃ (Mark 15,34a), which appears to be an anticipated echo of the "great cry" in *a* (Luke 23,46a). Green, while denying that there is any influence between John and the synoptics, nonetheless admits that the general content and sequence of the fourth gospel represents a primitive narrative of Jesus' passion similar to the Marcan version.[64] An examination of this similarity reveals that, although John may not borrow from the synoptics, Mark does adopt some material from a Johannine source *b*, namely the contents and the framework for this first cry from the cross.

---

[61] N.b. the verb ἐπιφώσκω in Luke 23,54, a verb which can be interpreted in two ways. Does it strictly refer to "dawn" (so C. H. Turner, "Note on ἐπιφώσκειν," *JTS* 14 [1913] 188-195), or can it also mean the approach of a conventional day (so F. C. Burkitt, "Ἐπιφώσκειν," *JTS* 14 [1913] 538-46).

[62] This point in Luke is developed below in Chapter Five.

[63] This point is developed below in Chapter Five.

[64] Green, *Death* 133.

John 19,28-30

John 19,28-30

²⁸ᵃΜετὰ τοῦτο εἰδὼς ᵇὁ Ἰησοῦς ᶜὅτι ἤδη πάντα τετέλεσται, ἵνα τελειωθῇ ἡ γραφή, ᵈλέγει, Διψῶ. ²⁹ᵃσκεῦος ἔκειτο ὄξους μεστόν· σπόγγον οὖν μεστὸν τοῦ ὄξους ᵇὑσσώπῳ περιθέντες ᶜπροσήνεγκαν αὐτοῦ τῷ στόματι. ³⁰ᵃὅτε οὖν ἔλαβεν τὸ ὄξος [ὁ] ᵇἸησοῦς εἶπεν, τετέλεσται, ᶜκαὶ κλίνας τὴν κεφαλὴν παρέδωκεν τὸ πνεῦμα.

The only word which John shares with the synoptics in describing the moment of death is πνεῦμα; there is no other term in these verses remotely resembling φωνὴ μεγάλη. Can the idea then that φωνὴ μεγάλη/πνεῦμα recounts the most primitive death narrative be upheld? The answer is a qualified affirmative.

On a literary plane, verse 28 is an elaboration of a cry at the last moments of a tortured death; everything except ὁ Ἰησοῦς... λέγει, Διψῶ is a late redaction. Whether the statement Διψῶ reflects an early account is debatable; it can also be seen as a redactor's specification of a loud cry. On the other hand, the statement itself can very well reflect an account at its simplest level. For someone undergoing an agonizing death to cry out in thirst is not unusual,[65] and despite the theological overtones Brown sees in Διψῶ,[66] for Jesus to say he is thirsty, and for that statement to be remembered among the believing community is highly plausible.

Verse 29ac is the response to the statement Διψῶ; the use of ὕσσωπος, because of its paschal coloring,[67] indicates a late redaction. When compared to the sponge episode in Mark or even Matthew, the Johannine account is less elaborate and thus the more primitive. Acknowledging that ὑσσώπῳ περιθέντες is a later redaction shows that v 29ac is more than likely an historical detail;[68] without the hyssop, the verse has little theological significance. If 29ac is an historical detail, it entered the narrative very early.

Therefore, it is difficult to agree with Neirynck that the synoptic gospels themselves and not the traditions behind them are the sources for the fourth

---

[65] Military chaplains on a battlefield often speak of trying to satisfy the unquenchable thirst of a dying soldier before saying prayers or administering the rites.

[66] Raymond E. Brown considers vv 28-30 to be the fourth episode in the crucifixion scene, a scene which has a chiastic structure. As such, Jesus' thirst and handing over the spirit parallel the description of the seamless tunic in vv 23-24 (*The Gospel According to John, 13-21*, vol. 2. [Anchor Bible 29a; Garden City, New York: Doubleday and Company, Inc, 1970] 911).

[67] Cf. above.

[68] Brown holds that the ὄξος was *posca*, a "diluted, vinegary wine drunk by soldiers and laborers" (*John* 2; 909). In this case, it is not at all unusual that ὄξος would be nearby and that someone would offer it to a dying man.

evangelist.[69] If this were so, it would be necessary to explain why John would delete the quotation from MT Ps 22,2 as found in Mark 15,34 (or Matt 27,46 for that matter) and substitute in its stead διψῶ (John 19,28). It makes far more sense to acknowledge that the synoptic account is a redaction and elaboration of the primitive *b* source.[70] This retouching was done because of the potentially scandalous nature of material found in John 19,28: The concerns of the Son of God at the moment of death were the same as any other's -- physical relief.

John in v 30b shares the phrase Ἰησοῦς εἶπεν with the Lucan parallel. In the Lucan gospel, 23,46 represents the earliest synoptic death account, a conclusion which hinges on the fact that Luke describes only one cry from the cross. The parallel account in John 19,28.30 appears to have two cries, Διψῶ (v 28b) and τετέλεσται (v 30b). If, however, τετέλεσται is considered a later redaction, then the Johannine account, like the Lucan one, also features only one cry from the cross, a cry described in a manner which is a prolongation of the final moments.

That this Johannine account (vv 28-30) is actually an extended cry is a conclusion based on the verbs employed. The verb τελέω has only two occurrences in John's gospel, 19,28.30. The first of these at v 28 is the work of a later editor; it draws attention to the completion of Jesus' life's work. The synonymous term τελειόω,[71] a verb which follows τελέω in v 28, reiterates the point, and its textual tradition suggests a later addition.[72]   On this basis, τετέλεσται which Ἰησοῦς εἶπεν introduces in John 19,30, like the citation from LXX Ps 30,6 in Luke 23,46, is interpolated material from a later period; the textual analysis of v 30 substantiates this point as well.[73]   This Johannine quotation completes the theme of fulfillment and accomplishment that runs throughout all John's gospel.   Excising all the explanatory and interpolated material from vv 28-30 leaves the primitive Johannine death account,

28bὁ Ἰησοῦς ᵈλέγει, Διψῶ. ²⁹ᵃσκεῦος ἔκειτο ὄξους μεστόν· σπόγγον οὖν μεστὸν τοῦ ὄξους ᶜπροσήνεγκαν αὐτοῦ τῷ στόματι. ³⁰ᶜκαὶ κλίνας τὴν κεφαλὴν παρέδωκεν τὸ πνεῦμα.

---

[69] Neirynck, "John" 398.

[70] Neyrey believes that the verb διψῶ in John 19,28 may be a reference to Ps 22,15 (*Passion* 146-7). If so, this explains how a Marcan redactor could be inspired to rely on MT Ps 22,2 for the dying words of Jesus.

[71] τελειόω, *complete, bring to an end, accomplish* (BAGD 809-10), is securely Johannine vocabulary. It occurs eight times in the gospels and Acts, five times in John, 4,34; 5,36; 17,4; 17,23; 19,28 (*VKGNT* 1/2; 1247-48). Three of these instances occur in the events after the triumphal entry into Jerusalem. τελέω, *bring to an end, complete, accomplish, fulfill* (BAGD 810-11), has a slightly different nuance but in certain cases can be interchangeable with τελειόω. John seems to employ it in the death account to underscore the notion of Jesus death as fulfillment and accomplishment.

[72] Cf. above.

[73] Cf. above.

Although this Johannine version does not contain all the vocabulary of the Lucan φωνὴ μεγάλη/πνεῦμα sequence, thematically, it conveys the same concept, a cry, possibly loud, followed by expiration.

The fact remains, however, that the Johannine description, though similar to the Lucan account in 23,46, is not identical, and there are two possibilities which can explain this difference. One is that John 19,28d.30c is a very early rewriting of the φωνὴ μεγάλη/πνεῦμα pattern; the phrase Διψῶ clarifies the Lucan φωνὴ μεγάλη. Another is that these Johannine verses represent a source just as primitive as φωνὴ μεγάλη/πνεῦμα but slightly different; this conclusion has two supporting facts. First, someone suffering the trauma of crucifixion would be thirsty and indeed express the same. Second, unlike the elaborations of the φωνὴ μεγάλη/πνεῦμα seen in Mark 15,34, Matt 27,46, and even Luke 23,46b, Διψῶ is rather pedestrian. The second possibility, that this Johannine account is a primitive version of the death of Jesus which parallels the one in Luke 23,46, is the more likely. On the basis that it notes an historical detail, verse 29ac is also part of the original Johannine death narrative.

Boismard, while noting the parallel between Mark 15,33-39 and Luke 23,44a-47, believes that for Luke 23,46, the final Lucan redactor borrowed from John 19,30; the Johannine verb παρέδωκεν prompted Luke to utilize LXX Ps 30,6 (παρατίθεμαι) for Jesus' last words.[74] Nonetheless, because the final Lucan redactor does not borrow any other material from the Johannine death account, the view that both Luke and John adapt material from a common tradition is preferable.

Brown speculates that MT Psalm 22,16 or possibly MT Psalm 69,22 is the referential point for John 19,28d; he also maintains that the purpose clause points both forward and backward.[75] On this basis, according to Brown, the subject Ἰησοῦς and the main verb λέγω encompass all the clauses in v 28. This was the reconstruction of a later redactor.

Summary

Both sources, *a* and *b*, can lay claim to being regarded as primitive; more than likely they both originated from a common tradition,[76] and as such, were adaptations of a "fixed point". Mark combined these two sources in forming the death narrative for the second gospel; the notification about the ninth hour (Mark

---

[74] Boismard, *Marc* 227.

[75] Brown, *Messiah* 2; 1072-4.

[76] Throughout this study, *source* signifies a written document whereas *tradition* represents the handing down of information more than likely by oral means. The most important distinction between the two terms is that it is possible to reconstruct a source but nearly impossible to do so for a tradition. The only exception to these definitions is found in quotations from other works and in the phrase *textual tradition*, a term which describes the history of scriptural manuscripts and witnesses.

15,34) forms the redactional seam. In redacting the two pieces, the second evangelist reworked the Διψῶ from the *b* account into a quotation from MT Ps 22,2a. That this citation displays evidence of an Aramaic if not Hebrew origin is testimony to its venerability, but whether this citation is simply the work of a Marcan editor or is based on some other early source is difficult to say.

Mark also takes the sponge episode from *b* but portrays it as a deed of cruel mockery. The refashioning of the cry from Διψῶ (John 19,28) to the psalm quotation (Mark 15,34) necessitated altering the sponge sequence. After the cry of abandonment, for the second evangelist to keep the Johannine version of the sponge pericope would make no sense. The Marcan redactor solves the problem by exaggerating the vocal similarity between the divine name, Eloi (ελωι), and the prophet, Elijah (ηλιας). The editor of this recension is no doubt drawing on the messianic overtones inherent in the name of Elijah, who was supposed to return to usher in the final age; such theological coloring is characteristic of a later redaction.

The *L* redactor knows about the vinegar but does not include it in the actual death narrative. In Luke 23,36 the soldiers, having joined the crowd in mockery, offered Jesus the drink; Mark does not have a parallel to this. Mark relates, however, that before the nails were hammered into Jesus' limbs, the soldiers gave him a wine mixture as an anesthetic which he refused,[77] and this is absent in Luke. Hence, Luke 23,36 exhibits elements of both Mark 15,23 and 15,36, though the sponge is missing from the Lucan account.

The mocking offer of wine by the soldiers is, for Fitzmyer, an historical detail added by Luke. Observing that Luke does not include a passage where the wine is given either as an anesthetic or as a response to a cry of abandonment, Fitzmyer concludes that it is unclear why Luke writes it in v 36.[78] If this is an historical detail peculiar only to Luke, however, it can be ascribed to *a*, a point further substantiated by the fact that the third gospel contains no exact parallel to the Marcan or Johannine sponge episode. Since the *a* source contains the vinegar sequence earlier in the account, the *L* redactor does not incorporate it at the cross because to do so would be a superfluous duplication of material.

Assuming that there are two sources, *a* and *b*, situating *b* before *a* would be the only way to combine the two stories. This is what Mark does. He then polishes the narrative by transposing the tearing of the temple curtain from before the death to after.

Luke 23,47-49

This second half of the Lucan death narrative displays redactional problems in which the delineation of a specific Lucan source is not as evident as in the first.[79]

---

[77] Mark 15,23 shows this as ἐσμυρνισμένον οἶνον.

[78] Fitzmyer, *Luke* 2; 1505. Boismard, however, explains that this event was present in proto-Luke and that final Luke placed it at 23,36-37 (*Synopse* 2; 426).

[79] The brackets [ ] represent *a*; parentheses ( ), *L*'s reworking of Marcan

Luke 23,47

47a[Ἰδὼν δὲ ὁ ἑκατοντάρχης τὸ γενόμενον ἐδόξαζεν τὸν θεὸν] b{λέγων},
(Ὄντως ὁ ἄνθρωπος οὗτος δίκαιος ἦν).

Mark 15,39

39aἸδὼν δὲ ὁ κεντυρίων ὁ παρεστηκὼς ἐξ ἐναντίας αὐτοῦ ὅτι οὕτως
ἐξέπνευσεν bεἶπεν, ἀληθῶς οὗτος ὁ ἄνθρωπος υἱὸς θεοῦ ἦν.

Verse 47

The Lucan pericope of the centurion in v 47 contains several deviations
from the Marcan account of which Luke's reading, ἑκατοντάρχης, is one of the
most notable. Fitzmyer states that Luke, avoiding the "Latinism of Mark 15,39,"
holds to his word choice of 7,2.6, the healing of the centurion's servant;[80] so
also Green.[81] Boismard, however, seeing this verse as an addition to the Marcan
text, attributes it to the Marcan-Lucan redactor.[82]

Several facts contest the position that Luke merely translates into Greek an
original Marcan reading of κεντυρίων. First, Mark witnesses κεντυρίων only
three times in his gospel, and although each of these occurs in the passion and
death account, only 15,39 has a parallel in Luke and Matthew.[83] Second, Mark
has no parallel to Luke 7,2.6 while there is one in Matthew 8,5.8.13 which, like
the Lucan pericope, employs ἑκατοντάρχης/ος.[84] In addition, Luke utilizes
ἑκατοντάρχης/ος throughout the Acts.[85] These points raise two important
questions. First, if Luke is really avoiding Mark's latinism, it must be on the
basis that, for whatever reason, Luke prefers Greek, or at least avoids Latin. Is
this a sturdy argument, particularly when Luke uses the Latin Αὐγοῦστος in 2,1
instead of the Greek Σεβαστός?[86] Second, if Luke 23,47 follows Mark 15,39,

---

material; uppercase brackets { }, *L*'s interpolation.

[80] Fitzmyer, *Luke* 2; 1519.

[81] Green, *Death* 99.

[82] Boismard, *Marc* 228. This notes a change in Boismard's opinion, however.
For the account of the centurion in the third gospel, Boismard had previously
maintained that the Lucan version could only have been late material on the
grounds that the proto-Luke source portrays the Jews alone as participating in the
crucifixion; the centurion episode entered the text through Intermediate Mark
(*Synopse* 2; 427).

[83] Mark 15,39.44.45 are the sole three occurrences of κεντυρίων in the NT
(*VKGNT* 1/1; 688). ἑκατοντάρχης/ος never occurs in the second gospel.

[84] The parallel in John 4,46b-54 reads Βασιλικός.

[85] Thirteen times in Acts: 10,1.22; 21,32; 22,25.26; 23,17.23; 24,23;
27,1.6.11.31.43; the Byzantine tradition also witnesses it at 28,16 (*VKGNT* 1/1;
363).

why does the third evangelist not continue with the Marcan account in which a centurion appears five verses later in 15,44.45?

If Mark is always the earlier account as is so often assumed, it is necessary to explain why Luke would omit the historical detail in which Pilate summons a centurion to verify whether Jesus is dead (Mark 15,44-45), especially when Luke includes the soldiers mocking Jesus in 23,36 which, as Fitzmyer argues, is an historical item.[87] In addition, Matthew lacks the episode as well. The answer can only be that Mark 15,44-45 is a late interpolation, a conclusion corroborated by two facts. First, none of the other three evangelists includes this account, and second, the apologetic intrusion of the subject matter itself betrays a later redaction; the Marcan narrative counters the argument that Jesus' disciples rescued him before he died,[88] a theme paralleled in John 19,31-35. The hand which added Mark 15,44-45 is the same one which changed ἑκατοντάρχης/ος to κεντυρίων in 15,39 on the grounds of maintaining consistency; this change, incidentally, may well reflect a "Roman" influence on the composition of the second gospel.

The centurion's quotation forces another issue on the redaction of this verse. Luke 23,47b differs from Mark 15,39b. Without the quotation itself, v 47a makes perfect sense: Ἰδὼν δὲ ὁ ἑκατοντάρχης τὸ γενόμενον ἐδόξαζεν τὸν θεόν. It is impossible, however, to separate the words of the centurion in Mark 15,39b from their introduction in v 39a. Since v 47a in Luke is a simple declarative sentence, whereas v 39a in Mark features a genitive absolute, with a noun clause as its accusative, it seems that Luke manifests the more primitive reading, *lectio brevior*. Undeniably, however, the individual citations in the second and third evangelist are very similar, and this must be taken into account. Quotations are usually inserted in response to a community's demand for specific detail.

It is possible that Mark somehow received Luke 23,47a. Mark then elaborated it by adding the quotation ἀληθῶς οὗτος ὁ ἄνθρωπος υἱὸς θεοῦ ἦν (v 39b). This redacted Marcan version then passed back to Luke, who altered the word order of the quotation and changed υἱὸς θεοῦ to δίκαιος. Another possibility is that Luke here has rewritten original Marcan material. Three arguments can be proposed in favor of this latter solution. First, the Lucan account exhibits vocabulary common to Mark and Matthew throughout v 47.[89]

---

[86] Σεβαστός, meaning *revered, worthy of reverence*, is a translation of the Latin Augustus, an appellation for Octavian as well as a generic designation of the Roman Emperor (BAGD 745). In addition, Luke employs Καῖσαρ 17 times throughout L-A (*VKGNT* 1/1; 663-4) which is also a latinism (BAGD 395).

[87] Fitzmyer, *Luke* 2; 1505.

[88] Brown, who believes that vv 44-45 are part of original Mark, challenges this interpretation on linguistic, grammatical, and syntactic grounds (*Messiah* 2; 1220-1). I do not agree. The final redactor polished and honed an intermediate Marcan gospel, thus the fine points. Secondly, verse 43 leads into v 46 quite well without a notice that Pilate gave Joseph the body, and finally, the Marcan centurion account could have entered the second gospel when intermediate Mark redacted the *b* death cry and sponge episode.

[89] Both Luke 23,47 and Mark 15,39 are introduced by Ἰδὼν δὲ ὁ. Both

Second, introducing this centurion's quotation ἐδόξαζεν τὸν θεὸν is a reworking
of Mark 15,39a, thereby reflecting Luke's desire to polish Mark's *lectio
difficilior*.   Third, the statement Ὄντως ὁ ἄνθρωπος οὗτος δίκαιος ἦν,
particularly in light of the first point, evidences the rewriting of Mark's οὗτος ὁ
ἄνθρωπος υἱὸς θεοῦ ἦν.

Each of these two arguments hinges on whether Mark's *lectio difficilior* is
preferable to Luke's *lectio brevior*.   But does Mark really witness the more
difficult reading? Certainly 15,39 is more complex, but it is not enigmatic. It
seems that Mark elaborates Luke rather than that Luke simplifies Mark.   In
addition, this solution addresses the issue of specificity.   In this case, a general
statement in Luke, Ἰδὼν δὲ ὁ ἑκατοντάρχης τὸ γενόμενον ἐδόξαζεν τὸν θεὸν (v
47a) becomes a quotation in Mark, ἀληθῶς οὗτος ὁ ἄνθρωπος υἱὸς θεοῦ ἦν (39b).
Such a refinement is a sign of late redaction.   This solution also acknowledges
Luke's dependence on Mark, albeit at a later stage.   Furthermore, it reconciles
the Marcan reading of κεντυρίων with ἑκατοντάρχης/ος of Luke and Matthew; a
Marcan redactor altered ἑκατοντάρχης/ος after the account returned to Luke. On
this basis, Luke 23,47a is the primitive narrative which passed on to Mark.

The presence of the accusative τὸ γενόμενον in v 47a precludes an
explanation relying solely on the interplay between Mark and Luke at this verse;
the parallel account in Matthew 27,54b shows τὰ γενόμενα.   Two possibilities
can explain this similarity between Luke and Matthew.   The first is that Luke
borrows from a primitive Matthean account. This, according to Boismard, is the
only way to justify the centurion's confession of faith, after witnessing the cosmic
events, that Jesus is the Son of God.[90]   This interpretation also accounts for the
reprise of τὰ γενόμενα in Luke 23,48b; the crowd witnesses the cataclysmic
events as well.[91]   The Lucan reading is thus an example of how the third
evangelist truncates a primitive text, in this case, a Matthean one.

An alternative view to Boismard's is the second possibility that τὸ
γενόμενον (47a) in Luke represents the primitive text which at a very early stage
a Matthean redactor copied from *a*.   Matt 27,51ac-52 is a fine literary
construction, the details of which betray a late redaction.[92]   Hence, it is
necessary to explain why a Lucan (or a Marcan) redactor would omit it.
Furthermore, according to Boismard's theory, Intermediate Matthew's influence
upon proto-Luke exists in material outside the passion and resurrection narratives;
for these, proto-Luke relies on Document C.[93]   On this basis, it is possible that,
at an early stage, a Matthean redactor copied the phrase τὸ γενόμενον from the *a*
account; this participle then became the cause of later elaborations in the first
gospel, elaborations such as the splitting of rocks, opening of tombs, and the

---

contain the third person imperfect of εἰμί, the pronoun οὗτος, and the nouns
ἄνθρωπος and θεός.   Jeremias sees Ἰδὼν δὲ ὁ as redactional (Jeremias, *Sprache*
308).

[90] Boismard, *Marc* 228. Cf. also *Quête* 144.

[91] Boismard, *Marc* 228.

[92] Cf. above.

[93] Boismard, *Synopse* 2; 16. Cf. also *Marc* 8.

raising of the dead. This same Matthean editor reconstituted the ὄχλος from Luke 23,48 into καὶ οἱ μετ᾽ αὐτοῦ (Matt 27,54b).

Why does Luke change τὸ γενόμενον to τὰ γενόμενα in such a short space? The solution hinges upon identifying the antecedents of τὸ γενόμενον in Luke 23,47a and τὰ γενόμενα in v 48b. One possibility is that the antecedent of τὸ γενόμενον in Luke 23,47a can be the death itself, and of τὰ γενόμενα in v 48b, the death *and* the centurion's confession, thus the switch from singular γενόμενον to plural γενόμενα in the Lucan narrative. Another possibility, and the most likely, is to assume that they share the same antecedents. In the first case, τὸ γενόμενον can be translated as *event*, that is, the death itself and everything leading up to it. In the second instance, *happenings* is a valid translation, and like the former example, it can refer to everything from the trial to the crucifixion. Although there is nothing in the grammar at v 48b demanding a plural object, that τὰ γενόμενα stands between the plural participles θεωρήσαντες and τύπτοντες may have influenced the final Lucan redactor to write τὰ γενόμενα purely for stylistic reasons. In this case, τὰ γενόμενα is indicative of a redactional seam.[94]

When Mark received this account, he amplified it by appending ἀληθῶς οὗτος ὁ ἄνθρωπος υἱὸς θεοῦ ἦν (15,39b) at which point Matthew copied from Mark while the pericope reverted to the Lucan redactor. At this juncture, L altered the syntax and substituted δίκαιος for υἱὸς θεοῦ.

Verses 48-49

Luke 23,48-49

48a καὶ πάντες οἱ συμπαραγενόμενοι ὄχλοι b ἐπὶ τὴν θεωρίαν ταύτην, θεωρήσαντες τὰ γενόμενα, c τύπτοντες τὰ στήθη d ὑπέστρεφον. 49a Εἰστήκεισαν δὲ πάντες οἱ γνωστοὶ αὐτῷ ἀπὸ μακρόθεν b καὶ γυναῖκες αἱ συνακολουθοῦσαι αὐτῷ ἀπὸ τῆς Γαλιλαίας, c ὁρῶσαι ταῦτα.

John 19,25

25a Εἰστήκεισαν δὲ παρὰ τῷ σταυρῷ τοῦ Ἰησοῦ b ἡ μήτηρ αὐτοῦ καὶ ἡ ἀδελφὴ τῆς μητρὸς αὐτοῦ, Μαρία ἡ τοῦ Κλωπᾶ καὶ Μαρία ἡ Μαγδαληνή.

Mark 15,40

40a Ἦσαν δὲ καὶ γυναῖκες ἀπὸ μακρόθεν θεωροῦσαι, b ἐν αἷς καὶ Μαρία ἡ Μαγδαληνὴ καὶ Μαρία ἡ Ἰακώβου τοῦ μικροῦ καὶ Ἰωσῆτος μήτηρ καὶ Σαλώμη,

The seams of the Lucan redaction in vv 48-49 indicate the influence of Mark at v 48b in the description of the spectacle and at v 49b with the inclusion

---

[94] Crump's argument, that τὸ γενόμενον can refer only to the death (*Jesus* 89-90), is untenable. For the interpretation that τὸ γενόμενον refers to a series of events from the trial to the crucifixion, cf. Karris (*Artist* 110) and Donald Senior, C.P. (*The Passion of Jesus in the Gospel of Luke*, [Wilmington: Michael Glazier, 1989] 147). Fitzmyer limits the reference to vv 43 and 46, Christ's words to the penitent criminal and his prayer to the Father (*Luke* 2; 1519).

of the women from Galilee; an *L* interpolation is evident at 48c. Redactional also is the omission of the women's names.

The vocabulary common among the synoptics in this case, θεωρέω, ἀκολουθέω, γυνή, Γαλιλαία is limited to the synoptic accounts concerning the women followers from Galilee. When the passage about the Galilean women and its attendant words are excised from the Lucan text, two comprehensible sentences remain, καὶ πάντες οἱ συμπαραγενόμενοι ὄχλοι...ὑπέστρεφον and Εἱστήκεισαν δὲ πάντες οἱ γνωστοὶ αὐτῷ ἀπὸ μακρόθεν. Likewise, when this material on the bystanders and the acquaintances is removed, the report about the women followers is also capable of standing independently if the participle συνακολουθοῦσαι is rewritten as a finite verb and the whole phrase is connected to the participle of θεωρέω, as it is in Mark.

The difficulties in this section are intertwined between vv 48 and 49. First, the phrase τὴν θεωρίαν ταύτην, θεωρήσαντες τὰ γενόμενα (v 48b) betrays an inelegant conflation. As a cognate noun of the verb θεωρέω, this only occurrence of the term θεωρία in the whole NT[95] appears as if the redactor did not know what else to do with it. In addition, the wording is a thematic doublet which obfuscates rather than clarifies the narrative; either the nominative or the participial expression would suffice, whereas both together hinder the story line. The second difficulty, ὁρῶσαι ταῦτα, (v 49c), by being a phrase synonymous with θεωρήσαντες τὰ γενόμενα, bears the stamp of a typical reprise; because the redaction separated the subject γυναῖκες (v 49b) from its original object θεωρήσαντες τὰ γενόμενα (v 48b), the editor had to write a new one, ὁρῶσαι ταῦτα.

Either v 48ad bears evidence of *a* or stands only as *L*'s later interpolation into Marcan material. While Matera attributes this verse to Lucan creativity,[96] Green rightly considers this passage to be a Lucan redaction based on a non-Marcan source.[97] Furthermore, Boismard holds to Lucan influence on Mark 15,40-41 and assigns the material in these two verses to the Marcan-Lucan redactor.[98]

The *a* source seems to be absent from Matthew and Mark. Traces must be found elsewhere. The only hint that this additional material in v 48ad had wider circulation exists in the Latin and Syriac codices which show the reading from the early second century *Gos. Pet.* 7,[99] a circumstance which suggests that the material represented by *a*, as it appears in v 48ad, pre-dates the canonical gospel. This is Green's opinion too.[100] H. B. Swete makes the observation that this citation seems to be an interpretation based on an amalgam of several Old

---

[95] *VKGNT* 1/1; 530.

[96] Matera, "Death" 484.

[97] Green, *Death* 99-101.

[98] Boismard, *Marc* 230. Boismard considers Luke 23,48ad part of proto-Luke (*Quête* 145).

[99] Cf. editor's comment in the *Gospel of Peter* (*Akhmim Fragment*) 12 n 4.

[100] Green, *Death* 100.

and New Testament references and quotations: LXX 3 Kgs 13,30; Isa 3,9; Dan 9,2.26; Luke 21,20; Rev 18,10.19.[101]

In citing the similarity between the *Gos. Pet.* and an Old Syriac version, Green suggests that such a convergence provides good evidence of a pre-Lucan reading.[102] If so, the material in g[1] sy[s.c] is not part of an early Lucan account. The phrase from the *Gos. Pet.* entered these witnesses after the final Lucan redaction;[103] hence, the origin of the passage is still unresolved.

The third evangelist is singular in including the bystanders (v 48a) and the acquaintances (v 49a) with the Galilean women (v 49b). The passion narrative, however, at least provides a context for the bystanders. This Lucan addition of the crowd is a continuation of an episode in 23,27-28 where Luke mentions Ἠκολούθει δὲ αὐτῷ πολὺ πλῆθος τοῦ λαοῦ καὶ γυναικῶν αἳ ἐκόπτοντο καὶ ἐθρήνουν αὐτόν, a sentence without any parallel in the other gospels.[104] Although this information from 23,27-28 says nothing about the acquaintances, it introduces the multitude who follow Jesus to the crucifixion. They appear again in v 35; in verse 48a Luke is being consistent.[105] Moreover, the people to whom Enoch is talking when the angels come for him, "...looked and they understood how Enoch had been taken away. And they glorified God. And they went away into their homes" (*2 Enoch* 67,3);[106] this verse from Enoch also suggests that the reading τύπτοντες τὰ στήθη in v 48c enters at the final Lucan redaction.[107] By reason of this literary echo and earlier date,[108] *2 Enoch* 67 rather than the *Gospel of Peter* influences Luke 23,48.

---

[101] Cf. editor's comment in the *Gospel of Peter (Akhmim Fragment)* 12 n 4.

[102] Green, *Death* 100.

[103] Cf. above.

[104] It is not clear whether the multitude *and* the women are lamenting; the relative pronoun αἳ can have as its antecedent both groups in which case it is feminine plural by attraction to γυναικῶν, or it can refer to γυναικῶν exclusively. Jesus' address, θυγατέρες Ἰερουσαλήμ, in v 28 seems to indicate that only the women are mourning, and as Fitzmyer notes, they are not necessarily disciples and should not be confused with those in v 49 (*Luke* 2; 1497).

[105] Verse 35 reads Καὶ εἰστήκει ὁ λαὸς θεωρῶν. The similarity of the vocabulary in this verse with that in vv 48-49 is evident. Brown observes the gradual progression of the multitude toward sympathy with Jesus in vv 27.35.48 (*Messiah* 2; 919).

[106] *OTPseud* 1; 195.

[107] The role of *2 Enoch* 67 in v 48 is further developed in Chapter Five below.

[108] Although no manuscripts of 2 Enoch older than the fourteenth century are known to exist, Andersen comments, "[i]n spite of its evident biblical style, there is no point at which it can be shown to depend on the text of the New Testament" (*OTPseud* 1; 95).

Verse 49a presents a different case. The inclusion of Εἰστήκεισαν δὲ πάντες οἱ γνωστοὶ αὐτῷ ἀπὸ μακρόθεν is peculiar to this verse. The two terms, μακρόθεν and ἀπό are part of the synoptic vocabulary. The adverb μακρόθεν is the only word from this vocabulary list which Friedrich Rehkopf attributes to pre-Lucan *Sprachgebrauch*.[109] Rehkopf evidently grounds this position on the fact that among the synoptics, six of the eleven instances of μακρόθεν occur in parallel accounts of the passion narratives, Matt 26,58; 27,55; Mark 14,54; 15,40; Luke 22,54; 23,49.[110] Fitzmyer notes that since Luke never recounts the flight of the disciples, they may be numbered among the γνωστοί.[111] There is no reason to dispute his conclusion, but the identification of the γνωστοί, as well as the reason for their inclusion, has still to be resolved.

The parallel account in John 19,25 introduces the passage about the women at the cross with a construction identical to that of Luke 23,49a, εἰστήκεισαν δὲ. This is not a frequent construction; these verses in Luke and John comprise two of its four occurrences in the gospels.[112] In addition, Boismard observes the same parallel and concludes that John follows a Lucan-Johannine tradition.[113]

The Johannine account does not mention Galilee whereas the synoptics do. Luke is, however, the only gospel which does not list the names of the women in the death narrative. These facts underscore two observations: First, Luke exhibits the *lectio brevior*, and second, although the common opening phrase in both Luke and John suggests another tradition outside the synoptic one,[114] the possibility nonetheless exists that John 19,25 is not original to *b* and may reflect influence from Mark, for neither does John include the γνωστοί. A comparison of Luke with Mark resolves some of these problems.

Luke 23,49 and Mark 15,40-41

Unlike Luke's use of ἵστημι in 49a, the parallel account in Mark opens with Ἦσαν δέ (15,40), and although ἵστημι is both a transitive and intransitive verb, it very often has a stative sense, especially when a preposition indicates place,[115] as in Luke 23,49a (ἀπὸ) and John 19,25 (παρά). On this basis there is little if any difference in meaning between Luke 23,49a and Mark 15,40; εἰμί and ἵστημι are synonyms, and there would be no reason to search for traces of a source outside Mark for this verse were it not that Luke is the only evangelist to

---

[109] Rehkopf, *Sonderquelle* 95.

[110] *VKGNT* 1/2; 757.

[111] Fitzmyer, *Luke* 2; 1520.

[112] *VKGNT* 1/1; 571-2.

[113] Boismard, *Marc* 231.

[114] While Jeremias holds the whole verse to be Lucan redaction, he considers οἱ γνωστοί to be Lucan tradition (*Sprache* 309).

[115] BAGD 382.

include γνωστοί in this scene. On this basis, it seems that in 23,49a Luke is not copying and editing Mark but is drawing upon another source. The redactor *L* interpolates into 23,49b the reading from Mark 15,40a.41. The origin of this Marcan reading, however, is still unknown. The Lucan phrase ἀπὸ μακρόθεν is a possible indication, that at some point, Mark copied *a* for the witness account.

The conflation of *a* with Mark in Luke 23,49 is quite apparent despite the differences between the second and third evangelist. Although Luke mentions that the women followed Jesus from Galilee, unlike the other three evangelists, Luke does not cite the names of these women at the cross. Why he excludes them is a debated question.

Fitzmyer's solution, that Luke omits the names of the women because he includes them in 8,2-3, is certainly one explanation.[116] Because Luke 8,2-3 has no parallel, Fitzmyer's explanation is probably correct for this Lucan pericope; his conclusion is not sufficient, however, to establish the origins of the account of the women witnesses, for which it is necessary to analyze the Johannine parallel, 19,25-27.

Luke 23,49 and John 19,25-27

Luke 23,49

49aΕἰστήκεισαν δὲ πάντες οἱ γνωστοὶ αὐτῷ ἀπὸ μακρόθεν bκαὶ γυναῖκες αἱ συνακολουθοῦσαι αὐτῷ ἀπὸ τῆς Γαλιλαίας,cὁρῶσαι ταῦτα.

John 19,25-27

25aΕἰστήκεισαν δὲ παρὰ τῷ σταυρῷ τοῦ Ἰησοῦ bἡ μήτηρ αὐτοῦ καὶ ἡ ἀδελφὴ τῆς μητρὸς αὐτοῦ, Μαρία ἡ τοῦ Κλωπᾶ καὶ Μαρία ἡ Μαγδαληνή. 26aἸησοῦς οὖν ἰδὼν τὴν μητέρα bκαὶ τὸν μαθητὴν παρεστῶτα ὃν ἠγάπα, cλέγει τῇ μητρί, γύναι, ἴδε ὁ υἱός σου. 27aεἶτα λέγει τῷ μαθητῇ, ἴδε ἡ μήτηρ σου. bκαὶ ἀπ᾽ ἐκείνης τῆς ὥρας ἔλαβεν ὁ μαθητὴς αὐτὴν εἰς τὰ ἴδια.

Mentioning witnesses at the cross is common among all four evangelists. Brown, although he does not suggest copying between John and the synoptics, nonetheless admits that this is a reference to a pre-gospel tradition.[117] Luke's opening phrase Ειστήκεισαν δέ in 23,49a, seen also in John 19,25a, reflects a trace of the common tradition which Luke and John share.[118] Furthermore,

---

[116] Fitzmyer, *Luke* 2; 1520-1.

[117] Brown, *Messiah* 2; 1195.

[118] Boismard also credits the reading in Luke 23,49 and John 19,25 to a common Lucan-Johannine tradition (*Marc* 231).

In addition to the literary evidence outlined above, a similar connection can be seen in Μαρία ἡ τοῦ Κλωπᾶ in 19,25b and the other disciple travelling with Κλεοπᾶς in Luke 24,13. Moreover, the two additional occurrences of εἰστήκεισαν δέ in Luke and John are found in the passion narrative (Luke 23,10; John 18,18).

The noun γνωστός points to another link Luke has with John. This term occurs in Luke 2,44; 23,49 and in John 18,15.16. As with εἰστήκεισαν δέ in

whereas the Lucan version still reflects this primitive source, the Johannine account underwent an early redaction; the Marcan recension, a conflation of the primitive Lucan and Johannine narratives, is the recension which L copied.

Verse 49a constitutes an early description of those standing at the cross; verse 49b consists of interpolated material from Mark 15,40a.41a. Boismard notes that the background for this verse, as well as for John 19,25-26, is LXX Psalm 37,12, an echo of which exists in Mark 15,39, ὁ παρεστηκὼς ἐξ ἐναντίας.[119] Boismard sees in this Marcan reading confirmation of the Marcan-Lucan redactor.[120] Thus, there is redactional material at this point which affects all four gospels.

In terms of the redactional history, a series of questions arise. Does a represent the more primitive source which somehow entered the b narrative (v 25) before the L recension; does b influence a; or do a and b, though sharing a common tradition, represent two different but parallel strains?

An investigation into whether b represents a source similar to but independent of a, resolves the issue. This prospect must justify the presence of those mentioned in John 19,25b. If Jesus' mother, his mother's sister, Mary the wife of Klopas, and Mary Magdalene are part of the primitive narrative, a problem emerges in v 26b with τὸν μαθητὴν...ὃν ἠγάπα; the beloved disciple is not standing by the cross with those listed in v 25. His presence here appears to be late interpolation. Verses 26-27, however, have their own internal unity and read well without v 25b. Moreover, that v 27 contains an address from the cross, a sentence devoid of any sign of pain, and that this verse also contains a reprise of μήτηρ point to a late redaction. The more primitive Johannine account lies in v 25.

Although there are similarities between John 19,25 and Luke 23,49, there are four differences of note. First, Luke states that the women are from Galilee, a specification John does not include. Second, John names the women; Luke does not. Third, Luke mentions the γνωστοί, a term absent in John. Fourth, Luke uses the adverbial phrase ἀπὸ μακρόθεν whereas John employs παρά plus the dative τῷ σταυρῷ. A tradition common to both the Lucan and Johannine readings, a "fixed point," is nonetheless evident.

The first and second differences are a result of L redaction; the designation of Galilee in the third gospel is Marcan material, while the list of women in Luke is placed at 8,2-3. The third item is close to the second; John's list of women may be a substitution for γνωστοί. The noun γνωστός signifies *acquaintance, friend, intimate*,[121] but it is masculine. If γνωστοί were originally the Johannine reading, referring to the male disciple in v 26b as determining the noun's gender is not a permissible solution, for verses 26-27 are a late redaction.

John, γνωστός also occurs in the pericope dealing with Peter's denial. There are 11 other occurrences of γνωστός in the NT, ten in Acts and one in Romans (*VKGNT* 1/1; 190).

[119] Boismard, *Marc* 230.

[120] Boismard, *Marc* 230.

[121] BAGD 164.

Examining the presence of the women in the four death pericopes best explains how the masculine noun γνωστοί was replaced by the list of women in John.

An investigation into the Johannine narrative reveals several points concerning the women witnesses. If *b* follows *a* in naming the women, the only list available is that found at Luke 8,2-3, and from that list, Μαρία ἡ Μαγδαληνή is the only person common to both the third and fourth evangelists; indeed, it is the only female name shared among all four evangelists. The textual tradition also shows how this lack of agreement among the gospels concerning the other names has puzzled scribes and editors almost from the beginning.

This fact helps to explain the reason for the discrepancy among the gospels in citing the women witnesses. There are only two constants among the evangelists: first, women were present, and second, one of them was Mary Magdalene; the other names were added or edited according to the importance a particular personage had for the community. Since γνωστοί in *a* is a generic term lacking specificity, the possibility that it is a primitive reading is great.[122] Whenever and however the *b* account received the tradition of women witnesses, the redactor substituted the list for the γνωστοί. Luke's omission of the flight of the apostles is well known, but the anonymous γνωστοί is the only record of their presence. If a Johannine redactor wanted to name the acquaintances, there appears to have been no list for him to use. A list of women witnesses was, however, available. Replacing the γνωστοί with the named women solved the problem. Not to be missed is a trace of the γνωστοί tradition in v 26b with τὸν μαθητὴν παρεστῶτα ὃν ἠγάπα; though part of a late redaction, it may reflect a reworking of an older reading.[123]

In addition, Brown investigates whether Luke had a specific group of individuals in mind with the inclusion of the γνωστοί. He discounts the possibility that it refers to the Eleven (Twelve minus Judas) on the ground that such an obscure reference would serve no purpose.[124] The most plausible suggestion for Brown is that γνωστοί refers to a group of Jesus' friends beyond the Twelve, possibly the seventy-two sent out during the Galilean ministry.[125] Brown's findings can be broadened to the extent that his conclusion reflects the tradition common to *a* and *b*.

The fourth point, the differences in adverbs between Luke and John, is a result of the *J* redactor. When vv 26-27 were added in John, the adverb had to be changed in order to give sense to the late interpolation of Jesus' address from the cross.

Before an intermediate Marcan redactor[126] conflated the *a* and *b* accounts

---

[122] It seems that the similarity in this parallel account, coupled with the frequency of γνωστός in the Johannine passion narrative, suggests a common tradition or "fixed point" for *a* and *b* in Luke 23,49 and John 19,25. Cf. above.

[123] Brown notes this similarity between the third and fourth Gospels as well but does not develop the point (*Messiah* 2; 1173).

[124] Brown, *Messiah* 2; 1172.

[125] Brown, *Messiah* 2; 1173.

[126] N.b. Boismard's theory of the Marcan-Lucan redactor (*Marc* 230).

of the cry from the cross, a Marcan editor combined the *a* and *b* versions of the witness narratives. This the editor did by a) replacing Εἰστήκεισαν δέ with the synonymous phrase Ἦσαν δέ, b) acknowledging the flight of the disciples by choosing the *b* list of women over the *a* reading of γνωστοί, and c) including special Marcan material by noting Galilee and rewriting the names of the women. This Marcan redaction was copied into the final Lucan recension with the list of women edited and transferred to 8,2-3 by *L*.[127] In sum, the list of women originated in John and entered Luke and Matthew through Mark. The plausibility of this theory is enhanced by the fact that it accounts for the mention of Galilee in the third gospel, explains Luke's singularity in containing γνωστοί, and acknowledges the presence of the women witnesses while respecting the differences of their names among the four evangelists.

Johannine arrangement

John is unique in placing the witness episode (vv 25-27) before the expiration. In all likelihood, the positioning of this account from after the death to before is connected with a redaction later than the *b* substitution of the women for the γνωστοί in v 25b. This is especially evident in one peculiarity of the Johannine narrative: Jesus' words to his mother and the beloved disciple.

Verses 26-27 represent the final *J* redaction. The elegant manner in which Jesus speaks contrasts sharply with the cry of thirst in v 28d; indeed, there is a chiastic structure: λέγει τῇ μητρί, γύναι, ἴδε ὁ υἱός σου (v 26c) and λέγει τῷ μαθητῇ, ἴδε ἡ μήτηρ σου (v 27a). Lest there be any doubt what this command means, the *J* redactor develops the idea in v 27b. Of course, this part of the narrative could only be situated before the death. Not only is such a position the sole logical possibility, but it also underscores the moment of death; τετέλεσται (v 30b) is true literally and figuratively. The evident editorial nature of vv 25-27 dictates that the Johannine placement of these verses does not reflect the order of the primitive *b* account; it is part of the final *J* redaction.

Summary

The examination thus far has probed the possibility that Luke's death account may exhibit not only another source, but one which also influenced the second evangelist; Luke is not simply copying and editing Mark. The analysis has presented two halves of the Lucan pericope. The first section, vv 44-46, while containing Marcan material, also reveals an earlier stage of the death account, *a*. Another ancient source, *b*, is similar to *a* and is evident in John 19,28-30. In a redaction of "death accounts" Mark combines these two sources, themselves a development of a "fixed point," to elaborate the cry from the cross. Matthew copies the "death account" from Mark .

The second half of Luke, vv 47-49, the "witness accounts," is further divided into two sections, v 47 and vv 48-49. Verse 47 originates with Luke. Simultaneously but independently, a Matthean and Marcan redactor receive this

---

[127] Boismard, however, believes that the mention of the women enters the account with proto-Luke (*Quête* 145).

centurion account; a later Matthean editor elaborates τὸ γενόμενον into a cosmic and apocalyptic event and reworks ὄχλος into καὶ οἱ μετʼ αὐτοῦ. At a later period, the *L* editor obtained the Marcan version and edited Marcan v 39 to form the final recension of 23,47. This same redactor conflated the Marcan vv 40-41 with *a* material in Lucan vv 48-49. A parallel to the *a* is the *b* account in John 19,25. Although *a* and *b* share a common tradition, on a redactional level there appears to be no contact between them. Mark also borrows from *a* and *b* at this point to write vv 40-41 in the second gospel; *L* then utilizes this redacted Mark in writing the final recension of vv 47-49.

Much of this discussion has depended upon the apparent similarity between *a* and *b*, particularly in the witness account, Luke 23,47-49. Referring to a common tradition for *a* and *b* is one explanation which allows for such closeness while respecting the visible differences between the two. The appeal to a common tradition for both primitive texts also supports the findings of Bailey, Boismard, Collins, Dauer, Dunn, and Schniewind. Of particular importance for this analysis is the idea of an oral tradition influenced by written accounts, a concept which Dauer and Bailey particularly develop. If indeed the origin of *a* and *b* lay in the "fixed point" of an oral tradition, such a tradition would be impossible to reconstruct; its traces in the form of *a* and *b* are all that remain today.

Overview

Stages of development

Marcan priority, while one explanation for the similarities in the death narratives among the synoptics, is visible only in the later redactions; both Matthew and Luke copy from the second evangelist at a time before their final recensions. When discussing earliest gospel sources and readings, however, it falls short; too many questions are glossed over and left unanswered. The idea whereby gospel pericopes developed from "fixed points"[128] solves many redactional problems[129] among the four evangelists while it acknowledges the preponderant role Mark has had in shaping the synoptic gospels. This theory, applied by Boismard in his analysis of the transfiguration,[130] taken up by Murphy-O'Connor,[131] and then developed by Reid, is also applicable to the death

---

[128] Dunn, "John" 351-79.

[129] N.b. Reid who sees "layers of development of the same basic tradition rather than the fusing of entirely separate traditions" (*Transfiguration* 86). At least for parts of the fourth gospel, even Brown admits to detecting pre-gospel stages in the formation of the narrative (*Messiah* 2; 1197).

[130] Boismard, *Synopse* 2; 250ff.

[131] Murphy-O'Connor, "Transfiguration," 8-21.

accounts in the gospels.

Behind Luke 23,44-49 and John 19,25-30 lie two written primitive narratives, *a* and *b*, which were originally independent and parallel, even though both reflect elements of a common, oral tradition concerning the last moments of Jesus. These two narratives form the core for the development of the death pericope among the four gospels, a development which has six major stages.

The death itself and the presence of witnesses are two "fixed points" which are slightly varied in the primitive *a* and *b* narratives. These written accounts comprise stage A.

Mark receives *a*; the *b* narrative soon replaces the γνωστοί with a list of the women witnesses, stage B.

Matthew and Mark then conflate the *a* and *b* accounts of the witnesses, the women, and the centurion. Simultaneously, Mark adds 15,39b.40.41, stage C.

Luke utilizes this redacted Marcan version for the last recension of the third gospel; Luke 23,44-49 takes its present form. The list of women is set at 8,2-3. A Matthean redactor elaborates this witness material by interpreting τὸ γενόμενον as apocalyptic events and rewriting the Lucan ὄχλος (24,48) as καὶ οἱ μετ' αυτοῦ (27,51b.52.53.54a), stage D.

A Marcan editor then copies the *b* account of Jesus' death and conflates it with the *a* version already present in the second gospel; Matthew copies Mark at this point, stage E.[132]

John undergoes a major redaction. Jesus' address to his mother and the beloved disciple is interpolated while this whole second part (vv 25-27) is placed before the cry of thirst; the redactor adds the phrase ὑσσώπῳ περιθέντες to v 29. The κεντυρίων reading enters Mark 15,39 with the episode in 15,44-45, stage F.

A more detailed exposition follows.

Stage A: Primitive narratives

Primitive source *a* is represented by Luke 23,44.45b.46ac.47a.48ad.49a, and primitive source *b*, by John 19,25a.28bd.29ac.30c;[133] these form the basis for Mark.

a

Cf. Luke 23,44Καὶ ἦν ἤδη ὡσεὶ ὥρα ἕκτη καὶ σκότος ἐγένετο ἐφ' ὅλην τὴν γῆν ἕως ὥρας ἐνάτης 45bἐσχίσθη δὲ τὸ καταπέτασμα τοῦ ναοῦ μέσον. 46aκαὶ φωνήσας φωνῇ μεγάλῃ ὁ Ἰησοῦς 46cἐξέπνευσεν. 47aἸδὼν δὲ ὁ ἑκατοντάρχης τὸ γενόμενον ἐδόξαζεν τὸν θεόν. 48aκαὶ πάντες οἱ συμπαραγενόμενοι ὄχλοι 48dὑπέστρεφον. 49aΕἰστήκεισαν δὲ πάντες οἱ γνωστοὶ αὐτῷ ἀπὸ μακρόθεν.

---

[132] This would be Boismard's proto-Mark (*Marc* 226-31). Cf. also Collins' pre-Marcan passion narrative ("Noble" 503).

[133] Brackets [ ] represent a reconstruction of the verse in *b*.

b

Cf. John 19,28b ὁ Ἰησοῦς ᵈλέγει, Διψῶ. ²⁹ᵃσκεῦος ἔκειτο ὄξους μεστόν· σπόγγον οὖν μεστὸν τοῦ ὄξους ᶜπροσήνεγκαν αὐτοῦ τῷ στόματι. ³⁰ᶜκαὶ κλίνας τὴν κεφαλὴν παρέδωκεν τὸ πνεῦμα. ²⁵ᵃΕἰστήκεισαν δὲ [γνωστοί αὐτῷ ἀπὸ μακρόθεν]

Stage B: Intermediate Mark - I; Intermediate John

Mark receives *a* material in some form while the γνωστοί in *b* are distinguished and rewritten as the women witnesses.

Intermediate John[134]

Cf. John 19,28b ὁ Ἰησοῦς ᵈλέγει, Διψῶ. ²⁹ᵃσκεῦος ἔκειτο ὄξους μεστόν· σπόγγον οὖν μεστὸν τοῦ ὄξους ᶜπροσήνεγκαν αὐτοῦ τῷ στόματι. ³⁰ᶜκαὶ κλίνας τὴν κεφαλὴν παρέδωκεν τὸ πνεῦμα. ²⁵ᵃΕἰστήκεισαν δὲ [ἀπὸ μακρόθεν] ᵇἡ μήτηρ αὐτοῦ καὶ ἡ ἀδελφὴ τῆς μητρὸς αὐτοῦ, Μαρία ἡ τοῦ Κλωπᾶ καὶ Μαρία ἡ Μαγδαληνή.

Stage C: Intermediate Mark - II; Intermediate Matthew - I

Matthew and Mark conflate the *a* and *b* witness narratives (stage A). Mark includes special material.[135]

Intermediate Mark - II

Cf. Luke 23,44 [Καὶ ἦν ἤδη ὡσεὶ ὥρα ἕκτη καὶ σκότος ἐγένετο ἐφ᾽ ὅλην τὴν γῆν ἕως ὥρας ἐνάτης ⁴⁵ᵇἐσχίσθη δὲ τὸ καταπέτασμα τοῦ ναοῦ μέσον. ⁴⁶ᵃκαὶ φωνήσας φωνῇ μεγάλῃ ὁ Ἰησοῦς ⁴⁶ᶜἐξέπνευσεν. ⁴⁷ᵃἸδὼν δὲ ὁ ἑκατοντάρχης τὸ γενόμενον] Cf. Mark 15,39b {εἶπεν, ἀληθῶς οὗτος ὁ ἄνθρωπος υἱὸς θεοῦ ἦν}. ⁴⁰ᵃ{Ἦσαν δὲ καὶ γυναῖκες} [ἀπὸ μακρόθεν] {θεωροῦσαι, ᵇἐν αἷς} (καὶ Μαρία ἡ Μαγδαληνή) {καὶ Μαρία ἡ Ἰακώβου τοῦ μικροῦ καὶ Ἰωσῆτος μήτηρ καὶ Σαλώμη, ⁴¹αἲ ὅτε ἦν ἐν τῇ Γαλιλαίᾳ ἠκολούθουν αὐτῷ καὶ διηκόνουν αὐτῷ, καὶ ἄλλαι πολλαὶ αἱ συναναβᾶσαι αὐτῷ εἰς Ἱεροσόλυμα}.

---

[134] Brackets [ ] represent a reconstruction of the verse.

[135] The display of stage C is an approximation. Brackets [ ] represent stage A, *a* material; parentheses ( ), stage A, *b*; uppercase brackets { }, Marcan or Matthean redaction.

Intermediate Matthew - I

Cf. Luke 23,44[Καὶ ἦν ἤδη ὡσεὶ ὥρα ἕκτη καὶ σκότος ἐγένετο ἐφ' ὅλην τὴν γῆν ἕως ὥρας ἐνάτης ⁴⁵ᵇἐσχίσθη δὲ τὸ καταπέτασμα τοῦ ναοῦ μέσον. ⁴⁶ᵃκαὶ φωνήσας φωνῇ μεγάλῃ ὁ Ἰησοῦς ⁴⁶ᶜἐξέπνευσεν]. ⁴⁷ᵃ[ὁ ἑκατοντάρχης {καὶ ὄχλοι ἰδόντες τὸ γενομενον } ἐδόξαζεν τὸν θεὸν] ⁴⁹ᵃΕἰστήκεισαν δὲ πάντες οἱ γνωστοὶ αὐτῷ ἀπὸ μακρόθεν`

Stage D: Final Luke; Intermediate Matthew - II

A later editor of Luke, borrowing from the Marcan redaction, added 23,45a to 45b, rewrote the quotation for 47b, and, while including 48c, conflated Mark 15,40-41 with Luke 23,48-49. This redactor or another transferred the Marcan list of women to Luke 8,2-3. Stage D is the final Lucan revision. A Matthean recension elaborates ὄχλος and τὸ γενόμενον.

Final Luke 23,44-49[136]

Cf. Luke 23,44Καὶ ἦν ἤδη ὡσεὶ ὥρα ἕκτη καὶ σκότος ἐγένετο ἐφ' ὅλην τὴν γῆν ἕως ὥρας ἐνάτης ⁴⁵ᵃ(τοῦ ἡλίου ἐκλιπόντος), ᵇἐσχίσθη δὲ τὸ καταπέτασμα τοῦ ναοῦ μέσον. ⁴⁶ᵃκαὶ φωνήσας φωνῇ μεγάλῃ ὁ Ἰησοῦς ᵇ(εἶπεν, πάτερ, εἰς χεῖράς σου παρατίθεμαι τὸ πνεῦμά μου. τοῦτο δὲ εἰπὼν) ᶜἐξέπνευσεν. ⁴⁷ᵃἸδὼν δὲ ὁ ἑκατοντάρχης τὸ γενόμενον ἐδόξαζεν τὸν θεὸν ᵇ(λέγων), {Ὄντως ὁ ἄνθρωπος οὗτος δίκαιος ἦν}. ⁴⁸ᵃκαὶ πάντες οἱ συμπαραγενόμενοι ὄχλοι ᵇ[ἐπὶ τὴν θεωρίαν ταύτην, θεωρήσαντες τὰ γενόμενα], ᶜ{τύπτοντες τὰ στήθη} ᵈὑπέστρεφον. ⁴⁹ᵃΕἰστήκεισαν δὲ πάντες οἱ γνωστοὶ αὐτῷ ἀπὸ μακρόθεν ᵇ[καὶ γυναῖκες αἱ συνακολουθοῦσαι αὐτῷ ἀπὸ τῆς Γαλιλαίας], ᶜ(ὁρῶσαι ταῦτα).

{Marcan text (15,40b) reworked and placed at Luke 8,2-3: Μαρία ἡ Μαγδαληνὴ καὶ Μαρία ἡ Ἰακώβου τοῦ μικροῦ καὶ Ἰωσῆτος μήτηρ καὶ Σαλώμη}.

Intermediate Matthew - II[137]

Cf. Luke 23,44[Καὶ ἦν ἤδη ὡσεὶ ὥρα ἕκτη καὶ σκότος ἐγένετο ἐφ' ὅλην τὴν γῆν ἕως ὥρας ἐνάτης ⁴⁵ᵇἐσχίσθη δὲ τὸ καταπέτασμα τοῦ ναοῦ μέσον. ⁴⁶ᵃκαὶ φωνήσας φωνῇ μεγάλῃ ὁ Ἰησοῦς ᶜἐξέπνευσεν].

---

[136] Brackets [ ] represent conflated Marcan and Lucan material; parentheses ( ), L interpolation; uppercase brackets { }, L reworking of Marcan reading; text without any of these marks, a material.

[137] The display of stage D is an approximation. Brackets [ ] represent stage A, a material; uppercase brackets { }, Matthean redaction.

Cf. Matt 27,51c{ἡ γῆ ἐσείσθη καὶ αἱ πέτραι ἐσχίσθησαν, ⁵²καὶ τὰ μνημεῖα ἀνεῴχθησαν καὶ πολλὰ σώματα τῶν κεκοιμημένων ἁγίων ἠγέρθησαν, ⁵³καὶ ἐξελθόντες ἐκ τῶν μνημείων μετὰ τὴν ἔγερσιν αὐτοῦ εἰσῆλθον εἰς τὴν ἁγίαν πόλιν καὶ ἐνεφανίσθησαν πολλοῖς} Cf. Luke 23,47a[ὁ ἑκατοντάρχης] Cf. Matt 27,54b{καὶ οἱ μετ᾽ αὐτοῦ τηροῦντες τὸν Ἰησοῦν} [ἰδόντες] {τὸν σεισμὸν καὶ} [τὰ γενόμενα] {ἐφοβήθησαν σφόδρα} [ἐδόξαζεν τὸν θεόν]. Cf. Luke 23,49a[Εἱστήκεισαν δὲ πάντες οἱ γνωστοὶ αὐτῷ ἀπὸ μακρόθεν]

Stage E: Intermediate Mark - III; Final Matthew

A subsequent redactor of the second gospel copied and redacted the cry of thirst and the sponge episode (John vv 28-29) and interpolated them at Mark 15,34-36. This Marcan redactor transferred the rending of the temple curtain to v 38 and specified the referent of *a*'s τὸ γενόμενον (v 39). Shortly after, a Matthean editor, receiving the Marcan narrative, made similar changes, and while harmonizing the account with Mark's, understood Mark as recording two separate cries (Matt 27,45-56).

Intermediate Mark - III[138]

Cf. Mark 15,33Καὶ γενομένης ὥρας ἕκτης σκότος ἐγένετο ἐφ᾽ ὅλην τὴν γῆν ἕως ὥρας ἐνάτης. ³⁴ᵃ[καὶ τῇ ἐνάτῃ ὥρᾳ ἐβόησεν ὁ Ἰησοῦς φωνῇ μεγάλῃ, ελωι ελωι λεμα σαβαχθανι; ᵇὅ ἐστιν μεθερμηνευόμενον ὁ θεός μου ὁ θεός μου, εἰς τί ἐγκατέλιπές με; ³⁵καί τινες τῶν παρεστηκότων ἀκούσαντες ἔλεγον, ἴδε Ἠλίαν φωνεῖ. ³⁶ᵃδραμὼν δέ τις καὶ γεμίσας σπόγγον ὄξους περιθεὶς καλάμῳ ἐπότιζεν αὐτὸν λέγων, ᵇἄφετε ἴδωμεν εἰ ἔρχεται Ἠλίας καθελεῖν αὐτόν]. ³⁷ὁ δὲ Ἰησοῦς ἀφεὶς φωνὴν μεγάλην ἐξέπνευσεν. ³⁸(Καὶ τὸ καταπέτασμα τοῦ ναοῦ ἐσχίσθη εἰς δύο ἀπ᾽ ἄνωθεν ἕως κάτω). ³⁹ᵃἸδὼν δὲ ὁ ἑκατοντάρχης (ὁ παρεστηκὼς ἐξ ἐναντίας αὐτοῦ ὅτι οὕτως ἐξέπνευσεν) ᵇεἶπεν, ἀληθῶς οὗτος ὁ ἄνθρωπος υἱὸς θεοῦ ἦν. ⁴⁰ᵃἮσαν δὲ καὶ γυναῖκες ἀπὸ μακρόθεν θεωροῦσαι, ᵇἐν αἷς καὶ Μαρία ἡ Μαγδαληνὴ καὶ Μαρία ἡ Ἰακώβου τοῦ μικροῦ καὶ Ἰωσῆτος μήτηρ καὶ Σαλώμη, ⁴¹αἳ ὅτε ἦν ἐν τῇ Γαλιλαίᾳ ἠκολούθουν αὐτῷ καὶ διηκόνουν αὐτῷ, καὶ ἄλλαι πολλαὶ αἱ συναναβᾶσαι αὐτῷ εἰς Ἱεροσόλυμα.

---

[138] Brackets [ ] represent Marcan conflation and rewriting of *b*; parentheses ( ), Marcan rewriting of Lucan material; text without any of these marks, stage C material unchanged or with slight editorial alterations.

Final Matthew 27,45-56[139]

45Ἀπὸ δὲ ἕκτης ὥρας σκότος ἐγένετο ἐπὶ πᾶσαν τὴν γῆν ἕως ὥρας ἐνάτης. 46[περὶ δὲ τὴν ἐνάτην ὥραν ἀνεβόησεν ὁ Ἰησοῦς φωνῇ μεγάλῃ λέγων, Ηλι ηλι λεμα σαβαχθανι; τοῦτ' ἔστιν· Θεέ μου θεέ μου, ἱνατί με ἐγκατέλιπες; 47τινὲς δὲ τῶν ἐκεῖ ἑστηκότων ἀκούσαντες ἔλεγον ὅτι Ἡλίαν φωνεῖ οὗτος. 48καὶ εὐθέως δραμὼν εἷς ἐξ αὐτῶν καὶ λαβὼν σπόγγον πλήσας τε ὄξους καὶ περιθεὶς καλάμῳ ἐπότιζεν αὐτόν. 49οἱ δὲ λοιποὶ ἔλεγον, ἄφες ἴδωμεν εἰ ἔρχεται Ἡλίας σώσων αὐτόν]. 50ὁ δὲ Ἰησοῦς (πάλιν) κράξας φωνῇ μεγάλῃ ἀφῆκεν τὸ πνεῦμα. 51a[Καὶ ἰδοὺ τὸ καταπέτασμα τοῦ ναοῦ ἐσχίσθη bἀπ' ἄνωθεν ἕως κάτω εἰς δύο] καὶ cἡ γῆ ἐσείσθη καὶ αἱ πέτραι ἐσχίσθησαν, 52καὶ τὰ μνημεῖα ἀνεῴχθησαν καὶ πολλὰ σώματα τῶν κεκοιμημένων ἁγίων ἠγέρθησαν, 53καὶ ἐξελθόντες ἐκ τῶν μνημείων μετὰ τὴν ἔγερσιν αὐτοῦ εἰσῆλθον εἰς τὴν ἁγίαν πόλιν καὶ ἐνεφανίσθησαν πολλοῖς. 54aὉ δὲ ἑκατόνταρχος bκαὶ οἱ μετ' αὐτοῦ τηροῦντες τὸν Ἰησοῦν ἰδόντες τὸν σεισμὸν καὶ τὰ γενόμενα ἐφοβήθησαν σφόδρα, c(λέγοντες), [ἀληθῶς θεοῦ υἱὸς ἦν οὗτος]. 55[Ἦσαν δὲ] (ἐκεῖ) γυναῖκες πολλαὶ ἀπὸ μακρόθεν [θεωροῦσαι], (αἵτινες) [ἠκολούθησαν τῷ Ἰησοῦ ἀπὸ τῆς Γαλιλαίας διακονοῦσαι αὐτῷ· 56ἐν αἷς ἦν Μαρία ἡ Μαγδαληνὴ καὶ Μαρία ἡ τοῦ Ἰακώβου] (καὶ Ἰωσὴφ μήτηρ καὶ ἡ μήτηρ τῶν υἱῶν Ζεβεδαίου).

Stage F: Final John and Mark

The final Johannine redactor interpolated Jesus' address from the cross, vv 26.27, which necessitated transferring the account of the witnesses to before the cry of thirst. This editor also added v 29b, ὑσσώπῳ περιθέντες, and elaborated the cry of thirst in v 28a to include material stressing the completion (τελέω, τελειόω) of Jesus' life; v 30b was redacted accordingly while v 30a was added.

Final John 19, 25-30[140]

25aΕἱστήκεισαν δὲ (παρὰ τῷ σταυρῷ τοῦ Ἰησοῦ) bἡ μήτηρ αὐτοῦ καὶ ἡ ἀδελφὴ τῆς μητρὸς αὐτοῦ, Μαρία ἡ τοῦ Κλωπᾶ καὶ Μαρία ἡ Μαγδαληνή. 26a[Ἰησοῦς οὖν ἰδὼν τὴν μητέρα bκαὶ τὸν μαθητὴν παρεστῶτα ὃν ἠγάπα, cλέγει τῇ μητρί, γύναι, ἴδε ὁ υἱός σου. 27aεἶτα λέγει τῷ μαθητῇ, ἴδε ἡ μήτηρ σου. bκαὶ ἀπ' ἐκείνης τῆς ὥρας ἔλαβεν ὁ μαθητὴς αὐτὴν εἰς τὰ ἴδια. 28aΜετὰ τοῦτο εἰδὼς] bὁ Ἰησοῦς c[ὅτι ἤδη πάντα τετέλεσται, ἵνα τελειωθῇ ἡ γραφή], dλέγει, Διψῶ. 29aσκεῦος ἔκειτο ὄξους μεστόν· σπόγγον οὖν μεστὸν τοῦ ὄξους b[ὑσσώπῳ

---

[139] Brackets [ ] represent Matthean copying and editing intermediate Mark-II; parentheses ( ), Matthean special material; text without any of these marks, stage C and D material unchanged or with slight editorial alterations.

[140] Brackets [ ] represent interpolated Johannine material; parentheses ( ), reediting of stage B; text without any of these marks, stage B material.

περιθέντες] ᶜπροσήνεγκαν αὐτοῦ τῷ στόματι. ³⁰ᵃ[ὅτε οὖν ἔλαβεν τὸ ὄξος ὁ ᵇἸησοῦς εἶπεν, τετέλεσται], ᶜκαὶ κλίνας τὴν κεφαλὴν παρέδωκεν τὸ πνεῦμα.

At some point the final Marcan redaction occurs with the interpolation of 15,44-45 into the narrative and the subsequent writing of the latinized κεντυρίων at v 39.

Final Mark 15,33-41[141]

³³Καὶ γενομένης ὥρας ἕκτης σκότος ἐγένετο ἐφ᾽ ὅλην τὴν γῆν ἕως ὥρας ἐνάτης. ³⁴ᵃκαὶ τῇ ἐνάτῃ ὥρᾳ ἐβόησεν ὁ Ἰησοῦς φωνῇ μεγάλῃ, ελωι ελωι λεμα σαβαχθανι; ᵇὅ ἐστιν μεθερμηνευόμενον ὁ θεός μου ὁ θεός μου, εἰς τί ἐγκατέλιπές με; ³⁵καί τινες τῶν παρεστηκότων ἀκούσαντες ἔλεγον, ἴδε Ἡλίαν φωνεῖ. ³⁶ᵃδραμὼν δέ τις καὶ γεμίσας σπόγγον ὄξους περιθεὶς καλάμῳ ἐπότιζεν αὐτὸν λέγων, ᵇἄφετε ἴδωμεν εἰ ἔρχεται Ἡλίας καθελεῖν αὐτόν. ³⁷ὁ δὲ Ἰησοῦς ἀφεὶς φωνὴν μεγάλην ἐξέπνευσεν. ³⁸Καὶ τὸ καταπέτασμα τοῦ ναοῦ ἐσχίσθη εἰς δύο ἀπ᾽ ἄνωθεν ἕως κάτω. ³⁹ᵃἸδὼν δὲ ὁ [κεντυρίων] ὁ παρεστηκὼς ἐξ ἐναντίας αὐτοῦ ὅτι οὕτως ἐξέπνευσεν ᵇεἶπεν, ἀληθῶς οὗτος ὁ ἄνθρωπος υἱὸς θεοῦ ἦν. ⁴⁰ᵃἮσαν δὲ καὶ γυναῖκες ἀπὸ μακρόθεν θεωροῦσαι, ᵇἐν αἷς καὶ Μαρία ἡ Μαγδαληνὴ καὶ Μαρία ἡ Ἰακώβου τοῦ μικροῦ καὶ Ἰωσῆτος μήτηρ καὶ Σαλώμη, ⁴¹αἳ ὅτε ἦν ἐν τῇ Γαλιλαίᾳ ἠκολούθουν αὐτῷ καὶ διηκόνουν αὐτῷ, καὶ ἄλλαι πολλαὶ αἱ συναναβᾶσαι αὐτῷ εἰς Ἱεροσόλυμα.

Mark 15,44-45

[⁴⁴ὁ δὲ Πιλᾶτος ἐθαύμασεν εἰ ἤδη τέθνηκεν καὶ προσκαλεσάμενος τὸν κεντυρίωνα ἐπηρώτησεν αὐτὸν εἰ πάλαι ἀπέθανεν· ⁴⁵καὶ γνοὺς ἀπὸ τοῦ κεντυρίωνος ἐδωρήσατο τὸ πτῶμα τῷ Ἰωσήφ].

The investigation into the textual, source, and redactional history of the Lucan death account shows that Luke 23,44-49 can be divided into two halves, the death itself and the witness account; there are two different versions of each, a and b. Traces of the former exist in the final Lucan version; the latter, in the final Johannine one. Both a and b influenced Mark, and secondarily, Matthew. Thus, a and b can be considered the first written accounts of a "fixed point" from the oral tradition concerning Jesus' death.

The development of the Lucan death account follows a series of stages which were altered as reflection on the mystery of Christ's death led to new conclusions. This reflection incorporated both an old and new understanding of canonical and non-canonical OT literature as well as the lived experience of the

---

141 Brackets [ ] represent Marcan interpolation and rewriting of stage E material; text without any marks, stage E material unchanged or with slight editorial alterations.

primitive Christian community. By the time of the final redaction, Luke saw the death as Christ's victorious battle against Satan and his minions in a war for the world. Moreover, in this victory, Luke not only set Christian salvation, but he also made the same soteriology a primary focus of the third gospel and the Acts. How this is done is addressed in Part Three.

Part Three

Synthesis

Throughout Luke's gospel Christ is contesting Satan and his forces. This battle increases in intensity in the passion, but the fight itself is from the cross. In constructing the scene, Luke employs various elements developed from other parts of the PN as well as the earthly ministry. These converge in the death account when Christ's battle with the *diabolical force* reaches its climax. Christ becomes identified with the *ministering angel* as understood in the late tradition.[1] Christ is victorious over Satan and is transfigured into glory; in addition, he extends that same glory to humanity.

Chapter Five

The Death Account; Luke 23,44-49

Luke crafts the death of Jesus into an event which sees both Satan's downfall and the Lord's visitation. The evangelist does this with references to *hour, darkness, eclipse, veil,* φωνὴ μεγάλη, *glorify, just,* and *crowds* as well as with allusions to the OT, deuterocanonical, and intertestamental works, especially *2 Enoch* 67.

The role of 2 Enoch 67

There is an apparent affinity between *2 Enoch* 67 and Luke 23,44-49.[2]

2 Enoch 67[3]
> [1]While Enoch was talking to his people, the Lord sent darkness onto the earth, and it became dark and covered the men who were standing with Enoch. [2]And the angels hurried and [the angels] grasped Enoch and carried him up to the highest heaven, and the Lord received him and made him stand in front of his face for eternity. And the darkness departed from the earth, and it became light.
> [3]And the people looked, and they understood how Enoch had been taken away. And they glorified God. And they went away into their homes.

---

[1] Particularly *T. Dan* 6,1-10; *T. Levi* 18,2-14; *T. Sim* 6,5-6; *T. Zeb* 9,8; *Jub* 15,30-32 (*OTPseud* 1; 782-828).

[2] For other selections from pseudepigraphic literature and their influence on Luke, cf. Chapter Two; for the redactional issues, cf. Chapter Four.

[3] *OTPseud* 1; 195 (shorter recension [A]). The parallel in the longer recension [J] contains the same material (*OTPseud* 1; 194).

Placing *2 Enoch* 67,1-3 in a parallel with Luke 23,44-49 yields several points of contact: temporary darkness (*2 Enoch* 67,1-2; Luke 23,44), presence of witnesses (*2 Enoch* 67,1.3; Luke 23,48), a glorification of God (*2 Enoch* 67,3; Luke 23,47), and a return home (*2 Enoch* 67,3; Luke 23,48).

Because this text is known only in a Slavonic translation and contains Christian glosses, it is not at first sight easy to see how *2 Enoch* could have influenced the Lucan account. On the other hand, F.I. Andersen, the principal specialist in the study of *2 Enoch*, regards it as "basically a midrash,"[4] thus a Jewish composition; moreover, Andersen holds that there are Hebrew or Aramaic sources behind the Greek version.[5] It was most probably written at the turn of the era[6] and could, therefore, have been known to the first Christians. That *1 Enoch* influenced the composition of the NT is generally admitted,[7] and Andersen observes *2 Enoch*'s "extensive connection" with *1 Enoch* which "can hardly be denied".[8]

Because of the multiple affinities between them, I propose to see *2 Enoch* 67 as a literary and theological model which played a prototypical role in the development of the Lucan death account.[9] To be precise, I suggest that the early Christian community drew upon *2 Enoch* 67 and used it in formulating the *a* source. In the final redaction, Luke too was aware of this text and took account of it as he reshaped the *a* source and reinterpreted it according to the growth in the community's understanding of the resurrection.

As with the analysis of the Lucan redaction, this discussion is divided into two halves, the death and the witness account.

---

[4] Andersen, *OTPseud* 1; 91.

[5] Andersen, *OTPseud* 1; 94.

[6] Andersen, *OTPseud* 1; 96. Andersen also places the "original nucleus" of *2 Enoch* "early rather than late" and in a "Jewish rather than Christian" community (*OTPseud* 1; 97).

[7] Cf. B. Brinkmann, S.J., ("Unterschiede zwischen der Lehre des hl. Paulus von der Parusie und den Anschauungen des Buches Henoch," *Bib* 13 [1932] 318-34 and 418-34); P. Grelot, ("Hénoch et ses Écritures," *RB* 82 [1975] 481-500); and even Emil Trenkle, ("Beitrag zur Zahlentypologie bei Lk 3,21-38 und Mt 1,1f. [Heer, Stammbäume] aus dem Buch Henoch," *BZ* 8 [1910] 262).

[8] *OTPseud* 1; 94.

[9] A.W. Zwiep, however, sees "close agreements" between *2 Enoch* 67,1-3 and the ascension accounts in Luke 24,50-53 and Acts 1,9-12 (*The Ascension of the Messiah in Lukan Christology* [New York: Brill, 1997] 49-51]). Cf. below.

The Death

Luke 23,44

⁴⁴Καὶ ἦν ἤδη ὡσεὶ ὥρα ἕκτη καὶ σκότος ἐγένετο ἐφ᾽ ὅλην τὴν γῆν ἕως ὥρας ἐνάτης

This Lucan reading is nearly an exact parallel to *2 Enoch* 67,1, but with one major difference: in *2 Enoch* the Lord sends the darkness; in Luke, the darkness is attributed to Satan. Noteworthy is that the ascension of Enoch is enclosed by the arrival and departure of darkness; once he is in heaven, light reappears. If Luke is following *2 Enoch*, why would the evangelist change darkness from an accident of divine action to a seemingly diabolical characteristic?

A frequent interpretation of the gospel verse is that Luke rearranged the Marcan material in order to join the rending of the temple veil to the darkness; thus, these two signs reflect God's wrath. According to Raymond Brown, Luke wishes to concentrate the negative aspects before the moment when Jesus would commit his spirit to the Father.[10] An investigation of the pericope, however, shows that rather than stressing the wrath of God, Luke is emphasizing divine visitation, a point clarified by the time in which darkness occurs.

Sixth and ninth hour

The two adjectives ἕκτος and ἔνατος modify the noun ὥρα. These times are often associated with the hours of prayer in L-A,[11] and here they are modifying ὥρα. The term ὥρα can mean both a specific point in the day or a time of eschatological revelation. There are several examples.[12]

In Luke 1,10.11 there is a coupling of the people praying ὥρᾳ τοῦ θυμιάματος with the appearance of ἄγγελος κυρίου to Zechariah. Anna the prophetess speaks to those looking for the redemption at αὐτῇ τῇ ὥρᾳ (2,38). Luke weaves together the two levels of time at 12,39.40.46. The example of the householder's vigilance concerning a thief in the night, a passage preceded by the master returning from the wedding feast, is juxtaposed with Jesus' statement ᾗ ὥρᾳ οὐ δοκεῖτε ὁ υἱὸς τοῦ ἀνθρώπου ἔρχεται (12,40). A similar concept is related in the parable of the Great Banquet (14,15-24; specifically v 17).

This melding of secular time with eschatological revelation reaches a climax in the passion and resurrection narratives (22,14.53; 24,33) which, of

---

[10] Brown, *Messiah* 2; 1038.

[11] ἕκτος identifies the month in Luke 1,26.36 and the hour in 23,44 and Acts 10,9 (*VKGNT* 1/1; 373). With the exception of 23,44, ἔνατος is used solely for the hour of prayer in Acts 3,1; 10,3.30 (*VKGNT* 1/1; 409).

[12] Exceptions to this statement are found in Luke 22,59; Acts 2,15; 5,7; 16,18; 23,23. Cf. above, Chapter Two.

course, have bearing on the meaning of ὥρα in 23,44. At the Last Supper (22,14-38), the *hour* (v 14) for sitting at the table is further explained in vv 15.16 where Jesus connects it to the kingdom of God, an echo of the Great Banquet in 14,15-24. Although ἡ ἐξουσία τοῦ σκότου is a negative, eschatological reference, with its coupling to ὥρα at 22,53, it is viewed within the same frame as the kingdom of God. Hence, at this point, the dominion of darkness begins to undergo its judgment. Indeed the darkness in 23,44, three hours of suffering leading to death, is the high tide of Satan's empire. With ὥρα functioning as a link between the passion, death, and resurrection, the Emmaus narrative (24,13-35) combines the elements of the heavenly banquet with revelation; it is at the breaking of the bread that Kleopas and the unnamed disciple recognize the traveler as Jesus who, in 23,44-49 died on the cross, and, who in 24,34, is called κύριος. At that ὥρα, they return to Jerusalem.

In the Acts, the dimension of the heavenly banquet is less pronounced with regard to the revelational character of ὥρα; the eschatological element is, however, present. The descent of the Holy Spirit at pentecost occurs at the third hour (2,15). The healing of the man lame from birth (3,1-10) occurs at the ninth hour (v 1); this is done in the name of Ἰησοῦ Χριστοῦ. The Peter and Cornelius pericope (10,1-33) gives explicit references to the sixth and ninth hours (vv 3.9). In each case, both receive a vision, the resolution of which is the descent of the Holy Spirit upon the Gentiles who subsequently receive baptism in vv 44-48. Likewise, the jailer and his household at Philippi are baptized ἐν ἐκείνῃ τῇ ὥρᾳ τῆς νυκτὸς (16,33). Saul's conversion (9,3-9) as well as his own accounts of it (22,6-16; 26,12-18) are replete with images of sight. Saul sees Ananias αὐτῇ τῇ ὥρᾳ (22,13) when the latter commissions the apostle to be a witness of all ἑώρακας καὶ ἤκουσας (22,15). Thus, ὥρα has here a revelatory dimension in the conversion accounts.

It seems, then, that ὥρα in L-A describes the moment of eschatological revelation, and that in Luke 23,44, the three-hour period of darkness is a frame for the manifestation of the eschaton. To be sure, the interval between the sixth and ninth hours is a measurable period of time, but the fact that Luke so often invests secular time with revelatory and eschatological meaning gives the three hours on the cross the same coloring.

Lucan shift

This Lucan emphasis on revelation explains the evangelist's understanding and use of *darkness*, a shift from that of *2 Enoch*. Although in *2 Enoch* the darkness is portrayed as part of the divine intervention in carrying away Enoch, after which light reappears, in the Lucan gospel, divine visitation or revelation is always depicted as light. Throughout the Lucan corpus, *light* represents the divine while *darkness*, the diabolical. These literary allusions, moreover, reflect the development of the *diabolical force* and *ministering angel* traditions.

In the canonical OT, Satan does not appear in terms of absolute evil; only in the pseudepigraphic works does a dualistic view of good and evil arise.[13] In the qumranic literature, the line of demarcation between the powers of light and the forces of darkness becomes even more pronounced. Luke, now incorporating

---

[13] Cf. Chapter Two.

the "fixed points" of the earliest Christian era, takes the separation further. To do this, the evangelist draws on the tradition reflected in the *Visions of Amram*, the *War Scroll* (1QM xiii), and Dan 12,3,[14] in which light, and never darkness, is considered a divine attribute.[15] It would be both an artistic and theological impossibility for Luke to have the Lord send in the darkness, Enoch's ascension notwithstanding.

The whole purpose of Jesus' life is to dispel the darkness (1,79). This he does by his death; light is reinterpreted as the light of revelation and it returns with the resurrection, the ultimate divine visitation.[16]

Temple cult

The eschatological character of the death is highlighted by the time of day. The specification that it occurs between the sixth and ninth hours draws attention to the temple cult. Both Exod 29,38ff and Num 28,4ff mention the morning and evening temple sacrifice, but they do not recount the specific hours of each. Josephus adds that at Passover, the sacrifices occurred from the ninth to the eleventh hour.[17] According to the *Tamid*, in the regular temple service, the concluding afternoon offering was slaughtered after half past the eighth hour and offered up at half past the ninth hour.[18] This regulated order was altered slightly at the Passover to accommodate the paschal sacrifices. On this occasion, the victim for the final, daily burnt-offering was slain at half past the seventh hour and was offered up an hour later; the slaughter of the Passover lambs then began.[19] Insofar as the *Tamid* regulation roughly coincides with Josephus' description, it can be considered a dependable witness for the temple cult here.

Since Luke records that the Last Supper took place on the day of Unleavened Bread, the same day on which the paschal lamb had to be sacrificed (22,7), he implies that the crucifixion and death occurred when the *Tamid* returned to its regular schedule.[20] In this case, if Christ dies at the ninth hour, the death roughly coincides with the slaughter of the concluding afternoon *Tamid*.

---

[14] Cf. Chapter Two.

[15] Indeed, in the *War Scroll* (1QH XI; 1QM XIV 14ff), the Just One, a creature of dust and ashes, participates in the eternal inheritance *in light* and in the company of angels (Puech, *Croyance* 479). Cf. Chapter Two.

[16] The treatment of darkness at the crucifixion in the *Gos. Pet.* is similar to the ascension account in *2 Enoch*, a matter which corroborates the fact that Luke is reinterpretating a "fixed point".

[17] Josephus, *J War* 6,9,3 (LCL 3; 498.423).

[18] Tractate Pesahim 5,1 in *Die Mischna*, Traktat Pesachim (ed. Georg Beer, 2,3; Gießen: Verlag von Alfred Töpelmann, 1912) 140-1.

[19] Tractate Pesahim 5,1 (*Die Mischna*, Beer 2,3; 140).

[20] But cf. John 12,1; 13,1; 19,14.31.42.

Hence, Luke would be drawing a parallel not so much to the paschal nature of the crucifixion as to the Jewish cultic practice: His death is similar to the temple sacrifice.[21]

Judgment of darkness

The word σκότος marks a further development of the crucifixion's eschatological significance. The negative connotation of σκότος in the Lucan corpus never varies.[22]   As the absence of light, darkness symbolizes the *diabolical force* in Luke 11,35; 22,53 and Acts 26,18. It is a punishment for working against the plan of the Lord in Acts 13,11. With the word σκότος, the citations in Luke 1,79 and Acts 2,20 display the prophetic element inherent in Jesus' life and death; this particularly comes to bear on Luke 23,44. The child addressed in 1,76, among other things, is called to enlighten τοῖς ἐν σκότει καὶ σκιᾷ θανάτου καθημένοις (v 79). The mention of darkness in Acts 2,20 is part of a quotation from LXX Joel 3,1-5a, an apocalyptic prophecy. It refers back to the crucifixion as it addresses the phenomena at pentecost. In Luke 23,44, σκότος acts as a point where both evil and the old order end and meet their judgment.

Précis

The specification of the ὥρα has two levels of meaning. The first is the hour of the day. That Christ dies about or at the ninth hour associates his death with the afternoon *Tamid*. This sacrifice leads to the second level of meaning. The ὥρα is the time of revelation which, during three hours of darkness, passes judgment on evil and on the old order.

Luke 23,45a

45a τοῦ ἡλίου ἐκλιπόντος, b ἐσχίσθη δὲ τὸ καταπέτασμα τοῦ ναοῦ μέσον.

Lagrange observes that there could not have been an eclipse at the time of the Passover;[23] a solar eclipse is impossible during a full moon, and in any case none could last three hours. If the three hours of darkness did occur at the time of Jesus' death, they must have had some other cause. A *khamsin*, the hot, dusty, wind which blows in from the eastern desert in April and early May, could cause this phenomenon; in severe cases, darkening at midday would not be at all unusual. In any case, the darkness takes on symbolic meaning, and its attribution to a solar eclipse heightens the image. In the battle against the *diabolical force*,

---

[21] For Matthean/Marcan specification of the ninth hour, cf. above, Chapter Four.

[22] σκότος occurs seven times in L-A: Luke 1,79; 11,35; 22,53; 23,44; Acts 2,20; 13,11; 26,18 (*VKGNT* 1/2; 1206-7).

[23] Lagrange, *Luc* 592. Cf. also above, Chapter Four.

all of creation comes under Satan's sway.

Interpretation of the eclipse

John F. A. Sawyer, observing the *Sitz im Leben* of the eclipse, notes two factors bearing on this Lucan reading. First, there is the eclipse of 24 November AD 29; second, there are the eclipse reports themselves.[24] The eclipse of 24 November AD 29 was the only eclipse observable in the area during the first century.[25] It occurred at 11:15 am, lasted for 1.5 minutes, and was total for Byzantium, parts of Asia Minor, and Syria.[26] Sawyer suggests that Luke, as a youth in Asia Minor, witnessed this eclipse and later compared it to the crucifixion darkness of the tradition.[27] Sawyer addresses the impossibility of a three-hour long eclipse by studying eclipse reports in both antiquity and modern times. Throughout history and as recently as 1927, witnesses of a solar eclipse have tended to exaggerate its duration.[28] Finally, Sawyer comments that the use of ὡσεί in v 44 may be evidence of the author's recollection of the eclipse in AD 29; 11:15 am would be between the fifth and sixth hours.[29] In addition, Brown notes Luke's liberal use of Augustan edicts and regional census reports for composing the worldwide enrollment in 2,1-4, and believes it plausible that the evangelist could have applied the same principle to his account of the eclipse.[30] Such a use of historical material, as Justin Taylor illustrates, is also evident in Acts 11,28 regarding the famine.[31] On this basis, Luke's editing of an historical detail in 23,45a is most probable, and the occurrence of a *khamsin* could have recalled the event to mind.[32]

Of course, Luke utilizes these events to make a theological point. The noun ἥλιος is often coupled with the noun σκότος in L-A.[33] Although sometimes

---

[24] John F.A. Sawyer, "Why is the solar eclipse mentioned in the Passion Narrative?" *JTS* 23 (1972) 126-7.

[25] Sawyer, "Why" 127.

[26] Sawyer, "Why" 127.

[27] Sawyer, "Why" 127.

[28] Sawyer, "Why" 128.

[29] Sawyer, "Why" 128.

[30] Brown, *Messiah* 2; 1040-1.

[31] Justin Taylor, S.M., *Les Actes des deux apôtres, commentaire historique (Act. 9,1-18,22), vol. 5* (EBib 23; Paris: J. Gabalda et Cie, 1994) 92-4.

[32] G. R. Driver also sees the *khamsin* as that act of nature responsible for the rending of the temple curtain ("Two problems in the New Testament," *JTS* 16 [1965] 334-6).

[33] ἥλιος occurs in Luke 4,40; 21,25; 23,45; Acts 2,20; 13,11; 26,13; 27,20

the setting sun simply describes the time of day (Luke 4,40), it also seems that Luke uses the approaching darkness as a time for demonic activity, thus playing on the idea of ἐξουσία τοῦ σκότους (22,53). With the demons proclaiming Jesus as the Son of God there is a nuance of revelation. In the Lucan apocalyptic (21,6-36) the disciples are informed that there will be signs in the sun (v 25). In Acts 2,20, the prophecy from LXX Joel 3,1-5a states that the sun will be turned into darkness. The inability to see the sun is part of the punishment Paul inflicts upon Elymas the magician in Acts 13,11. When Paul relates his conversion to Agrippa, he states that he saw οὐρανόθεν ὑπὲρ τὴν λαμπρότητα τοῦ ἡλίου περιλάμψαν με φῶς (Acts 26,13). The term ἥλιος is mentioned for the last time in Acts 27,20 where it has no eschatological significance.

From these examples, the Lucan apocalyptic (21,6-36) and the Joel prophecy in Acts 2,17-21 have the most bearing on the death account in 23,45; the sun's failure is recorded only by Luke. The mention of signs in the sun (Luke 21,25) foreshadows its eclipse in 23,45, while the use of the OT prophecy in Acts 2,20 recalls the same. By combining apocalyptic language with cultic terminology, Luke not only portrays the three-hour suspension on the cross as the heat of battle between Jesus and the *dominion of darkness*, but also as the end of the dark, old order and the beginning of the new, a point underscored by the tearing of the temple veil in the second half of the verse.

Luke 23,45b

The term σχίζομαι, as a passive, translates as *be divided, torn, split* or *become divided, disunited*.[34] The passive uses of σχίζομαι in the LXX, Exod 14,21; Zech 14,4; Isa 36,22; 48,21; Wis 5,11 and 1 Macc 6,45 have greater frequency than the occurrences of σχίζω, and these tend to be the divine passive.[35] In each of these cases, the tear or split described by σχίζομαι forms a path permitting passage through the middle.[36] This understanding is fortified by the adverbial use of μέσος.[37]

In Exod 14,21 and Zech 14,4 the verb relates a salvific action. The Exodus account notes the dividing of the waters through which the Israelites flee the pursuing Egyptians, and in apocalyptic language the Zechariah reading describes the coming of the Lord; the Mount of Olives on the east will split so that Jerusalem's inhabitants can escape while the Lord does battle against the nations. This is linked to Luke 21,21 where Jesus states that those inside the city should flee to the mountains when they see armies surrounding Jerusalem.

(*VKGNT* 1/1; 492-3). In four instances, it is found in the same pericope as σκότος: Luke 23,45; Acts 2,20; 13,11; 26,13.(cf. v 18).

[34] BAGD 797.

[35] Active voice of σχίζω in the LXX is found in Gen 22,3; 1 Kgs 6,14; Eccl 10,9; Isa 37,1; and Dan (Theo Sus) 55 [HR 1327-28].

[36] Isa 36,22 describes a torn garment.

[37] μέσος can mean *through the midst, between* (BAGD 507) Cf. LXX Gen 15,10; Exod 11,4; 14,22.23.27; 24,18; Josh 1,11; Amos 5,17; Ezek 9,4; 11,23;

Literary background

The term μέσος connects this understanding to another prophetic passage which shows great similarity to the Zechariah text above. LXX Ezek 11,23 describes the glory of the Lord ascending from the middle of the city and stopping on the mountain east of it;[38] the context of this passage is Ezekiel's announcement to captive Judah. In the following verses Ezekiel receives a vision which he recounts to all the exiles in Chaldea. He sees the divine glory returning to the temple from the East and through the east gate (43,2-4). Likewise, in the *Testament of Naphtali* (5,1ff), the Mount of Olives is the setting for the vision in which Levi seizes the sun and Judah the moon, thereby exalting themselves over all other nations.[39] Moreover, LXX Zech 14,7ff portrays that eschatological day as a time when there will not be "either cold or frost," and when there will be "continuous day...not day and not night, for at evening time there shall be light". The dominion of darkness, reaching its climax between the sixth and ninth hours, echoes the prophecy from Zechariah.[40]. To be noted is the reading from 2 *Enoch* 67,1, "...the Lord sent darkness on to the earth, and it became dark".

The relationship between the prophecies of Zechariah and Ezekiel has been noticed by others.[41] In addition to certain echoes between Ezekiel and Zechariah, the probability that Ezekiel was one of the immediate sources for Zechariah is strong.[42] Thus, Luke's situating the rending before the death takes full advantage of this prophetic tradition, a tradition which forms the context for the temple veil.

Through σχίζομαι and μέσος, Luke bases his interpretation of the tearing of the temple veil on these readings from Ezekiel, Zechariah, and to a lesser degree the *Testament of Naphtali*. Luke presents an apocalyptic scene of destruction and judgment in the spirit of Zechariah. It is Ezekiel 11,23 and 43,2-5, however, which complement the understanding.

Luke 4,30; 17,11; 21,21.

[38] N.b. LXX Ezek 10,19 mentions that the cherubim pause at the *east* gate with the glory of God hovering above them before they fly to the mountain east of the city in 11,23. That the glory makes its departure from the east gate is in keeping with the fact that the outer curtain of the temple faced East.

[39] *OTPseud* 1; 812.

[40] Zechariah's reference to "light" is addressed below.

[41] Cf. Jesus Asurmendi, "La gloire de Dieu sur la montagne qui est à l'Orient," *Le Monde de la Bible* 55 (Sept-Oct 1988) 7; Marco Nobile, "Ez 37,1-14 come costitutivo di uno schema cultuale," *Bib* 65 (1984) 476-484.

[42] Konrad Schaefer, O.S.B., "Zechariah 14: A Study in Allusion," *CBQ* 57 (Jan 1995) 89.

The temple

An issue which makes the interpretation of this verse especially difficult is the indeterminate role the temple plays in L-A. Although often seen in a positive light, the temple also has a negative connotation, particularly at the second half of Acts (21,27-36).[43] When Paul speaks about the temple after this point, he is making references to times past, and these usually have positive overtones.[44] Tyson believes that the prominence of the temple clashes with the contention that the Jewish leaders most responsible for Jesus' death are the chief priests; the temple involves the broader issue concerning rights of cult participation and teaching.[45] In addition, Tyson holds that the temple was both the scene and object of conflict, and thus Luke may use it as a symbol of the separation between Judaism and Christianity.[46]

Jerusalem, as the city of the temple's location, is often linked thematically with it. This association between the two is evident in the infancy narratives (Luke 2,22-46), and in the description of the early Jerusalem community (Acts 2,14.43-46); these instances and others paint both the temple and Jerusalem in a positive light. More often, a positive and negative connotation exist simultaneously; for example, Jesus enters Jerusalem triumphantly and dies there ignominiously five days later (19,29-40; 22,1ff).

The situation is similar with the temple; Christ overturns the money changers' tables in the precinct but then teaches there (Luke 19,45-48). The shift between positive and negative aspects of the temple and Jerusalem becomes even more evident two chapters later. The pericope of the widow's offering (21,1-4) precedes the passage on the temple's beauty (21,5) after which follows the Lucan apocalyptic (21,6-36). Furthermore, at the very next verse, Luke explains that Christ spent every day teaching in the temple, spent the night on the Mount of Olives, only to be in the temple the next day teaching once again (21,37-38).

Observing this fluctuation, Tyson concludes that "[t]he negative aspects of the treatment of Jerusalem are totally negative, while the negative aspects of the temple treatment seem more tentative."[47] Tyson's assessment should be nuanced. It is true, as the place of trial and crucifixion, Jerusalem is portrayed negatively. Jerusalem, however, witnesses the resurrection and pentecost, thus there is little difference in Luke's attitude toward the Holy City and to the holy place within the city. The relationship between the temple and Jerusalem is similar in Acts. Both are related rather positively from the period after the ascension until the Jews of Asia rouse the mob against Paul (Acts 21,27-36), and the Acts ends with

---

[43] For a discussion on the benevolent attitude which Luke displays toward the temple, cf. Matera, "Death". Cf. also Francis Weinert, "Luke, the Temple and Jesus' Saying about Jerusalem's Abandoned House (Luke 13:34-35)," *CBQ* 44 (1982) 68-76.

[44] Acts 22,17; 24,12.18; 25,8; 26,21.

[45] Tyson, *Death* 108.

[46] Tyson, *Death* 109.

[47] Tyson, *Death* 107.

Paul in Rome. Moreover, Luke's ambiguous treatment of the temple is similar to Ezekiel's treatment; the glory of the Lord leaves the temple (11,23) only to return (43,2-5).

On this basis, this contrast between teaching in the temple and reposing on the Mount of Olives frames the scene for the arrest. There at 22,53, Jesus tells his captors that he sat daily in the temple teaching and they did not lay hands on him; he also tells them that the present moment is "the power of darkness".

Of all these pericopes, Luke 21,37-38 and 22,53 are paramount for shedding light on the interpretation of the temple veil; by being associated with the Mount of Olives, these two episodes suggest an interpretation based on Ezek 10,18-19 and 11,23. In the former, the glory of the Lord ascends from the house, pauses above the cherubim, and they both stop at the east gate; in the latter, the glory rises from the middle of the city and stops on the mountain east of it.

Such an understanding in Luke may appear to be forcing the issue were it not for two facts. First, if one goes by LXX Psalm 26,4, the ideal is to live in the temple and to gaze upon the beauty of the Lord. That Luke is aware of this ideal is evident in the description of Anna; never leaving the temple, she fasted and prayed there night and day (2,37). Jesus' leaving the temple to pray on the Mount of Olives counters this understanding. Second, in both Luke 24,50 and Acts 1,12, the ascension takes place on the Mount of Olives.[48] Admittedly, the echo of the Ezekiel passage is tentative here, but the fact that in Acts 1,8 Christ charges the Apostles to be witnesses in Jerusalem and to the ends of the earth strikes a parallel with Ezekiel's proclamation to the captives in Chaldea (Ezek 11,24-25). The prophet's message, however, announces the exile whereas the apostles deliver good news. Hence, in the Lucan interpretation, it appears that God's visitation does not bring punishment but rather fulfillment. If the temple, and by extension Jerusalem, are symbols of the separation between Judaism and Christianity as Tyson suggests,[49] this split is not absolute but equivocal.

Throughout most of Acts the treatment of both the temple and Jerusalem is positive, or at least ambivalent. The rending of the temple veil at Luke 23,45b, therefore, does not emphasize apocalyptic doom; rather, it accentuates eschatological fulfillment. In the end times, the Lord's holiness leaves the temple and goes to a place where, as in Ezekiel, the revealed things can be related to all the nations.

This interpretation of divine visitation with universalist import is substantiated by Joel B. Green's social-cultural inquiry into the significance of the temple in Luke.[50] Historically, the temple correlated concepts of holiness with a system of restricted spaces.[51] Hence, it separated Gentile from Jew, Jewish female from Jewish male, Jewish priest from non-priest, and high priest from

---

[48] The gospel account reads πρὸς Βηθανίαν which can mean "toward Bethany". From Jerusalem it is approached, of course, via the Mount of Olives.

[49] Tyson, *Death* 109.

[50] Joel B. Green, "The Demise of the Temple in Luke-Acts," *RB* 101/4 (1994) 495-515.

[51] Green, "Temple" 507.

other priests.[52]   The rending of the temple veil symbolically destroys these
barriers.   By concentrating on the co-text surrounding v 45b, Green notes that
both the pagan centurion, (v 47) and the Jewish crowd (v 48), respond positively
to the rending of the veil.[53] This recalls Simeon's prophecy in 2,30-32, and thus
salvation embraces both Gentile and Jew.[54]
     Green sees two other aspects to Luke's portrayal of the temple.   First, it is
the center of teaching (Luke 19,47; 20,1; 21,37.38; 22,53; Acts 5,20.21.25.42)
and pious observance (Luke 2,37; 18,10; 19,46; Acts 3,1-10; 21,26; 22,17).[55]
Although it continues to be a place of prayer and teaching in Acts, with the
rending of the veil, it is the point of departure for a universal mission.[56]
Second, it is also the place of divine revelation (Luke 2,25-32; Acts 2,5-
11.21.39).[57] Paul's theophany (Acts 22,17-21) shows that Gentiles do not come
to the temple to find the Lord, rather, the Lord goes out, with witnesses like
Paul, to find them.[58]   Green emphasizes that the torn veil neutralizes the
"dominance of the temple as a sacred symbol of socio-religious power
predetermining insider and outsider".[59] In sum, for Green, the rending of the
veil in Luke is symbolic of the destruction of the *symbolic* world surrounding and
emanating from the temple, and is not symbolic of the destruction of the temple
itself.[60]

The rending of the veil

     The same desert wind or *khamsin* that plausibly is responsible for
conditions reminiscent of a solar eclipse is a possible historical explanation for
the tearing of the temple curtain as well.   While it is certainly possible that a
strong gust ripped the temple veil at the precise moment of Christ's death, it
seems unlikely; it would be physically impossible for someone to witness
simultaneously both the death of Jesus and the rending of the curtain.   In
addition, if there were such a coincidence, it would have been so etched in the

---

[52] Green, "Temple" 507.

[53] Green, "Temple" 504-5.

[54] Green, "Temple" 505.

[55] Green, "Temple" 511.

[56] Green, "Temple" 512.

[57] Based on the summary statements in Luke 24,53 and Acts 2,46 Green
believes the temple to be the setting for Pentecost (513 n 46). Also cf. above the
discussion on Jerusalem and the temple as synonymous terms.

[58] Green, "Temple" 513.

[59] Green, "Temple" 514.

[60] Green, "Temple" 514.

community's memory that, along with the multiple attestation in the synoptic accounts, one would expect to find other references as well as literary elaborations of the event within the whole NT corpus. More plausible is the possibility that, like census reports (Luke 2,1-5), the solar eclipse (Luke 23,45a), and the prediction of the famine (Acts 11,28), at some time within the history contemporaneous with Luke, a violent *khamsin* did tear the temple veil, and the evangelist recorded the event within the context of the death account. A parallel is provided by a passage in the *Jewish War*. Josephus records the spontaneous opening of the massive, brass doors to the temple.[61] The "learned," he explains, interpreted this event as a sign of the approaching desolation of the temple;[62] furthermore, the narrative continues that during a priestly procession, a voice announces, "We are departing hence."[63]

Luke's mention of the rending of the veil and Josephus' account of the opening of the temple doors suggest that there existed during the intertestamental period a tradition of portents presaging the temple's destruction. One of these was the departure of the divine presence expressed by the dissolution of temple barriers, be they doors or curtain. The concept of the desertion of the divine presence is grounded, no doubt, on OT prophetic literature, especially Ezek 10. In terms of the Lucan death narrative, it seems that the *a* source, in relating the death of Jesus, drew from this tradition,[64] and the final Lucan redactor followed suit.

Interpretation

There are several interpretations concerning the Lucan version of the rending of the curtain which the syntax of the passage helps to clarify. Acknowledging the ambiguity associated with the post-positive δέ (23,45b), Brown offers two possible understandings.[65] If δέ is read as a conjunctive, "And also," v 45b is joined to the preceding darkness and thus the rending of the temple veil is a sign of divine displeasure. On the other hand, if δέ is considered an adversative, "But," the rending is connected to the last words thereby becoming a positive reaction to the darkness; Jesus passes through to the Father. Brown makes a strong case favoring a negative interpretation for the rending of the veil.[66] First, the Lucan writer never uses the verb σχίζω as that action which forms a passageway.[67] Second, Brown notes that there is no evidence that Luke views Jesus in priestly terms. Thus, an interpretation of Jesus as a priest

---

[61] Josephus, *J War* 6,5,3 (LCL 3; 460.293).

[62] Josephus, *J War* 6,5,3 (LCL 3; 460-2.295-6).

[63] Josephus, *J War* 6,5,3 (LCL 3; 462.300).

[64] Reinforced by the curtain's tearing at some point during a *khamsin*?

[65] Brown, *Messiah* 2; 1103.

[66] Brown, *Messiah* 2; 1105-06.

[67] Cf. Luke 5,36*bis*; 23,45; Acts 14,4; 23,7.

proceeding into the sanctuary is faulty.[68] Without totally discarding the positive interpretation, Brown prefers the negative one, that like the darkness, the rending of the veil indicates God's wrath.[69]

Brown does not offer a totally persuasive argument, but his discussion opens another possibility. Luke's use of the verb σχίζω never has a positive connotation, thereby giving a basis for a negative interpretation. Of note, however, is that Luke most probably refers to the outer veil,[70] and places its rending before the death itself; this suggests a positive, or at least a less negative, meaning. To be noted is that the outer veil was decorated with an embroidery of the firmament symbolizing the elements of earth, air, fire, and water.[71]

To be sure, the darkness covering the earth and the violence inherent in the verb σχίζω depict the Day of the Lord and hence God's judgment, but the

---

[68] Brown, *Messiah* 2; 1105.

[69] Brown, *Messiah* 2; 1106.

[70] To be sure, a definitive answer to the question regarding the curtain to which Luke is referring is nearly impossible to make. Nonetheless, the possibility that it is the outer one is greatest.

Josephus describes a veil of Babylonian tapestry, symbolizing the elements of earth, air, fire, and water; this hung in front of the golden doors separating the vestibule from the cella, and its design depicted the heavenly bodies (*J War* 5,5,4 (LCL 3; 264.212-3).

Driver points out that although the LXX appears to use (κατα)κάλυμμα for the outer curtain of the tabernacle and καταπέτασμα for the inner, Josephus, a priest, uses καταπέτασμα for both ("Two problems in the New Testament," *JTS* 16 [1965] 335).

André Pelletier, S.J. however, examines the role of the temple curtain in the synoptics and early Christian writings by studying, among other things, the material and design of the veil ("La Tradition Synoptique du 'Voile Déchiré'," *RSR* 46 [1958] 161-80). Pelletier holds that this is the curtain to which Luke is referring.

Based on the accounts from Josephus as well as the observations of Driver and Pelletier, it seems most logical that, if a *khamsin* caused the curtain to rip, the one most likely to tear is the outer and not the inner veil; thus, Luke 23,45b refers to the outer curtain, the one between the vestibule and the ναός (For a discussion on temple vocabulary, cf. Paul Joüon, S.J. "Les Mots employés pour désigner 'Le Temple' dans l'Ancien Testament, le Nouveau Testament, et Josèphe," *RSR* 25 [1935] 329-43; S. Légasse, "Les Voiles du Temple de Jérusalem," *RB* 87 [1980] 580-81; L.-H. Vincent, O.P., *Jérusalem de l'Ancien Testament* [2; Paris: J. Gabalda et Cie 1956] 467). That it is the inner veil in front of the Holy of Holies is untenable. No one but the priests would know, and since they were part of those who had Jesus condemned to death (Luke 22,66; 23,18.24), most likely they would not tell anyone about a torn curtain at the Holy of Holies. Moreover, holding that natural explanations are to be preferred to supernatural ones, the arrival of a violent *khamsin* as that which is responsible for the rending of the curtain is to be preferred; such also harmonizes with the three hours of darkness.

[71] Josephus, *J War* 5,5,4 (LCL 3; 264.212).

other factors, namely the placement of the verse before the expiration, the death occurring at the hour of the afternoon *Tamid*, and the design of the veil itself portray the positive elements of God's visitation. It is true that Luke never uses σχίζω in a manner which suggests forming a passageway, but the passive voice suggests it anyway; if something is torn, passing through is a by-product.[72] Taking into account the syntactical ambiguity of δέ, the placement of v 45b before the death, the combining of σχίζομαι with μέσος, the OT and intertestamental prophecies, and the fabric and design of the outer veil, verse 45b describes an event which is both negative and positive with the positive element receiving the emphasis.

The apocalyptic atmosphere created by the darkness, the sense of judgment implied by ὥρα, along with the salvific overtones found in the combination of the verb σχίζομαι with the adverb μέσος seem to indicate that Luke 23,44-45 describes the Day of the Lord. Although Senior sees the rending of the curtain as foretelling the impending ruination of God's house in the final days,[73] the emphasis is not destruction, but the Lord's visitation. The ambiguity associated with various interpretations of the rending of the temple veil exists because the Lord's visitation entails both negative and positive features; apocalyptic destruction is concomitant with the eschaton. The reading from Ezek 10,18ff best expresses this concept. When the glory of the Lord leaves the temple (10,18-19; 11,22-23) and Israel is handed over to foreign enemies (11,8-12), there is still a promised restoration (11,17ff).

The divine presence quits the temple before Christ dies on the cross; it is the high point of the dominion of darkness. And the glory of the Lord which shines all around? This event occurs in the following verses.

Précis

The eclipse represents the totality and power of Satan's dominion of darkness. If a *khamsin* rends the temple veil, it is most probably an historical occurrence from another time, which like the eclipse, is rewritten into the death account. Both these events point to the apocalyptic prophecies. The veil tears moments before Christ, the final afternoon *Tamid* or prayer, dies, and it signifies the flight of the divine presence; the *diabolical force* has never been stronger. Although this action is not a negative judgment on the temple, it is ambiguous, thus reflecting both the destruction and restoration present in the Lord's visitation. The rending of the temple veil is part of the rising action leading to the climax -- the death itself.

Luke 23,46

⁴⁶ᵃκαὶ φωνήσας φωνῇ μεγάλῃ ὁ Ἰησοῦς ᵇεἶπεν, πάτερ, εἰς χεῖράς σου παρατίθεμαι τὸ πνεῦμά μου. τοῦτο δὲ εἰπὼν ᶜἐξέπνευσεν.

---

[72] An inexact but close analogy in English can be found with the verb *cut*: In active voice, "Someone cut a hole"; in passive, "A hole was cut". The latter implies that something can pass through.

[73] Senior, *Passion* 142.

Verse 46 has two sections. The first contains the φωνὴ μεγάλη/ἐκπνέω combination; the second, the paraphrase from LXX Psalm 30. This phrase (46a.c)[74] is further enriched by the material from LXX Psalm 30 in v 46b.

Prayer

In 23,46 Christ begins his prayer with πάτερ, thus recalling his relationship to God.[75] The use of the phrase φωνὴ μεγάλη here, as well as throughout most of L-A, then signals the divine sonship of Jesus which is further manifested in the works done in his name. With the expression in 23,46, Luke is also drawing upon OT apocalyptic passages as both Heribert Schützeichel[76] and Brown indicate.[77] In this verse, however, unlike all other instances, the phrase is on the lips of Christ who alone speaks. Jesus' words, a paraphrase of LXX Psalm 30, is peculiar to Luke. This quotation of the last words of Jesus from the cross focuses attention on the proclamation of Christ's divine sonship and ministry throughout L-A. The φωνὴ μεγάλη couplet occurs seven times in the Lucan gospel[78] and six times in Acts.[79] Eight of the instances are associated with a cry of thanksgiving or a proclamation of Christ's divine sonship.[80] With the exception of Luke 23,23, Acts 7,57, and 16,28, this word combination draws attention to Christ or his work. Specific examples make this clear.

The phrase describes Elizabeth's reaction to Mary's greeting in which she says καὶ πόθεν μοι τοῦτο ἵνα ἔλθῃ ἡ μήτηρ τοῦ κυρίου μου πρὸς ἐμέ (Luke 1,42.43). Thus, Elizabeth is the first to proclaim the Lordship of Christ. In 4,33.34, the unclean spirit in a φωνὴ μεγάλη calls Jesus ὁ ἅγιος τοῦ θεοῦ; similarly the Gerasene Demoniac Ἰησοῦ υἱὲ τοῦ θεοῦ τοῦ ὑψίστου (8,28). One of the lepers (17,15) returns δοξάζων τὸν θεόν in a loud voice. The crowds, rejoicing in a loud voice, acknowledge Jesus as ἐρχόμενος ὁ βασιλεὺς ἐν ὀνόματι κυρίου (19,38).

In the Acts, excluding 7,57 and 16,28, the use of φωνὴ μεγάλη is associated with the deeds done in Christ's name or as a reaction to the

---

[74] Cf. Chapter Four.

[75] Cf. LXX Psalm 30,6 where the address is κύριε ὁ θεὸς τῆς ἀληθείας.

[76] Schützeichel refers to MT passages featuring the voice of the Lord; the LXX parallels do not contain the φωνὴ μεγάλη combination: Amos 1,2; Joel 2,12; 4,16; Jer 25,30; Ps 29,7 ("Der Todesschrei Jesu," *TTZ* 83 [1974]) 4.

[77] Brown, *Messiah* 2; 1045.

[78] Luke 1,42; 4,33; 8,28; 17,15; 19,37; 23,23.46 (*VKGNT* 1/2; 1317-8).

[79] Acts 7,57.60; 8,7; 14,10; 16,28; 26,24 (*VKGNT* 1/2; 1317-8).

[80] Luke 1,42; 4,33; 8,28; 17,15; 19,37; Acts 7,60; 8,7; 14,10 (*VKGNT* 1/2; 1317-8).

proclamation of the resurrection. Stephen utters in the hearing of all κύριε, μὴ στήσῃς αὐτοῖς ταύτην τὴν ἁμαρτίαν (Acts 7,60). The spirits which cry out do so in reaction to the proclamation of the Messiah, though the content of their cries goes unspecified (8,7). When Paul and Barnabas are at Lystra, they command the cripple to rise *in a loud voice* (14,10). Hence, φωνὴ μεγάλη in L-A signifies the recognition of the divine presence.

Psalm 30

The Lucan writer uses the Greek verb παρατίθημι in one of two ways in L-A. In active, middle, and passive voices, παρατίθημι means *to set before another*; in middle voice, however, the verb also has the sense of *placing, depositing*, or *entrusting*.[81]

LXX Psalm 30 appears only in the Lucan death narrative. It opens as a lament and closes as a thanksgiving. The speaker first calls upon the Lord for help; the lament of physical and spiritual distress begins at v 10. It is not included in the *Tamid*. Indeed, it seems to have no cultic function at all, although individual worshipers may have recited lament psalms to accompany their expiatory sacrifices.[82] The Babylonian Talmud advises that a scholar recite MT Psalm 31,6 upon his bed at night.[83] The paraphrase of this particular psalm may also have been included in some early Christian liturgy. Not only does Luke change παρατίθημι from future to present, but he also employs the more intimate πάτερ as the term of address instead of κύριος. That Jesus speaks in a φωνὴ μεγάλη and employs the address, πάτερ, is an assertion of divine sonship.

Calling attention to Luke 9,44 where Jesus states that the Son of Man will be handed over (παραδίδοσθαι) into human hands, Brown notes that in 23,46 *Jesus places* his whole being (παρατίθεμαι τὸ πνεῦμά μου) into the hands of the

---

[81] BAGD 622-23. The Lucan occurrences are almost evenly divided in their usage with three instances showing παρατίθημι with food (Luke 9,16; 11,6; Acts 16,34) or even as food itself (Luke 10,8) [*VKGNT* 1/2; 1088]), and five cases where the term means *to place, deposit, entrust* (Luke 12,48; 23,46 and Acts 14,23; 17,3; 20,32 [*VKGNT* 1/2; 1088]). It is certainly possible that the Lucan writer is making a Eucharistic allusion in this verse, but several points suggest that such is not the case.

First, in the four cases where παρατίθημι appears in the middle voice, the context and grammar support the conclusion that this verb can only mean *entrust* or *place*. Second, in v 46 παρατίθημι is part of a paraphrase of LXX Ps 30,6 in which this verb appears as a future middle and where it signifies to *entrust* or *deposit*. Third, there is nothing in the psalm, either in the LXX or MT, to suggest anything concerning food. Fourth, the addressee is πάτερ for whom food is unnecessary. Hence, it seems that this verse has no Eucharistic overtones.

[82] H.H. Rowley, *Worship in Ancient Israel* (Philadelphia: Fortress Press, 1967) 179.

[83] *Babylonian Talmud*, Tractate Berakoth, 5a (ed. I. Epstein, 1; London: Soncino Press, 1961) 16.

Father; thus he brings his whole life and mission to their place of origin, the Spirit.[84] Furthermore, Brown holds that with the direct address, πάτερ, Luke maintains the level of Christ's trust in the Father's providence; Jesus makes the same appeal in his prayer on the Mount of Olives (22,42) and at the crucifixion (23,34). Brown sees this prayer as Luke's way of impressing upon Jesus' followers the proper sentiments as they face death.[85] But what are these sentiments?

The term πάτερ links three episodes, the agony, crucifixion, and death. Each of these scenes intensifies Jesus' ordeal, ranging from fear of the approaching death, through the tortured pain on the cross, to the death itself. At every moment there is not only a reliance on the Father, but also a steady refusal to succumb to the dominion of darkness. Jesus does not escape the Father's will (22,42), he forgives rather than curse his persecutors (23,34a), and he trusts rather than abandon all hope (23,46). In this manner, Jesus wages combat against the diabolical force, and herein lies the marrow of the whole Lucan corpus.

Christ the ministering angel

In employing LXX Psalm 30,6 for Jesus' final prayer and, in a sense, his final act, Luke reinterprets the *ministering angel* tradition. True, Jesus has fought the *diabolical force*; the darkness, the rending of the curtain, and eschatological imagery attest to the fact. On the other hand, there are no angelic hosts meeting the *diabolical force* on the battlefield. Instead, Luke attributes to Christ those qualities of the *ministering angel* described in the *T. 12 Patr*, a fact which hinges on the address, "Father". Christ becomes the mediator between God and humanity who opposes the enemy (*T. Dan* 6,2-3)[86], an enemy who wishes to "trip up" those calling on the Lord because he knows that on the day in which Israel does so, "the enemy's kingdom will be brought to an end" (*T. Dan* 6,4). This mediator, a new priest, binds Beliar (*T. Levi* 18,2-14).[87] Furthermore, in *Jub.* 15,30-32[88] the savior of Israel is identified as the Lord God alone.[89]

Noting the emphasis on Jesus' prayer and the imminence of his passion at the transfiguration, both Reid[90] and Murphy-O'Connor[91] observe the connection

---

[84] Brown, *Messiah* 2; 1068.

[85] Brown, *Messiah* 2; 1068.

[86] *OTPseud* 1; 810.

[87] *OTPseud* 1; 794-5. Cf. also Isa 24,21-23; *T. Sim.* 6,5-6 (*OTPseud* 1; 787); *T. Zeb.* 9,8 (*OTPseud* 1; 807).

[88] *OTPseud* 2; 87.

[89] Cf. Chapter Two.

[90] Reid also notes the sleepiness of the disciples as a literary thread (9,32; 22,45) [*Transfiguration* 96].

this event has with the agony on the Mount of Olives. The prayer in 23,46, therefore, also recalls the agony, and hence, hearkens back to the transfiguration. Satan's dominion of darkness has eclipsed the sun and cast a pall over the whole world. Yet, Satan cannot force Christ to curse or despair; rather, Christ trusts in the Father to the very end, and by doing so, he is transfigured. The witness account (23,47-49) supports this assumption.

Précis

Luke relies on a qumranic tradition in which the dualism between light and darkness is made absolute. Hence, unlike 2 *Enoch* 67, the Lord does not usher in the darkness. Throughout the Lucan corpus, the phrase φωνὴ μεγάλη is associated with proclamations of the divine sonship of Jesus or works done in his name. A scholar's bedtime prayer, according to the Babylonian Talmud, the quotation from LXX Psalm 30,6 may also have been part of an early Christian liturgy. The use of the direct address, πάτερ, shows Christ asserting divine sonship while maintaining trust in the Father's care; it is Jesus' weapon against the *diabolical force*. The prayer is also a reinterpretation of the *ministering angel* tradition. In addition, the address in the prayer serves to connect the death to the crucifixion, the agony, and most importantly, to the transfiguration.

The Witnesses

Luke 23,47

47a Ἰδὼν δὲ ὁ ἑκατοντάρχης τὸ γενόμενον ἐδόξαζεν τὸν θεὸν b λέγων, Ὄντως ὁ ἄνθρωπος οὗτος δίκαιος ἦν.

In 2 *Enoch* 67 the crowd glorifies God as it departs. In Luke, the crowd also departs, but the Roman official has the role of glorifying God.

The declaration of the Roman centurion constitutes the first reaction to the death of Jesus; proclaiming Jesus as *just* becomes an act of glorification, and at this verse, the Ezekiel and Zechariah prophecies, the readings from Wisdom, the ascension of Enoch, and the transfiguration all find their focus.

The centurion himself has a dual purpose in the story. On the historical level, the presence of Roman soldiers is to be expected; one can reasonably assume that the soldiers, who first appear in the passion narrative at 23,26, would be under the charge of a centurion. This foreign, pagan officer, in praising God, becomes a literary foil to the departing, breast-beating crowd of local Jews. On the theological level, in the Lucan corpus, centurions usually appear in a positive light,[92] an important fact for discerning the role of this Roman officer, who, as the representative of the occupying power, glorifies God by saying that a

---

[91] Murphy-O'Connor, "Transfiguration" 8-21, esp. 21.

[92] The only possible exception to this statement is Acts 27,11.

crucified man was δίκαιος.

That which the centurion observes, τὸ γενόμενον, extends to all the events of the passion for which the soldiers were present, the trial, the mockeries, the contact with the people, the crucifixion with the wrongdoers, the darkness, and most importantly, the death.[93]   These events, according to Luke, cause the centurion not simply to make a declaration but to glorify God,[94] a concept which is influenced by the OT.   Thus, several Hebrew terms convey three basic ideas which bear on ἐδόξαζεν τὸν θεόν in v 47.   The verbs, כבד (niph, piel),[95] and קדשׁ (niph)[96] are similar in that the concept of *honor* or *be honored* is part of their definition; אדר (niph),[97] נשׂא (niph),[98] and רוּם (pil)[99] signify *to be high* or *exalted*; and נוה (hiph)[100] and תִּפְאֶרֶת (cstr),[101] *to beautify* and *beauty*.   On this basis, δοξάζω means *to honor, exalt,* or *beautify*; the context in v 47 favors the former two.   The resolution of a much larger issue rests on whether δίκαιος signifies *innocent* or *just*.

δίκαιος: *Innocent or just?*

Brown delineates three possible ways to interpret the term δίκαιος, ways which are not mutually exclusive.[102]   The first is its use in the Book of Wisdom,

---

[93] For a grammatical and syntactical discussion on τὸ γενόμενον, cf. Chapter 4.

[94] Of the fourteen occurrences of the verb δοξάζω in L-A, the verb has θεός as its object eleven times, more than any other evangelist; it is a phrase peculiar to Luke (Luke 2,20; 5,25.26; 7,16; 13,13; 17,15; 18,43; 23,47; Acts 4,21; 11,18; 21,20; but cf. Luke 4,15; Acts 3,13; 13,48 [*VKGNT* 1/1; 258-259]).   By definition, δοξάζω signifies *praise, honor,* or *magnify* [BAGD 204], and whereas the MT uses 14 different verbs to describe *honor* or *praise*, the LXX employs only δοξάζω [HR 343-4].   In those ten instances in which the object of the verb δοξάζω is θεός or its referent, the Greek verb represents six Hebrew verbs and one noun (Exod 15,2.6; Lev 10,3; Judg 9,9; LXX 1 Kgs 2,30; Isa 5,16; 25,1; 43,23; 66,5 [HR 343-4]).

[95] BDB 457.

[96] BDB 873.

[97] BDB 12.

[98] BDB 671.

[99] BDB 926-7.

[100] BDB 627.

[101] BDB 802.

[102] Brown, *Messiah* 2; 1165-7.

particularly Wis 3,1.[103]   The second is the employment of δίκαιος as an early christological title based on the ideal king from the Davidic line[104] and its use in the description of the Suffering Servant in Isa 53,11.   The third is within the centurion's confession itself, which fits into a chain of conversions from considering Jesus as guilty to holding him innocent.   This chain begins with Pontius Pilate and Herod and continues through the symbolic portrayal of the Cyrenean carrying the cross and the request of one of the crucified wrongdoers; the centurion is the last of the conversions.[105]   In addition, Brown calls attention to Simeon's statement about Christ's being a light of revelation to the Gentiles (2,32).[106]   Thus, the pagan centurion in 23,47 becomes an example of one who has received the revelation.[107]

Tyson concludes that because the theme of innocence dominates the entire trial, the centurion declares Christ so in this verse.[108]   Hence, Tyson consistently translates δίκαιος as "innocent".   Tyson, preferring this reading, maintains that Jesus' innocence was recognized and affirmed by the Roman governor and by Herod but not by the Jewish leaders and people.[109]   Tyson's interpretation does not take into account the broader meaning associated with the term.   Lagrange, developing the juxtaposition of the pagan leaders with their Jewish counterparts, believes that δίκαιος is too strong a word for *innocent*, especially because Luke states that the centurion "glorified God".   Thus, Lagrange concludes that the centurion, believing a martyr's death to be glory to God, sees in Jesus the perfect, just one.[110]

According to Luke, the centurion honors God by his declaration.   The twofold, nearly identical, sense of the word δίκαιος, would seem like a negligible distinction[111] were it not for the literary tradition which informs each of its two meanings.

The Old Testament

The overwhelming use of צדק in the MT establishes a predominant concern with justice and righteousness[112] over innocence or guiltlessness (נָקִי,

---

[103] Brown, *Messiah* 2; 1165.

[104] Cf. Jer 23,5; LXX Zech 9,9; LXX Ps Sol 17,32.

[105] Brown, *Messiah* 2; 1166-7.

[106] Brown, *Messiah* 2; 1167.

[107] Brown, *Messiah* 2; 1167.

[108] Tyson, *Death* 137-9.

[109] Tyson, *Death* 137.

[110] Lagrange, *Luc* 593.

[111] Cf. Karris (*Artist* 110-1).

נְקִיא).[113] In the LXX, δίκαιος is used for both "just" and "innocent"; thus the distinction between the two, so evident in the Hebrew, is lost in the Greek.[114] Certain OT works, particularly but not exclusively the later ones, make this point clearer.

The LXX Job features two occurrences in which δίκαιος describes the innocence of the protagonist, 9,23; 17,8. The 36 other instances of δίκαιος emphasize justice or righteousness.[115] In chapter 9, Job speaks in terms of a lawsuit; in this case, no mortal can be just (v 2) before the Lord. This point is reiterated at vv 20 and 22 so that at v 23, Job is not speaking about himself personally. When he refers to the innocent, נְקִיִּם, he means that they, guiltless of any crime, may also be just. Similarly in 17,8, Job alludes to the outrage of the upright and innocent who view his condition; he does not call himself innocent.

Later works

The Wisdom of Solomon exists only in the LXX. The use of δίκαιος in this book is almost exclusively in terms of the *just*; most evident in this regard is Wis 2,10-3,1 where δίκαιος occurs five times. The description of the righteous individual, outlined in this section,[116] is echoed at more than one place in the PN: cf. Wis 2,12a and Luke 22,2; Wis 2,13.16d and Luke 22,70-71; 23,2; Wis 2,18 and Luke 23,35.39; Wis 2,20 and Luke 23,21.23; Wis 3,1 and Luke 23,46.

This last point, the parallel between Wis 3,1 and Luke 23,46, is most important. Christ's last words receive amplification from the centurion who glorifies God in v 47 by drawing attention to the righteous one who has placed himself in the hands of God and died which, as both Boismard[117] and Murphy-O'Connor indicate,[118] is specified in Wis 3,2 by the term ἔξοδος. Furthermore, according to Senior, that Luke shows Christ as true to God's plan to the end makes Jesus the just and faithful one described in Wis 3,9.[119]

Other verses from the Book of Wisdom elucidate the Lucan quotation.

---

[112] BDB 842-3.

[113] BDB 667.

[114] Twelve Hebrew terms in the MT, with derivatives increasing the total to eighteen, are translated by δίκαιος in the LXX (HR 330-2).

[115] LXX Job 34,10 shows δίκαιος as part of a construction expressing wrongdoing, ταράξαι τὸ δίκαιον. The parallel passage in the MT utilizes עָוֶל, injustice or unrighteousness.

[116] With particular attention to 2,12.16.18, and 3,1.

[117] Boismard, *Synopse* 2; 253.

[118] Murphy-O'Connor, "Transfiguration" 18.

[119] Senior, *Passion* 146.

Wisdom 2,12.13.18 not only reflect the accusations and mockeries leveled at Christ, but also provide a key to the logic of the Lucan quotation. The righteous one (2,12) claims to have knowledge of God and calls himself a child (παῖς) of God (2,13); the understanding in Wisdom is that God will deliver his child from the hand of adversaries.[120] Hence, for Luke, to be the just one is thereby to be the Son of God.[121]

Lucan usage

How Luke employs δίκαιος in other sections of his corpus[122] coincides with its application in the late OT, particularly septugintal literature. The use of δίκαιος in the parable of the Lost Sheep best explains its sense throughout L-A. In Luke 15,7, ninety-nine righteous persons are likened to one sinner. Such a comparison would seem to place δίκαιος in opposition to "sinner" and thereby give the meaning *innocent* to the term, but the context of the parable of the Lost Sheep precludes that possibility. This parable, as well as the following parables of the Lost Coin, Prodigal Son, Dishonest Steward, Rich Man and Lazarus are not situated in a discussion about the law. Indeed, Jesus explicitly states that the law and prophets were in effect until John came (16,16); hence, the legal measure of righteousness no longer exists. The new standard then, introduced by the Baptist, is one of character. One who is δίκαιος is not innocent of transgressing the law, although that is certainly a part of the picture, but is above legal calculation. Such is the meaning of *just* and *upright*. *To be just* is to have that quality which the angel, speaking to Zechariah about John, calls "...the mind of the righteous" (1,17); in this sense, more than in any other OT or septugintal work, Luke follows the understanding of δίκαιος found in the Book of Wisdom.[123]

---

[120] This is the significance behind the Matt/Mark versions of the derision on the cross (n.b. Matt 27,38-43 and Mark 15,27-32, but esp. Matt 27,40.43) as well as the centurion's statement in both Matt 27,54 and Mark 15,39. The point is that the Son of God will be protected by God.

[121] Brown develops this point as well (*Messiah* 2; 1165). Furthermore, I call attention to the notion of δίκαιος as developed in Maccabees, where the term is more closely associated with righteousness than with innocence (cf 2 Macc 1,24-25; 3 Macc 2,3.22; 4 Macc 2,23). Righteousness in turn becomes correct religious behavior (4 Macc 9,6; 13,24; 15,10; 18,15) and standard of a righteous life (4 Macc 16,21) as well as a divine attribute (2 Macc 12,6).

[122] Luke 1,6.17; 2,25; 5,32; 12,57; 14,14; 15,7; 18,9; 20,20; 23,47; 23,50; Acts 3,14; 4,19; 7,52; 10,22; 22,14; 24,15 (*VKGNT* 1/1; 250-1).

[123] Cf. also Craig A. Evans who draws attention to Luke 1,35 where the angel states that Jesus will be called the Son of God [*Luke and Scripture* (Minneapolis: Fortress Press, 1993) 39]; naturally, the Son of God would be just. It is also possible to see here another connection to Wis 2,13, παῖδα κυρίου ἑαυτὸν ὀνομάζει.

Lucan redaction

Luke rewrites the Marcan version of the centurion's statement, "Truly, this man is a son of God" (Mark 15,39) in order to reflect several concerns. First, on the apologetic level, δικαίος serves to underscore that Christ was innocent of any crime. Second, δικαίος reaffirms the connection Christ's death has with Wis 3,1-2; "...the souls of the righteous are in the hand of God..." though "...in the eyes of the foolish they seemed to have died". Indeed, δικαίος reinforces the connection with all of Wis 2,10-3,9. Third, with δικαίος, Luke alludes to OT issues of justice and righteousness present in the Hebrew צדק. Fourth, through the Book of Wisdom, the assertion of divine sonship, present in Mark/Matt, can be maintained, "...the righteous man...calls himself a child of the Lord" (Wis 2,12-13). By changing the Marcan quotation, Luke is able to assert Jesus' divine sonship as well as place Jesus' death within the broader context of the Book of Wisdom and the Old Testament figure of the righteous individual. These are the reasons Luke changes the quotation found in Mark 15,39.

δοξάζω

In all the Lucan instances, someone praises God or Jesus when there has been a revelation or experience of salvific power; in only three instances in the Lucan corpus does δοξάζω not have θεός as its object.[124] The centurion, then, after observing all the events from the trial to the crucifixion, undergoes a revelatory experience or epiphany.

The centurion's declaration represents an early christological statement. To be sure, Jesus is innocent of any crime; the interrogations before Pilate and Herod are indicative of that fact. Of greater importance is the portrayal of Jesus. As in the Book of Wisdom, Jesus is God's son because he acts as the Just One to the very end.[125] This is what the centurion observes, and because the centurion has received this revelation, in true Lucan form, he glorifies God.[126] This verse, however, cannot be removed from its historical context: A man innocent of any crime was put to death. On this purely historical level of understanding, the centurion is merely stating the obvious about a miscarriage of justice. Even here, however, an early Church apologetic is at work. If Christ were guilty of a capital crime, so also were his followers. G. D. Fitzpatrick demonstrates that declarations of innocence by all the leading Roman authorities obviate the charge.[127] Luke, developing this simple declaration of innocence into an

---

[124] Luke 4,15 shows "Jesus"; Acts 3,13, "Jesus," also referred to as τὸν παῖδα αὐτου; and Acts 13,48, λόγον τοῦ κυρίου.

[125] Cf. Luke 23,46 and LXX Wis 3,1. Cf. also above for the discussion on Mark 15,39 (Chapter Four).

[126] I think this explanation is preferable to Crump's which sees τὸ γενόμενον as a reference to Christ's prayer and as such is the reason the centurion declares Jesus "just" (90).

[127] G. D. Fitzpatrick, "A Theme of the Lucan Passion Story and Luke

assertion of human righteousness, by making allusions to the Book of Wisdom, also links it to divine sonship.

The centurion's declaration also provides the literary balance to the rending of the temple veil, which itself is influenced by OT prophecies. The reading from Zechariah describes the coming day of the Lord (14,4ff), while that from Ezekiel sees the glory of the Lord ascending from the middle of Jerusalem and resting on the Mount of Olives (11,23). Zechariah continues the prophecy with a description of a time when there will be "continuous day" (14,7ff). Ezekiel then depicts the returning of the same glory to the temple (43,2-4). Luke specifically states that the darkness lasts until the ninth hour; one can assume that the light returns at that moment.[128] Indeed, if 2 Enoch 67 is the prototype for Luke 23,44-49, then Luke implies as much.

Luke 23,44-45b portrays an apocalyptic vision of darkness; God's glory departs ($\sigma\chi\acute{\iota}\zeta o\mu\alpha\iota$). Christ cries out, $\phi\omega\nu\tilde{\eta}$ $\mu\varepsilon\gamma\acute{\alpha}\lambda\eta$, and ushers in the eschaton. This pattern, which Luke is following, parallels the presentation of the temple in Ezekiel where the divine presence leaves the temple temporarily (Ezek 10,4.18) only to be restored later (Ezek 40-48).[129] Luke also makes allusions to the final apocalyptic battle by drawing on Zech 14. Luke goes further than Ezekiel and Zechariah, however; the tearing of the temple curtain becomes a proclamation of a realized visitation -- good news for all people.

According to Ezek 43,2-4 and Zech 14,7ff, the eschaton sees God's glorification.[130] The Lucan text reads that the centurion glorified God. Is Luke referring to the glory which Peter, John, and James observe in Jesus at the transfiguration (9,31-32), when Moses and Elijah speak to him about his $\H\varepsilon\xi o\delta o\varsigma$ which according to Wis 3,2 is death?

Transfiguration

The use of the verb $\delta o\xi\acute{\alpha}\zeta\omega$ in 23,47 suggests that Luke interprets the death of Jesus through the transfiguration. When Jesus, Moses, and Elijah stand in glory, they speak about Jesus' departure to Jerusalem, the place of his death (9,30-32). The key for this interpretation rests with $\sigma\chi\acute{\iota}\zeta o\mu\alpha\iota$ and $\H\varepsilon\xi o\delta o\varsigma$. Boismard interprets the term $\H\varepsilon\xi o\delta o\varsigma$ in Wis 3,2 as *death*, a "passage through the land to God".[131] This point is further refined in Luke 9,51 with the term

---

23,47," *JTS* 52-3 (1941-42) 35.

[128] Why Luke does not specifically mention that the light returns, whereas it does in both 2 Enoch 67 and *Gos. Pet* 22, is treated below.

[129] Walthar Zimmerli outlines this restoration, *Ezechiel* (Neukirchen-Vluyn: Neukirchener Verlag, 1969) 976-1249. This point is underscored by Xavier Léon-Dufour, "Temple," *Vocabulaire de Théologie Biblique* (Paris: Les Éditions du Cerf, 1970) 1269.

[130] N.b. even Enoch is carried to heaven to gaze upon the face of God for all eternity (2 Enoch 67,2) [*OTPseud* 195].

[131] Boismard, *Synopse* 2; 253. Cf also Murphy-O'Connor, "Transfiguration" 18.

ἀνάλημψις,[132] where Jesus sets his face toward Jerusalem, the place of his death.[133]

In Wis 3,2 the term ἔξοδος may signify death, but the term also resonates with an event viewed as one of the most fundamental in Jewish history. The Exodus was a passage from death to life made possible when the sea was split in the middle (σχίζομαι, μέσος; LXX Exod 14,21-22). In addition, the Mount of Olives splits (σχίζομαι; LXX Zech 14,4) allowing the inhabitants of Jerusalem to escape to safety while the Lord battles the nations. Luke has developed this apocalyptic encounter into a war against the *diabolical force*,[134] a battle which reaches its highest pitch in 23,44-45. *Diabolical force* and passion imagery are also found in events surrounding the transfiguration, particularly in the commissioning of the twelve with power over demons (9,1), in the passage about Herod's search for Jesus (9,7-9), and in the notice about Jesus setting his face towards Jerusalem (9,31.51). Hence, when Christ cries out φωνῇ μεγάλῃ, he signals the day of the Lord when on earth the Lord's glory will shine all around (Ezek 43,2).

This link between the transfiguration and the death may seem to be implied more than explicit, but other factors undergird the connection. The centurion proclaims Jesus as *just* soon after seeing what had taken place (τὸ γενόμενον), the death. Thus, it is the death which glorifies God; the centurion is merely calling attention to the fact. Moreover, Reid notes, "...the transfiguration...answers the question posed in 9,9, 'Who is this?'"[135] The centurion responds to the same query. With the term δίκαιος, heavily influenced by the Book of Wisdom, the centurion declares Jesus as the Son of God,[136] a status confirmed after the death. Hence, Jesus is identified as the Son of God by his death because, by that same death, he is transfigured into glory. The remaining verses in the death account reflect such an understanding.

Elianic tradition

These allusions to the transfiguration also connect Jesus to Elijah, the other OT personage who is assumed into heaven (2 Kgs 2,11). Does Luke

---

[132] *Ascension* but also *death* (BAGD 57).

[133] Boismard, *Synopse* 2; 253.

[134] Cf. above, Chapter Two.

[135] Reid, *Transfiguration* 142-3. In addition, both Murphy-O'Connor ("Transfiguration") and Reid (*Transfiguration* 31-77) demonstrate that the redaction of Luke 9,28-36 reflects a weaving of Marcan and Lucan material in a manner similar to that outlined above in Chapter Four for the death account. Boismard in his analysis also distinguishes various levels of redaction in Luke 9, 28-36 incorporating material from Documents A, B, C, and proto-Luke (*Synopse* 2; 250-3).

[136] Cf. the passages parallel to Luke 23,47 in Mark 15,39 and Matt 27,54.

incorporate intertestamental works involving Elijah's ascension into his account of Christ's death? The evidence to date does not suggest so. O.S. Wintermute sees the *Apocalypse of Elijah* as a "composite work containing both Jewish and Christian materials".[137] David Frankfurter supports this view.[138] One can see this Jewish and Christian mix, for example, in *Apoc. Elijah* 4,27 which features both Enoch and Elijah, yet has at least one reference to Christ (4,27). In addition, Wintermute affirms that the martyrdom sequence is "strongly influenced" by the martyrdom described in Revelation 11,1-12.[139] In any case, there is no thematic or prototypical material in the *Apoc. Elijah* which even hints at an echo to the Lucan death account.

The Coptic text of the *Apoc. Elijah* undergirds Wintermute's opinion.[140] Not only is the Coptic version replete with references to Christ (12,10-20; 18,15-19,5; 20,5), but Albert Pietersma, relying on A.F. Shore, dates it to the end of the fourth or beginning of the fifth century AD.[141] Even the *Vita Eliae* is "Christian in authorship".[142] Furthermore, a collection of texts and fragments attributed to Elijah does not include descriptions of the prophet's ascension.[143]

One cannot deny, however, that there is an Elianic influence on L-A. Richard Dillon displays the bearing Elijah has on the Lucan narrative with particular attention toward the ascension accounts in the gospel (24,50-53) and Acts (1,6-11).[144] Dillon also observes that the language of Acts 1,9-11 is "borrowed" from the Elijah texts.[145] In addition, Thomas Brodie holds that if Luke is a Hellenistic writer, then Luke is true to the Hellenistic tradition by maintaining the procedure of *mimesis* or *imitatio* in following 1 Kgs 17,1-2 Kgs 8,15.[146] Brodie sees this *mimesis* particularly in Luke 4,16-30; 7,11-17 [1 Kgs

---

[137] Wintermute, *OTPseud* 1; 730.

[138] David Frankfurter, *Elijah in Upper Egypt; the Apocalypse of Elijah and Early Egyptian Christianity* (Minneapolis: Fortress Press, 1993) 18-20.

[139] Wintermute, *OTPseud* 1; 725.

[140] Albert Pietersma and Susan Turner Comstock with Harold W. Attridge, trans., *The Apocalypse of Elijah based on P. Chester Beatty 2018* (Chico, California: Scholars Press, 1981).

[141] Pietersma, *Elijah* 6.

[142] Michael Stone and John Strugnell, eds. and trans., *The Books of Elijah, Parts 1 and 2* (Missoula, Montana: Scholars Press, 1979) 99.

[143] Stone, *Elijah*.

[144] Richard Dillon, *From Eye-witnesses to Ministers of the Word* (AnBib 82; Rome: Biblical Institute Press, 1978) 177-82.

[145] Dillon, *Eye-witnesses* 177.

[146] Thomas Brodie, "Luke-Acts as an Imitation and Emulation of the Elijah-Elisha Narrative," *New Views on Luke and Acts* (ed. Earl Richard; Collegeville, Minnesota: The Liturgical Press, 1990) 79.

17,17-24]; 9,51-56 [2 Kgs 1,1-2,6]; Acts 6,9-14.7,58a [1 Kgs 21,8-13][147] where a "...systematic dependence on the Elijah-Elisha story is an important factor."[148] In fact, Brodie maintains that there is "direct dependence on the Elijah-Elisha story for Luke-Acts' overall plan."[149]

The influence of the Elijah-Elisha cycle on the Lucan narrative as outlined by both Dillon and Brodie is convincing. Of particular interest here is the Elianic role in the Lucan ascension account.[150] While Luke may have used 2 Kgs 2,11-12 in constructing the ascension accounts, the evangelist employs 2 *Enoch* 67 to connect them with the death narrative. With this *imitatio*, one from the pseudepigraphic corpus and the other from the canonical one, Luke draws on two venerable traditions and thus allows for greater resonance wherever the gospel is preached.

Précis

The first reaction to Christ's death comes from a pagan centurion, an historical note developed into a theological point. The declaration itself, δίκαιος, has two levels of meaning. The first, within the historical and forensic sphere, is *innocent*. The second and more important for L-A, based on the Book of Wisdom, is *just*, a fact which also establishes the claim to divine sonship. The septuagintal and intertestamental tradition, particularly through the terms ἔξοδος in Wis 3,2-3, and σχίζομαι in Exod 14,21 and Zech 14,4 as well as the thematic elements in Ezek 11,23; 43,2ff and Zech 14,7ff depict a death-yields-to-life paradox. The centurion glorifies God, a glorification which Luke foreshadows in Jesus' transfiguration (9,28-36), and which is realized in his death here. In addition, the transfiguration also highlights the Elianic tradition which influences the Lucan ascension accounts.

Luke 23,48

[48a]καὶ πάντες οἱ συμπαραγενόμενοι ὄχλοι [b]ἐπὶ τὴν θεωρίαν ταύτην, θεωρήσαντες τὰ γενόμενα, [c]τύπτοντες τὰ στήθη [d]ὑπέστρεφον.

The participle συμπαραγενόμενος, in addition to meaning *coming together*, also conveys *coming together to the aid of someone*.[151] That the Lucan writer specifies that the crowd had gathered to see the spectacle, however,

---

[147] Brodie, *Imitation* 80-1.

[148] Brodie, *Imitation* 82.

[149] Brodie, *Imitation* 85.

[150] Cf. Brodie's outline (*Imitation* 83).

[151] BAGD 779.

suggests that the participle here retains its primary definition. The following phrase underscores this fact. The crowd came together to see the spectacle, and once they saw *what had taken place*, they departed. The crowd itself, unique to Luke, is the second element in a tripartite structure which, as Brown notes, matches the three parties who react to Jesus on the way to his execution.[152] In 23,26-31 the three include Simon, a multitude, and the Daughters of Jerusalem; in 23,44-49 they are the centurion, the crowd, and the Galilean women.

The phrase τύπτοντες τὰ στήθη marks a redactional seam which calls attention to the ascension of Enoch (*2 Enoch* 67).

> [3]And the people looked, and they understood how Enoch had been taken away. And they glorified God. And they went away into their homes.[153]

In *2 Enoch*, the people *look, understand, glorify*, and *return*. In Luke 23,48, those in the crowd observe the spectacle and depart beating their breasts; they neither understand nor glorify. It is plausible that a primitive version of Luke's gospel ended at this point[154] with the crowd, as in *2 Enoch*, understanding the happenings (τὰ γενόμενα) and glorifying God as they return (ὑποστρέφω). Several factors make this proposition likely.

First, Luke 23,44-47, in the tradition of Ezekiel and Zechariah, relates a departure and a return of God's glory. Included in the narrative is a confessional statement in confirmation of divine sonship. Second, the φωνῇ μεγάλη construction ushers in the eschaton while Jesus' prayer connects the agony and death to the transfiguration. Third, ἔξοδος (9,31) and ἀνάλημψις (ascension) [9,51] connote death. Fourth, both the people in *2 Enoch* 67 and the centurion in Luke 23,47 glorify God after observing what has taken place. Fifth, people watch Jesus in both accounts of the ascension (Luke 24,52; Acts 1,9) and after the phenomenon, they return (ὑποστρέφω in each) to Jerusalem. At that moment they are either filled with joy (Luke 24,52), or are mystified and resort to prayer (Acts 1,10-14).

For the death and the ascension narratives, the characters are nearly parallel (witnesses to the passion, death, or resurrection), the setting (Jerusalem/Mount of Olives) is thematically linked (Ezekiel, Zechariah), and the action is exactly the same (return to Jerusalem). Furthermore, the phrase τύπτοντες τὰ στήθη is the only piece which gives a negative coloring to vv 48-49, and it is the subject of textual difficulties.[155] Therefore, Luke 24,52 and Acts 1,12 are a reprise of Luke 23,48; a primitive version of the third gospel viewed the crucifixion and death as the moment of Christ's glorification.[156] To

---

[152] Brown, *Messiah* 2; 1196.

[153] *OTPseud* 1; 195.

[154] Included in this statement is material from v 49.

[155] The same holds true for ὑποστρέφω; cf. Chapter Three.

[156] N.b. the similarity this understanding has with John 19,28-30. Zwiep rightly sees in the Lucan ascension accounts elements of Jewish rapture theology of which *2 Enoch* 67 is a prime example (*Ascension* 49-51).

be sure, the Lucan ascension pericopes seem to be a *mimesis* of Elijah's ascension in the whirlwind, but whereas Enoch's ascension is the cause of God's glorification, Elijah's is not. Here then, with the influence from *2 Enoch* 67, Luke makes a statement of Jesus' divine sonship.

Omission of the light

Why should a Lucan redactor add accounts of the burial, resurrection, and ascension? Although a thorough examination of these pericopes is beyond the scope of this study, it may be suggested briefly that the early community needed to elaborate the resurrection event, itself a "fixed point", and herein lies the explanation for why Luke does not specifically mention the light's return, although it does so in *2 Enoch* 67.

If the Lucan gospel, with its concomitant idea of glorification and transfiguration, at some point in its developmental history ended at 23,48-49, it soon became necessary for a successive generation to know fully the concepts of glorification and transfiguration. The resurrection and ascension accounts provided the material, and, to do this, it was necessary to re-write vv 48-49, hence the cumbersome style of v 48. The phrase τύπτοντες τὰ στήθη was added to open the narrative for the inclusion of the resurrection and ascension accounts, pericopes replete with the "light" of visitation and revelation. The resurrected Christ becomes the permanent light of the world.[157] The addition of τύπτοντες τὰ στήθη is not merely gratuitous, however; in noting that the people in the crowd depart beating their breast, Luke makes a theological statement.

Striking the breast

In the LXX, στῆθος occurs nine times;[158] the parallel passages in MT show three different terms matching the Greek word[159] which are not interchangeable. The physical and symbolic sense of the Hebrew term לֵב is characterized in Exod 28,29.30. The heart, besides being a physical organ, is

---

[157] Zwiep notes that Luke 24,50-53 and Acts 1,9-12, unlike *2 Enoch* 67, do not mention the presence of darkness. For this reason, he sees *2 Enoch* 67 and the Lucan ascension accounts as representing "two independent rapture traditions" (*Ascension* 50). It is the presence of the darkness in Luke 23,44-49, however, which grounds *2 Enoch* 67 as the literary and theological model for the Lucan death narrative. To be sure, Zwiep is correct in seeing a rapture christology in L-A for which the ascension plays a primary role, but that ascension comes at the death. In other words, at the earliest level of the tradition, the death of Jesus was originally interpreted as the rapture. In the final redaction, Luke explained that point by writing the ascension accounts.

[158] HR 1290.

[159] גָּחוֹן, belly (BDB 161); חֲזֵי, breast (Aramaic [BDB 1092]); לֵב, heart (BDB 524).

also the place of thought and emotion.[160]   The Greek στῆθος, while literally signifying *breast* and *chest*, is the *seat of inner life* as well.[161]   The στῆθος is distinct from κοιλία which represents the *body cavity* or the *innermost recesses of the human body*; though a variation between κοιλία and καρδία is possible, the nine occurrences of κοιλία in the Lucan corpus are restricted to *womb*.[162]   Thus an emotional element is highlighted when Luke speaks of the crowd beating their breasts: The physical chest is also the seat of inner life.

The verb τύπτω, *strike* or *beat*, most often expresses a physical attack against another.[163]   τύπτω parallels the meanings of the Hebrew verbs חלק (hiph), נגף, כרת, and נכה;[164] Luke employs it more frequently than the other evangelists.[165]   In the LXX, 1 Kgs 1,8, having no parallel in the MT, is the one septuagintal occurrence in which τύπτω signifies an emotional setback, figuratively, a blow to the heart.   The Lucan use, however, describes a physical strike in every case.   Only twice in the NT, and never in the OT, is τύπτω coupled with στῆθος, Luke 18,13 and 23,48.

The parable of the Pharisee and the Publican (Luke 18,9-14) provides the interpretation for the phrase, *striking the breast*.   The repentant tax collector, acknowledging his sinfulness, begs forgiveness and is justified.   That Luke 18,9-14 links beating the breast with acknowledgement of sinfulness and request for forgiveness strongly suggests a similar attitude for the crowd in 23,48.[166]   They depart from the crucifixion beating their breasts because they realize the sinfulness of their actions.   Verse 48 also unites the reaction to Jesus' death with his own prayer in 23,34.

In terms of the narrative, the Lucan writer has the people return; judging from the address to the Daughters of Jerusalem (Luke 23,27-31) the crowd presumably re-enters that city.   If so, Luke seems to be setting the stage for the crowds to be present there at pentecost.   As Peter explains the events of the past fifty days to the people in Jerusalem (Acts 2,14-36), he tells them to repent and to be baptized for the forgiveness of sins, which they do (Acts 2,41).   Luke 23,48, then is not exhibiting the reaction of a faithless people who have knowingly committed a wrong and resign themselves to their fate, nor is it a precursor to the destruction of Jerusalem.   The verse depicts, rather, a people

---

[160] BDB 525.

[161] BAGD 767.

[162] Cf. Luke 1,15.41.42.44; 2,21; 11,27; 23,29; Acts 3,2; 14,8; but Luke 15,16 (variant) where it means *belly* (*VKGNT* 1/1; 695).

[163] BAGD 830.

[164] HR 1378.

[165] Cf. Luke 6,29; 12,45; 18,13; 22,64 (variant); 23,48; Acts 18,17; 21,32; 23,2.3(bis).   Matthew witnesses it twice, 24,49; 27,30; and Mark once, 15,19 (*VKGNT* 1/2; 1270-1).

[166] Brown sees a similar parallel between this parable and 23,48 (*Messiah* 2; 1168).

who realize the sinfulness of their actions and now beg God's mercy which, in terms of the story line, is poured out at pentecost. As Henry Wansbrough observes, the theme of repentance and forgiveness permeates the Lucan death narrative.[167]

Précis

Verse 48, a redactional seam, echoes a similar passage in *2 Enoch* 67, and as such, underscores the presentation of Christ's death as transfiguration through glorification; it is plausible to state that Luke's gospel, at one stage in its development, ended at this point.

The crowd is unique to Luke and part of a tripartite structure within the passion narrative. Their breast-beating recalls the Parable of the Pharisee and the Publican (18,9-14). That the people return to Jerusalem is a literary thread connecting the death with the events of pentecost where mercy is poured out (Acts 2,41).

Luke 23,49

[49a]Εἰστήκεισαν δὲ πάντες οἱ γνωστοὶ αὐτῷ ἀπὸ μακρόθεν [b]καὶ γυναῖκες αἱ συνακολουθοῦσαι αὐτῷ ἀπὸ τῆς Γαλιλαίας, [c]ὁρῶσαι ταῦτα.

The noun γνωστός itself describes a relationship; it is often rendered as *acquaintance, friend*, or *intimate*.[168] That this verse juxtaposes γνωστός with the ὄχλος in v 48 suggests that *friend* is its meaning here. Those in v 48 are distinct from those here in v 49. First, although the crowd and the multitude are watching the happenings, the group in v 49 is standing at a distance. The third evangelist seems to stress that the friends and women are witnessing the death of someone they personally know. Second, the participial use of the verb ἀκολουθέω, intensified with the prefix σύν, reiterates the intimacy expressed by γνωστός. Because those who know him are portrayed in a positive light, Senior holds that there is no connection to LXX Psalm 37,12 where the aloofness of the friends is negative.[169] It seems more accurate to say, however, that Luke has tempered the reference to LXX Psalm 37,12. Certainly when compared to the Marcan treatment, Luke has an ambivalent attitude toward the friends or disciples; they do not flee, but neither are they models of courage.

Unlike the crowd in Jerusalem, the women have been with Jesus from Galilee. Brown asserts that this is a pericope which anticipates the work of the women in the early Church (Acts 16,14-15).[170] He highlights as well the fact

---

[167] Henry Wansbrough, O.S.B., "The Crucifixion of Jesus," *Clergy Review* 56 (1971) 251-61.

[168] BAGD 164.

[169] Senior, *Passion* 148.

[170] Brown, *Messiah* 2; 1169-70.

that, unlike the crowds, they do not return but remain at the site where they observe the burial and go on to prepare the spices; they will have a positive role in proclaiming the resurrection.[171] Robert Karris believes that Luke's reference to the women here is a flashback to Luke 8,1-3; they are both witnesses to Jesus' earthly life as well as witnesses to his death.[172] In addition, Brown believes that the women from Galilee are juxtaposed with the Daughters from Jerusalem; the former will be with the Eleven and the mother and brothers of Jesus at pentecost, and the latter, along with their children will meet God's judgment on the city.[173]

The interpretations of Brown, Karris, and Senior attest to the artistry of the final Lucan redactor; vv 48-49 mark a seam. Verse 49, without the notice about breast-striking (48c) and the women (49b), at an earlier redactional stage stood with v 48 as the conclusion to the third gospel.[174] The final redactor has a purpose for distinguishing between the crowds on one side and the friends and women on the other. This Lucan editor wishes to set in relief a group of witnesses who observe not only the crucifixion, but who are also aware of the context in which the crucifixion has occurred, specifically, Jesus' ministry. Hence v 49 becomes a thread stitching the crucifixion and resurrection accounts, "fixed points," with the rest of the gospel.

Literary borrowing

Enoch's ascension is first mentioned at Gen 5,24, "Enoch walked with God; then he was no more, because God took him". The reading in 2 Enoch 67 is an elaboration of the Genesis account which is similar to the description of Elijah's ascension (ἀναλαμβάνω, aor pass) in LXX 4 Kgs 2,10-11. Why Enoch and Elijah came to such an end is explained in the Book of Wisdom, "There were some who pleased God and were loved by him, and while living among sinners were taken up" (μετατίθημι, aor pass) [4,10]. These traditions also influenced the Gospel of Peter.[175] At the moment of his death, Jesus cries, "My power, my power, you have left me, and having said this, he was taken up" (ἀναλαμβάνω, aor pass) [5]. Moreover, the Gos. Pet. includes darkness overspreading Judea and the sun's return at the ninth hour (6).

The use of ἀναλαμβάνω in LXX 4 Kgs 2,10-11 and the Gos. Pet. calls to mind its cognate ἀνάλημψις employed by Luke as a term for Jesus' death (9,51). Although these readings raise questions too broad for this study, they provide a glimpse into the belief of the primitive church. At the moment of his death, Jesus commends his spirit to the Father. In a Hellenistic world, this statement could be mistaken as an understanding of the afterlife akin to the Greek concept

---

[171] Brown, Messiah 2; 1170-71.

[172] Robert J. Karris, O.F.M., "Women and Discipleship in Luke," CBQ 56 (1994) 13.

[173] Brown, Messiah 2; 1171.

[174] Cf. Chapter Four.

[175] For a discussion on the dating of the Gos. Pet., cf. Chapter Three.

in which the soul alone would survive.[176] The citation in Luke 9,51 (and the
Gos. Pet. for that matter), drawing on the ascension of Elijah and Enoch,
represents a Jewish corrective to the prevailing Greek thought.[177] In this sense,
the death of Jesus in Luke approaches a Johannine theme, that of the death of
Jesus as an elevation.

Précis

Unlike the crowds, the friends and women stand at a distance, neither
fleeing nor interceding on Jesus' behalf. The presence of the friends as well as
the crowd (v 48a.d), concluded the narrative. With the addition of the women at
the final redaction (v 49b), this verse situated the crucifixion within the confines
of Christ's ministry and prepared for the resurrection accounts.

Summary

The internal analysis of the Lucan death narrative brings to light several
points.
First, by combining apocalyptic language with cultic terminology, Luke
portrays the three-hour suspension on the cross as the end of the old order and the
beginning of the new.
Second, the mention of signs in the sun (Luke 21,25) foreshadows the
failure of the sun in 23,45, while the use of the OT prophecy in Acts 2,20 recalls
the same. The three-hour darkness, so powerful that the sun is eclipsed, is the
climax of the dominion of darkness; it also symbolizes the apocalyptic Day of the
Lord.
Third, the interpretation of the tearing of the temple veil, an element
which has a predominantly positive emphasis, stems from the Lucan apocalyptic
as well as from readings of Zechariah and Ezekiel. God leaves the temple and
the city; the eschaton has arrived, and it is universal in scope. The verb σχίζομαι
and the adverb μέσος highlight the salvific nature of the Day of the Lord.
Fourth, the phrase φωνὴ μεγάλη, from its use throughout most of L-A,
signals the divine sonship of Christ, and from its OT usage, it announces the
Lord's visitation. When Luke couples it with the quotation from LXX Psalm
30,6, he shows Jesus as asserting his relationship with the Father; Jesus cries in a
φωνὴ μεγάλη as he addresses, πάτερ.

---

[176] Cf. Fred W. Burnett, "Philo on Immortality: A Thematic Study of Philo's
Concept of παλιγγενεσία," *CBQ* 46 (1984) 447-70; Notker Füglister, "Die
biblische Anthropologie und die postmortale Existenz des Individuums," *ZRT* 22
(1980) 129-45; Carl A. Rubino, "'A Thousand Shapes of Death': Heroic
Immortality in the *Iliad*," *Arktouros* (ed. Glen W. Bowerstock, et al., New York:
Walter de Gruyter, 1979) 12-18; Eduard Schweizer, "Die hellenistische
Komponente im neutestamentlichen σάρξ-Begriff," *ZNW* 48 (1957) 237-53.

[177] The gospels in general seem to meld the biographical facts of Jesus' life
with the kerygmatic cross and resurrection. The former reflects the concerns of
the Jewish Christians and Gnostics while the latter emphasizes the kerygma
(Nodet and Taylor, *Origins* 10).

Fifth, with this cry, Luke reinterprets the *ministering angel* tradition by placing all its attributes on Christ, an action which suggests that the evangelist is relying on readings from the *T. 12 Patr.* Christ alone battles the *diabolical force.*

Sixth, the term πάτερ (23,46) links together the agony, crucifixion, and death, while the prayer itself connects the whole of Jesus' suffering and death to the transfiguration. The address also establishes Jesus' divine sonship.

Seventh, the pagan centurion's testimony is based on the prophecies of Ezekiel and Zechariah along with the *Testament of Naphtali* and *2 Enoch* 67. The Roman soldier observes the return of God's glory through the death of his son, now transfigured in glory; thus, in true Lucan form, he glorifies God. His pronouncement represents an early christological statement.

Eighth, the thematic and verbal references to the Book of Wisdom as well as the interrogations before Pilate and Herod dictate that δίκαιος be read as *just* or *righteous* over *innocent.* The Greek term also resonates with Christ's divine sonship.

Ninth, the Lucan redactor rewrites the return of the light at Enoch's ascension as the resurrection and ascension narratives; in the Lucan ascension accounts, there is also influence from the Elianic tradition.

Tenth, the phrase τύπτοντες τὰ στήθη, is a product of the final redaction and indicates that at a primitive stage the third gospel ended at vv 48-49. This redactional seam supports the interpretation that with Jesus' battle against the *diabolical force*, Jesus conquers death by forgiving, praying, and dying. Thus, Christ's death results in his glorification, which is elaborated in the successive resurrection and post-resurrection experiences delineated in L-A.

The redactional phrase, τύπτοντες τὰ στήθη, is elucidated through the parable of the Pharisee and the Publican (Luke 18,9-14). In the death account, when the crowd depart *beating the breast*, they are acknowledging their sinfulness while begging for forgiveness; in this way they too are justified. Luke also uses the crowds to connect the crucifixion with pentecost, an event with eschatological significance.

Eleventh, because the friends and women know the ministry which precedes the crucifixion, they are able to interpret the whole passion and death and thus be credible witnesses to the resurrection. They, too, are present at pentecost.

These observations paint a tense scene which, through the artistry of the final Lucan redactor, reaches a resolution in the resurrection, ascension, and pentecost, events fully elaborated in the Acts. Nonetheless, there is an internal unity within the death account. The darkness, eclipse, and temple veil build up to the climax -- the death -- which takes place at the end of three hours of darkness. The centurion's declaration, the reaction of the crowds, the silent response of the friends and women followers form the dénouement. The presence of the friends and women disciples connects the Gospel to the Acts where they proclaim and hasten God's visitation from Jerusalem to Rome -- the center of the known world.

The death of the Just One represents the Lord's visitation, which is characterized by transfigured glory. Christ's death is a time of revelation; the powers of evil meet their judgment. The three-hour darkness and the eclipse of the sun represent the fury of battle against Satan and are read within the background of OT prophecy, intertestamental works, and Peter's pentecost speech.   Coinciding with the afternoon *Tamid*, the crucifixion ushers in the eschaton. This moment, represented by the rending of the temple curtain, signals the Day of the Lord in which God's glory temporarily vanishes. The departed divine glory returns with the death, linked to the transfiguration by Jesus' prayer. Both the centurion's declaration and the redactional seams attest to this fact.

Conclusion

Part One of this study discusses the major themes running through the Lucan PN and selects the *diabolical force* and *ministering angel* traditions, "fixed points" for further investigation. Part Two provides the textual, source, and literary analysis of the death accounts among all four evangelists and shows the development of the "fixed points". The synthesis in Part Three concentrates solely on the Lucan death narrative and uncovers the soteriological aspect of the third gospel; Jesus, as the Son of God, assumes all the qualities of the *ministering angel* and is victorious over Satan, the *diabolical force*.

Stated in the introduction is Erich Auerbach's comment that within the gospel rests "...something which neither the poets nor the historians of antiquity ever set out to portray: the birth of a spiritual movement in the depths of the common people."[1] Christianity, however, is not unique in this respect. The canonical Old Testament and intertestamental literature attest that many other groups have made the same claim. Rather, Christ's death served as the nexus for the various religious currents running through intertestamental Palestine and was interpreted accordingly.

In Acts 26,18, Luke has fashioned an inexact parallel construction, "...turn from darkness to light and from the dominion of Satan to God..."; one would expect something more fluid such as "the dominion of Satan to the kingdom of God". This slip in literary elegance, maybe intentional, pinpoints Christian salvation. Redemption is not the attaining of a heavenly dwelling place; it is much more. Further on in the same verse one reads, "so that they may receive forgiveness of sins and a place among those who are sanctified by faith in me." Christ's victory over Satan and his dark dominion is through a glorified death. As disciples, Christians too are sanctified, transfigured into glory, indeed, divinized, when they, like their master, defeat the powers of darkness by forgiving and trusting to the very end.

---

[1] Auerbach, *Mimesis* 42-3.

Luke 23,44-49	John 19,25-30	Mark 15,33-41	Matt 27,45-56
[44]Καὶ ἦν ἤδη ὡσεὶ ὥρα ἕκτη καὶ σκότος ἐγένετο ἐφ' ὅλην τὴν γῆν ἕως ὥρας ἐνάτης [45a]τοῦ ἡλίου ἐκλιπόντος, [b]ἐσχίσθη δὲ τὸ καταπέτασμα τοῦ ναοῦ μέσον.		[33]Καὶ γενομένης ὥρας ἕκτης σκότος ἐγένετο ἐφ' ὅλην τὴν γῆν ἕως ὥρας ἐνάτης.	[45]Ἀπὸ δὲ ἕκτης ὥρας σκότος ἐγένετο ἐπὶ πᾶσαν τὴν γῆν ἕως ὥρας ἐνάτης.
		v 38	v 51
	[28a]Μετὰ τοῦτο εἰδὼς [b]ὁ Ἰησοῦς [c]ὅτι ἤδη πάντα τετέλεσται, ἵνα τελειωθῇ ἡ γραφή, [d]λέγει, Διψῶ.	[34a]καὶ τῇ ἐνάτῃ ὥρᾳ ἐβόησεν ὁ Ἰησοῦς φωνῇ μεγάλῃ, ελωι ελωι λεμα σαβαχθανι; [b]ὅ ἐστιν μεθερμηνευόμενον ὁ θεός μου ὁ θεός μου, εἰς τί ἐγκατέλιπές με;	[46]περὶ δὲ τὴν ἐνάτην ὥραν ἀνεβόησεν ὁ Ἰησοῦς φωνῇ μεγάλῃ λέγων, Ηλι ηλι λεμα σαβαχθανι; τοῦτ' ἔστιν· θεέ μου θεέ μου, ἱνατί με ἐγκατέλιπες;
		[35]καί τινες τῶν παρεστηκότων ἀκούσαντες ἔλεγον, Ἴδε Ἠλίαν φωνεῖ.	[47]τινὲς δὲ τῶν ἐκεῖ ἑστηκότων ἀκούσαντες ἔλεγον ὅτι Ἠλίαν φωνεῖ οὗτος.
	[29a]σκεῦος ἔκειτο ὄξους μεστόν· σπόγγον οὖν μεστὸν τοῦ ὄξους [b]ὑσσώπῳ περιθέντες [c]προσήνεγκαν αὐτοῦ τῷ στόματι.	[36a]δραμὼν δέ τις καὶ γεμίσας σπόγγον ὄξους περιθεὶς καλάμῳ ἐπότιζεν αὐτὸν λέγων,	[48]καὶ εὐθέως δραμὼν εἷς ἐξ αὐτῶν καὶ λαβὼν σπόγγον πλήσας τε ὄξους καὶ περιθεὶς καλάμῳ ἐπότιζεν αὐτόν.
		[36b]ἄφετε ἴδωμεν εἰ ἔρχεται Ἠλίας καθελεῖν αὐτόν.	[49]οἱ δὲ λοιποὶ ἔλεγον, ἄφες ἴδωμεν εἰ ἔρχεται Ἠλίας σώσων αὐτόν.

Luke 23,44-49	John 19,25-30	Mark 15,33-41	Matt 27,45-56
⁴⁶ᵃκαὶ φωνήσας φωνῇ μεγάλῃ ὁ Ἰησοῦς ᵇεῖπεν, πάτερ, εἰς χεῖράς σου παρατίθεμαι τὸ πνεῦμά μου. τοῦτο δὲ εἰπὼν ᶜἐξέπνευσεν.	³⁰ᵃὅτε οὖν ἔλαβεν τὸ ὄξος [ὁ] ᵇἸησοῦς εἶπεν, τετέλεσται, ᶜκαὶ κλίνας τὴν κεφαλὴν παρέδωκεν τὸ πνεῦμα.	³⁷ὁ δὲ Ἰησοῦς ἀφεὶς φωνὴν μεγάλην	⁵⁰ὁ δὲ Ἰησοῦς πάλιν κράξας φωνῇ μεγάλῃ
		ἐξέπνευσεν.	ἀφῆκεν τὸ πνεῦμα.
v 45b		³⁸Καὶ τὸ καταπέτασμα τοῦ ναοῦ ἐσχίσθη εἰς δύο ἀπ' ἄνωθεν ἕως κάτω.	⁵¹ᵃΚαὶ ἰδοὺ τὸ καταπέτασμα τοῦ ναοῦ ἐσχίσθη ᵇἀπ' ἄνωθεν ἕως κάτω εἰς δύο καὶ ᶜἡ γῆ ἐσείσθη καὶ αἱ πέτραι ἐσχίσθησαν,
			⁵²καὶ τὰ μνημεῖα ἀνεῴχθησαν καὶ πολλὰ σώματα τῶν κεκοιμημένων ἁγίων ἠγέρθησαν,
			⁵³καὶ ἐξελθόντες ἐκ τῶν μνημείων μετὰ τὴν ἔγερσιν αὐτοῦ εἰσῆλθον εἰς τὴν ἁγίαν πόλιν καὶ ἐνεφανίσθησαν πολλοῖς.
⁴⁷ᵃἸδὼν δὲ ὁ ἑκατοντάρχης τὸ γενόμενον ἐδόξαζεν τὸν θεὸν ᵇλέγων, ×Ὄντως ὁ ἄνθρωπος οὗτος δίκαιος ἦν.		³⁹ᵃἸδὼν δὲ ὁ κεντυρίων ὁ παρεστηκὼς ἐξ ἐναντίας αὐτοῦ ὅτι οὕτως ἐξέπνευσεν ᵇεἶπεν, ἀληθῶς οὗτος ὁ ἄνθρωπος υἱὸς θεοῦ ἦν.	⁵⁴ᵃΟ δὲ ἑκατόνταρχος ᵇκαὶ οἱ μετ' αὐτοῦ τηροῦντες τὸν Ἰησοῦν ἰδόντες τὸν σεισμὸν καὶ τὰ γενόμενα ἐφοβήθησαν σφόδρα, ᶜλέγοντες, ἀληθῶς θεοῦ υἱὸς ἦν οὗτος.

Luke 23,44-49	John 19,25-30	Mark 15,33-41	Matt 27,45-56
⁴⁸ᵃκαὶ πάντες οἱ συμπαραγενόμενοι ὄχλοι ᵇἐπὶ τὴν θεωρίαν ταύτην, θεωρήσαντες τὰ γενόμενα, ᶜτύπτοντες τὰ στήθη ᵈὑπέστρεφον.			
⁴⁹ᵃΕἱστήκεισαν δὲ πάντες οἱ γνωστοὶ αὐτῷ ἀπὸ μακρόθεν ᵇκαὶ γυναῖκες αἱ συνακολουθοῦσαι αὐτῷ ἀπὸ τῆς Γαλιλαίας, ᶜὁρῶσαι ταῦτα.	²⁵ᵃΕἱστήκεισαν δὲ παρὰ τῷ σταυρῷ τοῦ Ἰησοῦ ᵇἡ μήτηρ αὐτοῦ καὶ ἡ ἀδελφὴ τῆς μητρὸς αὐτοῦ, Μαρία ἡ τοῦ Κλωπᾶ καὶ Μαρία ἡ Μαγδαληνή.	⁴⁰ᵃῙΗσαν δὲ καὶ γυναῖκες ἀπὸ μακρόθεν θεωροῦσαι,	⁵⁵ῙΗσαν δὲ ἐκεῖ γυναῖκες πολλαὶ ἀπὸ μακρόθεν θεωροῦσαι,
	²⁶ᵃἸησοῦς οὖν ἰδὼν τὴν μητέρα ᵇκαὶ τὸν μαθητὴν παρεστῶτα ὃν ἠγάπα, ᶜλέγει τῇ μητρί, γύναι, ἴδε ὁ υἱός σου.	ᵇἐν αἷς καὶ Μαρία ἡ Μαγδαληνὴ καὶ Μαρία ἡ Ἰακώβου τοῦ μικροῦ καὶ Ἰωσῆτος μήτηρ καὶ Σαλώμη,	αἵτινες ἠκολούθησαν τῷ Ἰησοῦ ἀπὸ τῆς Γαλιλαίας διακονοῦσαι αὐτῷ·
	²⁷ᵃεῖτα λέγει τῷ μαθητῇ, ἴδε ἡ μήτηρ σου. ᵇκαὶ ἀπ᾽ ἐκείνης τῆς ὥρας ἔλαβεν ὁ μαθητὴς αὐτὴν	⁴¹ᵃῐ ὅτε ἦν ἐν τῇ Γαλιλαίᾳ ἠκολούθουν αὐτῷ καὶ διηκόνουν αὐτῷ, καὶ ἄλλαι πολλαὶ αἱ συναναβᾶσαι αὐτῷ εἰς Ἱεροσόλυμα.	⁵⁶ἐν αἷς ἦν Μαρία ἡ Μαγδαληνὴ καὶ Μαρία ἡ τοῦ Ἰακώβου καὶ Ἰωσὴφ μήτηρ καὶ ἡ μήτηρ τῶν υἱῶν Ζεβεδαίου.

Primary Sources

Classical Authors

Herodotus. *Books 1-2*. Trans. A. D. Godley. LCL 1; Cambridge: Harvard
University Press, 1975.

Josephus. *Jewish Antiquities, Books 5-8*. Trans. H.St.J. Thackeray and Ralph
Marcus. LCL 5; Cambridge: Harvard University Press, 1988.

_____. *The Jewish War, Books 1-3*. Trans. H.St.J. Thackeray. LCL 2;
Cambridge: Harvard University Press, 1989.

_____. *The Jewish War, Books 4-7*. Trans. H.St.J. Thackeray. LCL 3;
Cambridge: Harvard University Press, 1990.

Plutarch. *Moralia V: Obsolence of Oracles*. Trans. Frank Cole Babbitt. LCL 5;
Cambridge: Harvard University Press, 1969.

Jewish Literature

Babylonian Talmud. Ed. I. Epstein, 1; London: Soncino Press, 1961.

Mishnah

Tractate Pesahim in *Die Mischna*, Traktat Pesachim. Ed. Georg Beer. 2,3;
Gießen: Verlag von Alfred Töpelmann, 1912.

Tractate Tamid in *Die Mischna*, Traktat Tamid. Ed. Oscar Holtzmann. 5,9;
Gießen: Verlag von Alfred Töpelmann, 1928.

Judean Desert Literature

Dead Sea Scrolls Translated. Ed. Florentino García Martínez. 2nd Edition;
Leiden: E.J. Brill, 1996.

New Testament

Codex Vaticanus Graecus 1209 (Codex B), TA IEPA BIBΛIA. In Civitate
Vaticana 1965.

Matthäusevangelium. Itala Das Neue Testament in altlateinischer Überlieferung.
Hrsg. A. Jülicher. 1; Berlin: Walter de Gruyter 1972.

Novum Testamentum Graece, 27th Edition. Ed. Eberhard and Erwin Nestle,
Barbara and Kurt Aland. Stuttgart: Deutsche Bibelgesellschaft, 1993.

Synopsis Graeca Quattuor Evangeliorum. Ed. M.-É. Boismard, O.P. and A.
Lamouille. Leuven: Peeters, 1986.

Synopsis Quattuor Evangeliorum. Ed. Kurt Aland. 4/5; Stuttgart: Biblia-Druck, 1975.

United Bible Societies Greek New Testament, 4th Revised Edition. Ed. B. Aland, K. Aland, J. Karavidopoulos, C. M. Martini, and B. M. Metzger. Stuttgart: Deutsche Bibelgesellschaft, 1993.

Old Testament

Biblia Hebraica Stuttgartensia. K. Elliger and W. Rudolph, eds. Stuttgart: Deutsche Bibelgesellschaft 1977.

Septuagint. A. Rahlfs, ed. Stuttgart: Deutsche Bibelgesellschaft 1979.

Patristic Authors

Irénée de Lyon. *Contre les Hérésies.* SC 100; Paris: Les Éditions du Cerf 1965.

Justin. *Dialogue avec Tryphon.* Éd. Georges Archambault. Tome 2; Paris: Librairie Alphonse Picard et Fils, 1909.

Pseudepigraphic, Apocryphal, Gnostic, and Intertestamental Works

1 Enoch. Trans. E. Isaac in *The Old Testament Pseudepigrapha.* Ed. James H. Charlesworth, 1; London: Darton, Longman, and Todd, 1983; 13-89.

2 Enoch. Trans. F. I. Andersen in *The Old Testament Pseudepigrapha.* Ed. James H. Charlesworth, 1; London: Darton, Longman, and Todd, 1983; 102-213.

Apocalypse of Elijah. Trans. O.S. Wintermute in *Old Testament Pseudepigrapha.* Ed. James H. Charlesworth. 1; London: Darton, Longman, and Todd, 1983; 735-53.

Apocalypse of Paul. Trans. William R. Murdock and George W. MacRae in *Nag Hammadi Codices.* Ed. Douglas M. Parrott. NHS 11; Leiden: E.J. Brill, 1979; 58-61.

Apocrypha and Pseudepigrapha of the Old Testament. Ed. R.H. Charles. 2; Oxford: Clarendon Press, 1913.

Gospel According to Thomas. Trans. A. Guillaumont, *et al.* Leiden: E. J. Brill, 1976.

Gospel of Peter in *The Akhmim Fragment of the Apocryphal Gospel of Peter.* Ed. H.B. Swete. New York: Macmillan and Co, 1893.

Greek Versions of the Testaments of the Twelve Patriarchs. Ed. R.H. Charles. Oxford: Clarendon Press, 1908.

Jubilees. Trans. O. S. Wintermute in *The Old Testament Pseudepigrapha.* Ed. James H. Charlesworth, 2; New York: Doubleday and Company, Inc., 1985; 52-142.

Martrydom and Ascension of Isaiah. Trans. M. A. Knibb in *The Old Testament Pseudepigrapha.* Ed. James H. Charlesworth, 2; New York: Doubleday and Company, Inc., 1985; 156-76.

Testaments of the Twelve Patriarchs. Trans. H. C. Kee in *The Old Testament Pseudepigrapha* =(*OTPseud.*). 1; London: Darton, Longman, and Todd, 1983; 775-828.

Testament of Asher.	*OTPseud* 1; 816-8.
Testament of Benjamin.	*OTPseud* 1; 825-8.
Testament of Dan.	*OTPseud* 1; 808-10.
Testament of Levi.	*OTPseud* 1; 788-95.
Testament of Naphtali.	*OTPseud* 1; 810-4.
Testament of Reuben.	*OTPseud* 1; 782-5.
Testament of Simeon.	*OTPseud* 1; 785-8.
Testament of Zebulon.	*OTPseud* 1; 805-7.

Reference Works

Bauer, W., W. F. Arndt, F. W. Gingrich, and F. W. Danker. *A Greek-English Lexicon of the New Testament and Other Early Christian Literature.* Chicago: University of Chicago Press, 1979.

Blass, F., A. Debrunner, and Robert W. Funk. *A Greek Grammar of the New Testament.* Chicago: The University of Chicago Press, 1973.

Brown, F., S. R. Driver, and C. A. Briggs. *Hebrew and English Lexicon with an appendix containing the Biblical Aramaic.* Peabody, Massachusetts: Hendrickson Publishers 1979.

Hatch, Edwin and Henry Redpath. *Concordance to the Septuagint.* Oxford: Clarendon Press, 1897.

Joüon, Paul, S.J. *A Grammar of Biblical Hebrew.* Trans. T. Muraoka. 14 /1; Roma: Editrice Pontificio Istituto Biblico, 1991.

Koehler, L. and W. Baumgartner. *Lexicon in Veteris Testamenti libros.* Leiden: E. J. Brill, 1985.

Liddel, Henry George and Robert Scott. *Greek-English Lexicon.* 1 and 2;

Oxford: Clarendon Press, 1940.

Vollständige Konkordanz zum Griechischen Neuen Testament 1/1-2.   Ed. K.
Aland. Berlin: Walter de Gruyter, 1983.

Zerwick. Maximilian, S.J. *Biblical Greek.* Rome: Pontificio Istituto Biblico
1963, reprinted 1987.

Secondary Sources

Anonymous.   "Short Notes," *The New Testament Textual Research Update.* 2
(1994) 41-51.

Asurmendi, Jesus.   "La gloire de Dieu sur la montagne qui est à l'Orient," *Le
Monde de la Bible* 55 (Sept-Oct 1988) 7.

Auerbach, Erich. *Mimesis, the Representation of Reality in Western Literature.*
Princeton: Princeton University Press, 1953.

Bailey, John Amedee. *The Traditions Common to the Gospels of Luke and John.*
Leiden: E. J. Brill, 1963.

Bellinzoni, Jr., Arthur J., "The Source of the Agraphon in Justin Martyr's
Dialogue with Trypho 47:5," *VC* 17 (1963) 65-70.

Boismard, M. -É., O.P. *En Quête du proto-Luc.* EBib 37; Paris: J. Gabalda et
Cⁱᵉ, 1997.

_____. *Le Diatessaron de Tatien à Justin.* EBib 15; Paris: J. Gabalda et Cⁱᵉ,
1992.

_____. *L'Évangile de Marc, sa préhistoire.* EBib 26; Paris: J. Gabalda et
Cⁱᵉ, 1994.

_____.   *Moïse ou Jésus. Essai de christologie johannique.*   Leuven:
University Press, 1988.

_____. *Synopse des Quatre Évangiles.* 2; Paris: Les Éditions du Cerf, 1972.

_____., and A. Lamouille. *Synopse des Quatre Évangiles: L'Évangile de
Jean.* 3; Paris: Les Éditions du Cerf, 1977.

Botha, F. J. "'Umâs in Luke xxii. 31". *ExpTim* 64 (1952-53) 125.

Brinkmann, B., S.J. "Unterschiede zwischen der Lehre des hl. Paulus von der
Parusie und den Anschauungen des Buches Henoch," *Bib* 13 (1932) 318-
34 and 418-34.

Brodie, Thomas.   "Luke-Acts as an Imitation and Emulation of the Elijah-Elisha
Narrative, *"New Views on Luke and Acts.*   Ed. Earl Richard.
Collegeville, Minnesota: The Liturgical Press, 1990; 78-85.

Brown, Raymond E., S.S. · *The Death of the Messiah*. 1 and 2; New York: Doubleday, 1994.

_____. *The Gospel According to John, 13-21, vol. 2.* Anchor Bible 29a; Garden City, New York: Doubleday and Company, Inc, 1970.

Brun, Lyder. "Engel und Blutschweiß, Lc 22,43-44". *ZNW* 32 (1933) 265-76.

Büchele, Anton. *Der Tod Jesu im Lukasevangelium.* Frankfurt: Josef Knecht, 1978.

Bultmann, Rudolf. *The History of the Synoptic Tradition.* Oxford: Basil Blackwell, 1968.

Burkitt, F.C. "'Επιφώσκειν," *JTS* 14 (1913) 538-46.

Burnett, Fred W. "Philo on Immortality: A Thematic Study of Philo's Concept of παλιγγενεσία," *CBQ* 46 (1984) 447-70.

Charlesworth, James H. *The Old Testament Pseudepigrapha and the New Testament.* SNTSMS 54; New York: Cambridge University Press, 1987.

Collins, Adela Yarbro. "From Noble Death to Crucified Messiah," *NTS* 40 (1994) 481-503.

Conzelmann, Hans. "Historie und Theologie in den synoptischen Passionsberichten," *Zur Bedeutung des Todes Jesu.* Gütersloh: Gütersloher Verlagshaus Gerd Mohn, 1968; 35-53.

Cosgrove, Charles. "Justin Martyr and the Emerging Christian Canon," *VC* 36 (1982) 209-232.

Crump, David. *Jesus the Intercessor.* WUNT 2/49; Tübingen: J. C. B. Mohr (Paul Siebeck), 1992.

Dauer, Anton. *Die Passionsgeschichte im Johannesevangelium.* München: Kösel-Verlag, 1972.

Dillon, Richard. *From Eye-witnesses to Ministers of the Word.* AnBib 82; Rome: Biblical Institute Press, 1978.

Driver, G. R. "Two problems in the New Testament," *JTS* 16 (1965) 327-335.

Dunn, James D. G. "John and the Oral Gospel Tradition," *Jesus and the Oral Gospel Tradition.* Ed. Henry Wansbrough. Sheffield: Academic Press [= JSNTSup 64] 1991; 351-79.

Duplacy, Jean. "La préhistoire du texte en Luc 22:43-44," *New Testament Textual Criticism: Essays in Honour of Bruce M. Metzger.* Ed. Eldon Jay Epp and Gordon D. Fee. Oxford: Clarendon Press, 1981, 77-86.

Ehrman, B. D., and M. A. Plunkett, "The Angel and the Agony: The Textual

Problem of Luke 22:43-44," *CBQ* 45 (1983) 401-16.

Esler, Philip F. *Community and Gospel in Luke-Acts*. SNTSMS 57; Cambridge: Cambridge University Press, 1987.

Evans, Craig A. *Luke and Scripture*. Minneapolis: Fortress Press, 1993.

Farmer, W.R. *The Synoptic Problem: A Critical Analysis*. New York: Macmillan Company, 1964.

Feldkämper, Ludger, S.V.D. *Der betende Jesus als Heilsmittler nach Lukas*. Veröffentlichungen des Missionspriesterseminars St. Augustin bei Bonn 29; St. Augustin: Stelyer Verlag, 1978.

Fitzmyer, Joseph A., S.J. "Methodology in the Study of the Aramaic Substratum of Jesus' Sayings in the New Testament," *Jésus aux origines de la christologie*. Ed. J. Dupont, Leuven: Leuven University Press, 1975; 73-102.

_____. *The Gospel According to Luke, 1-9, vol. 1*. Anchor Bible, 28; Garden City, New York: Doubleday and Company, 1981.

_____. *The Gospel According to Luke, 10-24, vol. 2*. Anchor Bible 28a; Garden City, New York: Doubleday and Company, 1985.

Fitzpatrick, G. D. "A Theme of the Lucan Passion Story and Luke 23,47," *JTS* 52-3 (1941-42) 34-36.

Frankfurter, David. *Elijah in Upper Egypt; the Apocalypse of Elijah and Early Egyptian Christianity*. Minneapolis: Fortress Press, 1993.

Füglister, Notker. "Die biblische Anthropologie und die postmortale Existenz des Individuums," *ZRT* 22 (1980) 129-45.

Gaston, Lloyd. *No Stone on Another*. NovTSup 23; Leiden: E.J. Brill, 1970.

Grández, Rufino María, O.F.M. Cap. *Las Tinieblas en la Muerte de Jesus, Estudio sobre Lc 23,44-45a*. Jerusalem: Studium Biblicum Franciscanum, 1989.

Green, Joel B. "Jesus on the Mount of Olives," *JSNT* 26 (1986) 29-48.

_____. *The Death of Jesus*. WUNT 2/33; Tübingen: J.C.B. Mohr (Paul Siebeck) 1988.

_____. "The Demise of the Temple in Luke-Acts," *RB* 101/4 (1994) 495-515.

Grelot, P. "Hénoch et ses Écritures," *RB* 82 (1975) 481-500.

Grossfeld, Bernard. "Aramaic: the Targumim," *Encyclopedia Judaica*. 4; New York: The Macmillan Company, 1971; 842-51.

Hagner, Donald A. "The Sayings of Jesus in the Apostolic Fathers and Justin Martyr," in *Gospel Perspectives*. Ed. David Wenham. 5; Sheffield: JSOT Press, 1985; 233-268.

Harris, Rendel. "The Origin of a Famous Lucan Gloss," *ExpTim* 35 (1923-24) 7-10.

Havener, Ivan, O.S.B. *Q, The Sayings of Jesus*. Wilmington, Delaware: Michael Glazier, 1987.

Hills, Julian V. "Luke 10.18 -- Who Saw Satan Fall". *JSNT* 46 (1992) 25-40.

Jeremias, Joachim. *Die Sprache des Lukasevangeliums*. Göttingen: Vandenhoeck and Ruprecht, 1980.

Johnson, Sherman E. *The Griesbach Hypothesis and Redaction Criticism*. Atlanta: Scholars Press, 1991.

Joüon, Paul, S.J. "Les Mots employés pour désigner 'Le Temple' dans l'Ancien Testament, le Nouveau Testament, et Josèphe." *RSR* 25 (1935) 329-43.

Kähler, Martin. *The So-Called Historical Jesus and the Historic Biblical Christ*. Trans. Carl E. Braaten. Philadelphia: Fortress Press, 1964.

Karris, Robert J. O.F.M. *Luke: Artist and Theologian*. New York: Paulist Press, 1985.

_____. "Women and Discipleship in Luke," *CBQ* 56 (1994) 1-20.

Kelly, H. A., S.J. "The Devil in the Desert". *CBQ* 26 (1964) 190-220.

Kilgallen, John J., S.J. "The Return of the Unclean Spirit (Luke 11,24-26)" *Bib* 74 (1993) 45-59.

Klein, Günter. "Die Berufung des Petrus". *ZNW* 58 (1967) 1-44.

_____. *Rekonstruktion und Interpretation*. BEvT 50; München: Chr. Kaiser Verlag, 1969, 49-98.

Lagrange, M.-J., O.P. *Évangile selon Saint Luc*. EBib 15; Paris: J. Gabalda et Cie 1921.

Légasse, S. "Les Voiles du Temple de Jérusalem." *RB* 87 (1980) 560-89.

Léon-Dufour, Xavier. "Temple," *Vocabulaire de Théologie Biblique*. Paris: Les Éditions du Cerf, 1970; 1266-73.

Marshall, I.H. *Luke: Historian and Theologian*. Exeter: The Paternoster Press, 1978.

_____. *The Gospel of Luke*. Exeter: The Paternoster Press, 1978.

Matera, Frank J. "The Death of Jesus According to Luke," *CBQ* 47 (1985) 469-485.

McGinn, Bernard. *The Foundations of Mysticism*. 1; New York: Crossroad, 1992.

Metzger, Bruce M. *A Textual Commentary on the Greek New Testament*. New York: United Bible Societies, 1971.

_____. *A Textual Commentary on the Greek New Testament, 2nd Edition*. New York: American Bible Society, 1994.

Murphy-O'Connor, Jerome, O.P. "The Essenes and Their History," *RB* 81 (1974) 215-44.

_____. "What Really Happened at the Transfiguration," *Bible Review* 3/3 (1987) 8-21.

Murphy, Richard T. A., O.P. *The Dereliction of Christ on the Cross*. Washington, DC: Pontificium Institutum Angelicum, 1940.

Neirynck, Frans. "John and the Synoptics," *Evangelica: Gospel studies -- Études d'Évangile, collected essays*. Ed. F. van Segbroeck; Lueven: University Press (1982) 365-400.

New Revised Standard Version. Bruce M. Metzger, ed. New York: Collins Publishers 1989.

Neyrey, Jerome, S.J. *The Passion According to Luke*. New York: Paulist Press, 1985.

Nobile, Marco. "Ez 37,1-14 come costitutivo di uno schema cultuale," *Bib* 65 (1984) 476-484.

Nodet, Étienne, O.P. and Justin Taylor, S.M. *The Origins of Christianity, an Exploration*. Collegeville, Minnesota: The Liturgical Press, 1998.

O'Toole, Robert F., S.J. *The Unity of Luke's Theology*. Wilmington, Delaware: Michael Glazier, 1984.

Pelletier, André, S.J. "La Tradition Synoptique du 'Voile Déchiré'," *RSR* 46 (1958) 161-80.

Pietersma, Albert and Susan Turner Comstock with Harold W. Attridge. Trans. *The Apocalypse of Elijah based on P. Chester Beatty 2018*. Chico, California: Scholars Press, 1981.

Prete, Benedetto, O.P. *Il Primato e la Missione di Pietro*. Brescia: Paideia Editrice, 1969.

_____. "Le Preghiere di Gesù al Monte degli Ulivi e sulla Croce". *Atti della XXVII Settimana Biblica*. Brescia: Paideia Editrice, 1984. 75-96.

Puech, Émile. *La croyance des Esséniens en la vie future: immortalité, résurrection, vie éternelle? Histoire d'une croyance dans le judaïsme ancien.* EBib 22; Paris: J. Gabalda et Cie, 1993.

Rehkopf, Friedrich. *Die lukanische Sonderquelle, ihr Umfang und Sprachgebrauch.* Tübingen: J.C.B. Mohr (Paul Siebeck) 1959.

Rehm, Martin. "Eli, Eli lamma sabacthani," *BZ* 2 (1958) 275-78.

Reid, Barbara, O.P. *The Transfiguration: A Source- and Redaction- Critical Study of Luke 9,28-36.* CahRB 32; Paris: J. Gabalda et Cie, 1993.

Reinbold, Wolfgang. *Der Älteste Bericht über den Tod Jesu.* New York: Walter de Gruyter, 1994.

Rowley, H.H. *Worship in Ancient Israel.* Philadelphia: Fortress Press, 1967.

Rubino, Carl A. "'A Thousand Shapes of Death': Heroic Immortality in the *Iliad*," *Arktouros.* Ed. Glen W. Bowerstock, et al. New York: Walter de Gruyter, 1979.

Rudolph, Kurt. "Gnosticism," *Anchor Bible Dictionary.* Ed. David Noel Freedman. 2; New York: Doubleday, 1992, 1033-40.

Sawyer, John F.A. "Why is the solar eclipse mentioned in the Passion Narrative?" *JTS* 23 (1972) 124-8.

Schaefer, Konrad, O.S.B. "Zechariah 14: A Study in Allusion," *CBQ* 57 (Jan 1995) 66-91.

Schneider, Gerhard. *Die Passion Jesu nach den drei älteren Evangelien.* München: Kösel-Verlag, 1973.

_____. *Verleugnung, Verspottung und Verhör Jesu.* München: Kösel-Verlag, 1969.

Schniewind, Julius. *Die Parallelperikopen bei Lukas und Johannes.* Hildesheim: Georg Olms Verlagsbuchhandlung, 1958.

Schützeichel, Heribert. "Der Todesschrei Jesu". *TTZ* 83 [1974]) 1-16.

Schweizer Eduard. "Die hellenistische Komponente im neutestamentlichen σάρξ-Begriff," *ZNW* 48 (1957) 237-53.

Senior, Donald, C.P. *The Passion of Jesus in the Gospel of Luke.* Wilmington: Michael Glazier, 1989.

Squires, John T. *The Plan of God in Luke-Acts.* SNTSMS 76; Cambridge: Cambridge University Press, 1993.

Stone, Michael and John Strugnell, eds. and trans. *The Books of Elijah, Parts 1 and 2.* Missoula, Montana: Scholars Press, 1979.

Streeter, B. H. "On the Trial of Our Lord before Herod, a Suggestion," *Oxford Studies in the Synoptic Problem.* Ed. W. Sanday. Oxford: Clarendon Press, 1911, 229-31.

Tannehill, Robert C. *The Narrative Unity of Luke-Acts, A Literary Interpretation.* Philadelphia: Fortress Press, 1986.

Taylor, Justin, S.M. *Les Actes des deux apôtres, commentaire historique (Act. 9,1-18,22), vol. 5.* EBib 23; Paris: J. Gabalda et Cie, 1994.

Taylor, Vincent. *The Passion Narrative of St Luke.* SNTSMS 19; Cambridge: University Press, 1972.

Tiede, David L. *Prophecy and History in Luke-Acts.* Philadelphia: Fortress Press, 1980.

Treat, Jay C. "The Two Manuscript Witnesses to the *Gospel of Peter,*" *SBL Seminar Papers* (1990) 391-99.

Trenkle, Emil. "Beitrag zur Zahlentypologie bei Lk 3,21-38 und Mt 1,1f. (Heer, Stammbäume) aus dem Buch Henoch," *BZ* 8 (1910) 262.

Trevor, J. C. "Hyssop," *The Interpreter's Dictionary of the Bible.* 2; New York: Abington Press, 1962; 669-70.

Turner, C. H. "Note on ἐπιφώσκειν," *JTS* 14 (1913) 188-95.

Twelftree, Graham H. *Jesus the Exorcist.* WUNT 2/54; Tübingen: J.C.B. Mohr (Paul Siebeck), 1993.

Tyson, Joseph B. *The Death of Jesus in Luke-Acts.* Columbia: University of South Carolina Press, 1986.

Untergaßmair, Franz Georg. *Kreuzweg und Kreuzigung Jesu.* Paderborn: Ferdinand Schöningh, 1980.

Vincent, L.-H., O.P. *Jérusalem de l'Ancien Testament.* 2; Paris: J. Gabalda et Cie, 1956.

Viviano, Benedict T., O.P. "The High Priest's Servant's Ear: Mark 14:47," *RB* 96 (1989) 71-80.

Wansbrough, Henry, O.S.B. "The Crucifixion of Jesus," *Clergy Review* 56 (1971) 251-61.

_____. "Suffered Under Pontius Pilate," *Scripture* 18 (1966) 84-93.

Weinert, Francis. "Luke, the Temple and Jesus' Saying about Jerusalem's Abandoned House (Luke 13:34-35)," *CBQ* 44 (1982) 68-76.

Zimmerli, Walthar. *Ezechiel.* Neukirchen-Vluyn: Neukirchener Verlag, 1969.

Zwiep, A.W. *The Ascension of the Messiah in Lukan Christology.* New York: Brill, 1997.

OLD TESTAMENT

Genesis

4,8	54n.
5,24	175
6,2	55
15,10	150n.
19,1-15	65.73.75
21,17-19	65.73.75
22,3	150n.
28,12	65.73.75
31,11-13	65.73.75
40	42

Exodus

11,4	150n.
12,22 MT	104
12,22	104
14,21-27	150
14,21-22	168
14,21	170
15,2	162n.
15,6	162n.
24,18	150n.
28,29 MT	172
28,30 MT	172
29,38	147

Leviticus

10,3	162n.
14,4	104n.
14,6	104n.
14,49	104n.
14,51	104n.
14,52	104n.

Numbers

19,6	104
28,4	147

Deuteronomy

17,6-7	27
19,15	27
32,43	64n.66.73.75

Joshua

1,11	150n.

Judges

6,11-22	65
6,12-22	73.75
9,9	162n.

2 Samuel

15,19-21	7
15,21	60n.
15,30	8
17,13	59

1 Kings

1,8	173
2,30	162n.
5,13 MT	104n.
6,14	150n.
17-2 Kg 8,15	169
17,17-24 MT	169
19,5-7	65.73.75
21,8-13	170

2 Kings

1,1-2	170
1,6	170
2,11-12 MT	170
2,11 MT	168
19,35	66.73.75

T. Benj.

3,3   61.64

T. Dan

5,10-11   73
6,1-10   73.143n.
6,2-3   74.160
6,4   74.160

T. Levi

5,1-7   73
18,2-14   73.74n.143n.
             160
18,12   53

T. Naph.   177

3,5   73
5,1   151

T. Reub.

5,6   73

T. Sim.

6,5-6   74.143n.160n.

T. Zeb.

9,8   74.143n.160n.

Vitae Eliae   169

JOSEPHUS   64

J. Ant.

5,2,9   62n.

J War

1,20,4   31n.
5,5,4   156n.
6,5,3   155n.
6,9,3   147n.

JUDEAN DESERT LIT.

Vis. Amram   69.75.147

War Scroll   75

CD

II,6   68n.
V,18   68n.
VII,2   68n.
VIII,2   68n.
XVI, 5   68n.

1QH

XI   71.147n.
XI, 28-32   68n.
XIV   71
XVIII,10   70n.

1QM

I,1   67n.
I,11   67n.
I,13   67n.
I,15   67n.
III,3   67n.
IV,2   67n.
IX,15-X,11   67n.
X,8   67n.
XII,4   67n.70
XII,8   67n.
XIII   70.147
XIII,2   67n.
XIII,4   67n.70

graphic

F-87350 PANAZOL
N° Imprimeur : 9036043-99
Dépôt légal : Avril 1999

DATE DUE

			Printed in USA